[

A

)

NarcoDiplomacy

NarcoDiplomacy

Cornell University Pres

EXPORTING THE
U.S. WAR ON DRUGS

H. Richard Friman

ITHACA AND LONDON

First published 1996 by Cornell University Press.

Printed in the United States of America

Library of Congress Cataloging-in-Publication Data

Friman, H. Richard.
  NarcoDiplomacy : exporting the U.S. war on drugs / H. Richard Friman.
      p.   cm.
  Includes bibliographical references and index.
  ISBN 0-8014-3274-X (alk. paper)
  1. Narcotics, Control of.   2. Drug traffic.   I. Title.
HV5801.F75   1996
363.4'5'0973—dc20   96-18387

This book is printed on Lyons Falls Turin Book, a paper that is totally chlorine-free and acid-free.

CONTENTS

TABLES

PREFACE

While the world was greeting the end of the Cold War with euphoria, a war of much longer duration continued unabated. It appears that the twentieth century will end as it began, with the United States at battle against the international drug trade. The U.S. campaign against cocaine and heroin in the 1990s follows campaigns against cocaine in the 1980s, heroin and marijuana in the 1970s, marijuana in the 1960s, heroin and opium in the 1950s and 1940s, alcohol during the 1920s and early 1930s, and cocaine, opium, and manufactured narcotics from the early 1900s to the late 1930s. Through all this time, U.S. officials have seen illicit trafficking in drugs of abuse and addiction as a global problem with negative social, economic, and political consequences. Yet, U.S. efforts to win the support of other countries for the American agenda have met with highly inconsistent responses. This book explores why foreign compliance has been so unreliable.

In the United States foreign compliance with U.S. drug control efforts has often been linked to state capacity, that is, to the ability of a given state to meet the requirements involved. Lack of capacity expresses itself in two main ways: involuntary and voluntary failure to comply.[1] Thus, government officials may make good-faith pledges to carry out drug control measures but be prevented by weak state capacity from actually doing so. Or policy makers, recognizing domestic weaknesses but faced with international pressure, may agree to participate in international control efforts even though they have no intention of actually implementing them.

If capacity is the problem, it follows that increased U.S. involvement in the affairs of such countries is the solution. Specifically, the United States should increase pressure on foreign governments in order to deter deception and, at the same time, provide economic or military support or both to offset weak domestic capacity. Indeed, this has been U.S. strategy since the early 1900s.

Yet the actual dynamics of foreign cooperation with the U.S. agenda remain underexplored. Working in the context of the drug campaigns of the late 1980s and early 1990s, scholars have tended to focus on U.S. relations with primary source and transit countries such as Colombia, Bolivia, Peru, Myanmar (Burma), Thailand, and Mexico. Similar assumptions about the importance of state capacity underly recent scholarship on the emergence of East European countries and the successor states of the Soviet Union as new conduits and sources in the illicit drug trade.

In fact, however, U.S. beliefs about state capacity originated in drug campaigns waged during the early 1900s. In order to explore the validity of these beliefs, this book departs from the traditional focus to look at two countries now touted as staunch U.S. allies in the drug war. Both Germany and Japan before the 1940s were seen as central to the illicit trade in cocaine and manufactured narcotics such as heroin. Both countries came under strong U.S. influence after World War II. Both have pursued the U.S. agenda with varying degrees of enthusiasm since the 1950s.

The book is divided into two basic parts. The first explores German and Japanese responses to the American agenda from the early 1900s through each country's formal withdrawal from the international drug control efforts of the League of Nations. Chapter 2 examines German drug control policy, especially regarding cocaine, from 1909 to 1934, while the United States was trying to bring manufactured narcotics under the same sorts of controls applied to opium. Chapter 3 analyzes how Japanese drug control policy from 1906 to 1939 was influenced by U.S. charges of transshipment and Chinese narcotization. The second part of the book turns to the postwar Japanese and

German responses to the American agenda from 1945 through the early 1990s. Chapters 4 and 5 examine Japanese and German drug control policy during occupation and subsequent pressures to adhere to the Nixon and Reagan-Bush drug campaigns. Chapter 6 examines the relationship between state capacity and foreign compliance in light of the German and Japanese experience and outlines the ramifications of these findings for the future of U.S. drug control policy.

This book is the result of a five-year exploration of relations among developed countries concerned about the control of the illicit drug trade. Explorations incur debts, and this project has been no exception.

For helpful comments, suggestions, and reality checks along the way, I especially thank Judith Bailey, Hans-Georg Betz, Ralf Beke-Bramkamp, Philip Cerney, Robert Denemark, Alice Friman, Julie Friman, Virginia Haufler, Roger Haydon, Hirano Kenichiro, Robert Jervis, Peter Katzenstein, Barrett McCormick, Ethan Nadelmann, R. T. Naylor, T. J. Pempel, James Rosenau, Susan Strange, Duane Swank, Raju Thomas, Tamura Masayuki, Tsunekawa Keiichi, William Walker, and several anonymous reviewers. I am also grateful for the invaluable research assistance provided by Michael Abbey, Akiyama Tozen, Kamla Bhatt, Paul Bovee, Fuse Naomi, Lai Hongyi, Liu (Alvin) Qing, Mary Mabweijano, Maria Okuneva, Osaname Mitsue, and Tani Atsuko. (Here, as in the text, Japanese names are listed according to Japanese usage.) I also acknowledge the patience of my students at Marquette University and the stimulating feedback they gave me when they found themselves faced with a nontraditional subject and approach in their international relations and international political economy courses.

For access to the historical record, I am grateful to the staffs of the State Department Diplomatic Records Section of the National Archives, the Library of Congress, and the European Community Information Service Library (Washington, D.C.); the Political Archives of the German Foreign Office (Bonn), the Merck Firm Archives (Darmstadt), the German Central State Archive of Interior Ministry and Foreign Office Records (Potsdam), and the German Library (Frankfurt); the International House of Japan Library, the National Diet Library, the Diplomatic Records Office, the National Press

Center, the Foreign Correspondents Club, and the Tokyo Metropolitan Central Library (Tokyo); and the Inter-Library Loan Division of Marquette University.

For information about more recent aspects of drug control strategy, I thank more than fifty U.S., German, and Japanese policy makers and law enforcement officials who made time to speak with me. The book could not have been written without the cooperation of personnel from agencies including the U.S. State Department, Drug Enforcement Agency, and National Institute of Drug Abuse; the German Federal Criminal Office, Foreign Office, Federal Ministry of the Interior, and Federal Ministry for Youth, Family Affairs, Women, and Health; the Japanese National Police Agency, National Research Institute of Police Science, Ministry of Justice, Ministry of Health and Welfare, Ministry of Finance; and the United Nations Asia and Far East Institute for the Prevention of Crime and Treatment of Offenders. Because of the sensitive nature of recent deliberations over drug policy, especially the issue of compliance with the American agenda, I have refrained from identifying the individuals involved.

Financial assistance for this project was provided by the American Council of Learned Societies, the American Political Science Association, the Northeast Asia Council of the Association of Asian Studies, the Bradley Institute for Democracy and Public Values, and the Marquette University Graduate School and Committee on Research. I am grateful to these institutions for their support.

Earlier versions of portions of the book were published as "Neither Compromise nor Compliance: International Pressures, Societal Influence, and the Politics of Deception in the International Drug Trade," in David Skidmore and Valerie Hudson, eds., *The Limits of the State Autonomy: Societal Groups and Foreign Policy Formulation* (Boulder, Colo.: Westview Press, 1993), pp. 103–26, copyright © 1993 by WestviewPress, used by permission of WestviewPress; "International Pressures and Domestic Bargains: Regulating Money Laundering in Japan," *Crime, Law and Social Change* 21 (December 1994): 253–66, © 1994 by Kluwer Academic Publishers, used by permission of Kluwer Academic Publishers; "Awaiting the Tsunami? Japan and the International Drug Trade," *Pacific Review* 6 (January 1993), 41–50, adapted with permission of Routledge Journals; and "The United States, Japan, and the International Drug Trade: Troubled Partnership," *Asian Survey* 31 (September 1991): 875–90, © 1991 by the Regents of the University of California, adapted with permission of the University of California Press.

Finally, this book is dedicated to my grandparents, Helen and Jerry Pesner. After too many years, I now have a better sense of the origins of my interest, drive, and stubbornness in working out the puzzles.

H. RICHARD FRIMAN

Milwaukee, Wisconsin

NarcoDiplomacy

1

The Dynamics
of Defection

The status of Germany and Japan in the American war against drugs has changed considerably during the twentieth century. U.S. authorities viewed them as allies in the first campaign against the opium trade during the early 1900s. By 1911, however, U.S. policy makers had identified Germany as the primary obstruction to international control. By the late 1920s and especially during the 1930s, the German threat had faded and attention shifted to Japan as the source of the illicit trade not only in Asia but around the world. Military occupation after Word War II changed the status of both countries again, allowing direct intervention in both countries to bring drug laws into line with American wishes. Both countries have since been touted as allies in antidrug campaigns.

This book explores the dynamics of German and Japanese responses to the American agenda. What I have found is that in both countries both before and after the war these dynamics fail to support the basic premise of American drug control policy as applied by U.S. policy makers. German and Japanese policy responses have not always reflected the capacity of their leaders to deliver on international commitments. More important, where state capacity was at issue U.S. policy makers tended either to misinterpret the specific aspects of capacity at stake or to conceptualize them incorrectly.

Theda Skocpol defines state capacity as the ability of states "to implement official goals, especially over the actual or potential opposition of powerful social groups."[1] States are organizations of differentiated institutions and personnel which hold monopoly power over "binding rulemaking" within a given territory.[2] State capacity is generally shaped by basic factors such as territorial integrity ("stable administrative-military control of a given territory"), financial resources, and "loyal and skilled officials."[3] Scholarship, however, has tended to focus on aspects of state and societal structure.

Structural approaches to state capacity have generally emphasized the nature of state institutions. For example, Stephen Krasner suggests that power fragmentation among state institutions creates international as well as intranational variation in the policy instruments available to state leaders,[4] and in the opportunities for societal groups to influence policy. The state structure of the United States is commonly compared to that of Japan, particularly in the issue areas of international trade and monetary policy.[5] Those who focus on state institutions hold that the greater the institutional fragmentation of the state, the weaker the state capacity.

In contrast, Joel Migdal contends that aspects of societal structure can inhibit state capacity.[6] For example, Migdal notes that patterns of societal organization determine the kind and degree of social control. Specifically, societies distinguished either by highly centralized organization that "concentrates control at the top" (pyramidal) or by social control "spread through a number of fairly autonomous social organizations" (diffused) can seriously challenge state leaders.[7] Moreover, this pattern tends to hold unless societal organization is disrupted by disaster or crisis.[8] In short, the stronger the societal organization and, in turn, social control in a given country or issue area, the weaker the state capacity.[9]

Robert Putnam's work on the dynamics of two-level games suggests that such structural dynamics can lead to involuntary defection from negotiated international agreements. After making international commitments, policy makers may find themselves unable to garner the necessary domestic support for compliance.[10] That is, patterns in the organization, mobilization, and preferences of societal coalitions opposed to such agreements can increase the difficulty of gaining their ratification and subsequent enforcement. If power fragmentation necessitates the involvement of many state agencies in the ratification process, policy makers also may be forced to bargain.[11] Bargaining is not always possible, however, nor is it always successful. Thus, weak state capacity can increase the likelihood of involuntary defection.

The work of Skocpol, Putnam, and others suggests a theoretical framework for a second capacity argument. By virtue of their position within the state apparatus, policy makers must mediate societal, state, and international pressures. When external pressures are great and policy makers know that state capacity is weak, they are likely to turn to deception as a way to reconcile domestic and international considerations.[12]

Deception, according to the *American Heritage Dictionary* (1969), is the "deliberate concealment or misrepresentation of truth with intent to lead another into error or disadvantage" through the use of tactics such as cheating and ambiguity. Policy makers can negotiate ambiguity into formal and informal agreements and arrangements to facilitate action contrary to their intent, or they can cheat on such agreements by violating certain of their provisions.[13] Deception reduces the costs of compliance by misleading others into believing that they have gained more than is actually the case.

Deception, however, has the inherent flaw of untenability. As the deception is discovered, policy makers find the initial pressures renewed and compounded, moreover, by the possibility of retaliation. As Jon Elster notes, however, people tend to "attach less weight to future consumption or utility than to present."[14] The costs of deception are future costs, but policy makers who refuse to join an international agreement face immediate sanctions. When state capacity is weak and international pressure heavy, policy makers are likely to trade potential long-term costs for short-term gains through deception.

For all its history U.S. drug policy has been based on the dynamics of involuntary and voluntary defection, and not without reason. State capacity can affect foreign compliance. Policy makers can lack such preconditions as territorial and financial integrity, or they can find insurmountable obstacles in state and societal structure. Yet if the United States is to alter foreign behavior, policy makers must correctly identify the nature and the sources of the defection taking place. It is clear that in Germany and Japan the United States has not often done so.

Targets on the American Agenda

Among developed countries, the United States has adopted the strictest national control measures against illicit drugs and has played the most active role in international enforcement. Enforcement measures have included criminalization of drug production, trafficking, possession, and use, as well as drug eradication and interdiction and financial interdiction campaigns. Since the early 1900s, the United States has also used various pressure tactics to win international allies and convert adversaries in the war against drugs.

Among the many targets of U.S. pressure, Germany and Japan are unique. They are the only two countries that have historically been targeted as major producers, exporters, and traffickers, have had their domestic drug laws rewritten by U.S. authorities, and have evolved into major commercial and financial centers capable of laundering illicit drug profits and facilitating drug demand. Germany and Japan have had and retain the potential to derail U.S. efforts against the international drug trade.

German and Japanese attitudes toward drug control have been anything but consistent. Prior to 1945, Germany selectively resisted international control attempts, especially with regard to the cocaine trade, and introduced a weak domestic enforcement regime. At that time Japan strengthened already strict domestic enforcement measures and pledged to support international control efforts, while its policy makers tolerated illicit drug transshipment to the Far East and the United States and appeared to be actively promoting the narcotics trade into China. Since the 1940s, the two countries have continued to follow different paths, despite U.S. occupation policies on drug control. Germany has introduced strict domestic control measures while gradually shifting its emphasis from enforcement to prevention. Internationally, German policy makers have responded selectively to the enforcement agenda advocated by the United States. Japan's domestic control measures, in contrast, have been relatively weak compared to those of other developed countries, and its follow-through on broad pledges of international cooperation has often been limited.

Several important works have addressed the dynamics of German and, to a greater extent, Japanese responses to American pressure prior to 1945, but with few exceptions, these have not drawn on German or Japanese source materials.[15] For the period since 1945, there has been little systematic scholarship on relations between the United States and Germany or Japan. This book draws on public and private archival materials from Germany and Japan, U.S. and British archival collections, and secondary sources to trace the causal influence of capacity on the responses of German and Japanese policy makers. To help explain postwar German and Japanese responses the book also relies on interviews of American, German, and Japanese policy makers and law enforcement officials which I conducted from 1989 to 1991. What I am interested in here is the relationship of foreign compliance to state and societal structure, not to cognitive attributes of specific foreign policy makers. Thus, although I sometimes note the actions of key individuals, the individual level of analysis is not systematic or primary. Any research design must balance parsimony against possible gains in explanatory power. It is my hope that the historical case study analysis offered here, focused on prominent arguments about state capacity and the dynamics of defection, will highlight the basic premise of U.S. policy and permit assessment of its strengths and weaknesses.

The British Context

It is important to note at the outset that the policies followed in Germany and Japan during the early 1900s were partially shaped by the British response to U.S. drug control efforts. Scholarship on drug control policy in Great Britain and relations between Britain and the United States on this issue is extensive. I present a brief summary of the initial stages of this relationship here to set the context for German and Japanese policies. Specifically, the British efforts to deflect U.S. as well as domestic pressure on the issue of controlling the international opium trade helped to make Germany and Japan the primary targets of subsequent U.S. drug strategy.

During the 1800s the Americans and the British were both active in the opium trade with China, but Great Britain dominated it. The East India Company and later the British crown held a monopoly over the production and sale of Indian opium and used it to generate revenues for India's colonial government estimated at $50 million annually. When the Chinese government moved to halt the opium trade, strong British opposition resulted in the Opium War of 1839 and the legalization of opium imports under British pressure in 1858. The United States government formally withdrew support for American involvement in the Chinese opium trade during the 1880s, but by the early 1900s the British government had not followed suit.[16]

Concerned that the United States was being shut out of China and facing domestic pressure from missionaries, reform organizations, prohibition groups, and their congressional supporters, American policy makers began to exert pressure on Great Britain. The initial diplomatic overtures in 1905 and 1906 were limited to suggestions for international treaties to prohibit "the sale of intoxicants and opium to all uncivilized races."[17] On October 17, 1906, however, the U.S. ambassador approached the British foreign secretary to propose a joint international commission to investigate the Far East opium trade. The positive British response reflected changes in British domestic politics as well as the international pressures generated by the U.S. initiative.[18]

Domestically, the British general election of 1906 had marked a clear turning point on the opium issue. Antiopium forces such as the Anglo-Oriental Society for the Suppression of the Opium Trade had been working against the trade since the 1870s with limited results. In 1891 the society had failed to gain the requisite support for a parliamentary resolution. The Royal Commission established in 1893 as a compromise between antiopium and India Office supporters in Parliament vindicated the trade in its 1895 report (partly because the commission was mandated to explore its effects on India and England but not China).[19] Capitalizing on public dissatisfaction with Conservative party rule (1895–1906), antiopium forces threw their backing behind Liberal party candidates in exchange for formal pledges of support once in Parliament. The landslide victory by the Liberal party included 250 such candidates (out of a total of 333 seats won). More important, the new cabinet was distinguished by its antiopium views including those reputedly held by the secretary and undersecretary for India. In May 1906 antiopium supporters in Parliament reintroduced a version of the 1891 resolution declaring the Indo-Chinese opium trade "morally indefensible" and requesting that the government "take such steps as may be necessary for bringing it to a speedy close." This time the government supported the resolution, and it passed unanimously.[20]

The government's interpretation of this resolution, however, was different from that of the antiopium forces. Speaking before the House of Commons, Secretary for India John Morely had noted the decline in the relative importance of opium revenue to the Indian government as well as the finding of the U.S. Philippines Commission that the financial gains from opium could not compensate for the "evil" of its use. More important, Morely was unwilling to support opium prohibition and offered only "to restrict Indian production if the Chinese government would suppress poppy cultivation and its use."[21] British policy makers thus placed the burden of ending the trade on China. In September 1906 the Chinese government released an imperial declaration pledging a renewed attack on the opium problem, including new restrictions on opium use and a proposal for a ten-year phased reduction of opium imports. The latter was accepted by the British government in 1907.[22] The resulting Ten Year Agreement called for an annual reduction in Indian opium exports by 10 percent of the average annual export. Following a three-year trial period (1908–1910) to determine the patterns in imports and China's success in curtailing domestic production, the agreement was to be renewed for another seven years.[23]

As Morely had said, the relative importance of opium to India was slowly decreasing. Thus, phasing out the opium trade would reinforce an existing trend, avoiding the dislocations that rapid suppression might cause. Setting the base period at the higher 1901–1905 average, rather than a narrower, more recent base, would minimize the immediate impact on the Indian government and those individuals involved in opium production and trade. Moreover, as frustrated Chinese officials learned in 1910, the British were basing the annual reductions not on the average total Indian exports for 1901–1905 (67,000 chests) but on the exports taken by China during this period (51,000 chests). Relying on ambiguity negotiated into the agreement, British policy makers called for annual reductions of 5,100 chests instead of 6,700 chests per year. By 1910, therefore, the British would still be allowed to export 51,700 chests of opium from India, 700 more chests than the Chinese had imported prior to the Ten Year Agreement.[24] Finally, if China failed to curb consumption and production during the probationary period, a task made more difficult by the availability of Indian opium, Britain was no longer bound by the agreement.

The timing of events in 1906 suggests that the United States had extremely limited influence in gaining British compliance with the idea of an international investigative commission. As Arnold Taylor notes, the U.S. proposals of October 1906 would "most likely have been ignored or rejected" if it were not for the steps taken by China to impose control at home and the "anti-opium agitation in Great Britain."[25] Although British policy makers agreed to the U.S. proposals, to divert attention from India they added the conditions that China's domestic opium production be considered and that British participation hinge on the participation of other major powers. By the time the commission actually met the Ten Year Agreement was in place and domestic critics largely mollified, and British officials took steps that effectively removed the Indo-Chinese opium trade from the commission's agenda.

Efforts by the United States to expand the number of conference participants and the death of China's empress dowager delayed the first meeting of the Shanghai Opium Commission until February 1909.[26] Taking advantage of the delay and the upcoming British decision necessary to extend the Ten Year Agreement in 1910, the Foreign Office instructed Sir John Jordan, Britain's minister in China, to obtain an "expression of satisfaction" from the Chinese Foreign Ministry on the agreement. Unsurprisingly, Jordan's success raised concerns in the United States that American efforts to build an international consensus on a more restrictive solution to the opium problem would be wasted. Responding to urgent American entreaties, the British Foreign Office assured U.S. officials that China's satisfaction did not preclude discussion of the Indo-Chinese opium trade.[27]

Despite appearances, the British were not bowing to American concerns. Immediately before the commission met, the British delegation had sent an emissary to the viceroy of Nanking with a different message. Citing the statement of satisfaction from the Chinese Foreign Ministry, the emissary declared that the British intended to prevent discussion of the Ten Year Agreement at the Shanghai Commission.[28] Indeed, once the commission hearings began, resolutions introduced by the U.S. delegation affecting the Indo-Chinese opium trade were either severely modified or simply rejected by the British delegation. In addition, citing the Chinese expression of satisfaction, the British delegation refused to allow the commission to discuss the Ten Year Agreement.[29] Since the United States needed British cooperation to salvage the credibility of this first international conference on the drug trade, the American delegation chose not to reveal the British deception. As a result, the United States ended up with a Shanghai Commission whose nonbinding resolutions sanctioned the British program of gradual suppression.

After the experience at Shanghai, American policy makers began to work toward convening an international conference capable of producing a binding agreement on controlling the opium trade. Although British policy makers received the initial U.S. proposal for such a conference in September 1909 and domestic pressure calling for British participation emerged in March 1910, formal British acceptance did not come until September 1910. Again, however, rather than comply with the American proposals or work toward a simple compromise, British policy makers turned to deception.

The U.S. proposal contained several provisions that British policy makers found objectionable. During the Shanghai Commission the British had maintained that since different countries faced different drug situations, uniform regulations and controls as well as foreign review of existing drug treaties made little sense. In addition, such steps would infringe on the phased reduction of the Indo-Chinese opium trade. Now, the United States proposed to put these very points on the agenda of the new conference. Unsurprisingly, the initial communications among the British Foreign Office, the India Office, the Colonial Office, the Board of Trade, and the colonial government in India revealed strong opposition to the American proposals.[30] The British secretary of state of foreign affairs, Sir Edward Grey, however, insisted that it was better to have a deciding voice within an international conference than to "stand out alone and obstruct the convening of the proposed conference." He therefore called for an interdepartmental meeting to discuss the British response to the United States.[31]

On June 8, 1910, U.S. Ambassador Whitelaw Reid notified Grey that the U.S. proposal had won preliminary acceptance from six countries, including Germany, Japan, and the Netherlands, and he urged the British to follow suit. Two days later the Foreign Office passed on a copy of the note to the other executive departments and began to make arrangements for the interdepartmental meeting Grey had requested.[32] The drafting and approval of the formal reply to the United States delayed the British response until September.[33] Meanwhile, the British forestalled further pressure from the United States by intimating that a reply was forthcoming and that Britain was interested in addressing problems of morphine and cocaine as well.[34]

On September 17 Grey finally notified Reid of the formal British position on the Hague Conference. Grey specifically noted that the British government would be "ready . . . if satisfactory assurances can be given to them on certain points . . . to take part at a proper time in a conference . . . [to give] effect . . . [to the] resolutions of the Shanghai Commission." Britain must be assured, first, that all conference participants are willing to discuss fully the "restricting of manufacture, sale, and distribution" of morphine and cocaine as well as opium. Second, participants must collect data on the domestic production and trade patterns in these drugs and prepare preliminary studies. Third, the Ten Year Agreement and other existing treaties between Great Britain and China "should be excluded from consideration by the conference." Fourth, the British were not prepared to discuss the American proposals for allowing search of naval vessels, restricting the use of flags by naval vessels, or establishing an international body to implement agreements reached at the conference.[35] On October 14 Reid conveyed the U.S. government's acceptance of the British conditions.

Taylor and S. D. Stein maintain that the British insistence on the inclusion of morphine and cocaine was a deception. Taylor sees it as a delaying tactic, aimed at postponing the Hague conference until the negotiations between China and Great Britain over the Ten Year Agreement could be resolved. Stein, in contrast, believes that the primary motivation was to draw international attention away from the British colonies and the opium trade. More important, the Germans and Japanese, who had supported the United States on the Shanghai Commission, would be less likely either to rush into an international conference or, once the conference began, to align with the United States, for both were involved in morphine and cocaine production and trade.[36]

In fact, British policy makers did use deception but not in this manner or for these reasons. The conference would not jeopardize British negotiations with China, for the United States had already agreed to remove the Ten Year Agreement and all British treaties with China from the conference agenda. Nor is there any suggestion in the Foreign Office files that British policy makers were concerned that the pending Hague Conference would affect these negotiations. Broadening the focus of the conference, moreover, was likely to draw more rather than less attention to Great Britain, for Britain and Germany were the two largest exporters of morphine. In addition, by early 1910 British policy makers were being pressured by local authorities in the crown colonies to do something about the morphine and cocaine trade and growing problems of addiction. The British feared that unilateral action to restrict the morphine trade would merely open the foreign market to competitors such as Germany and, to a lesser degree, Japan.[37]

The crux of the deception was the demand for "satisfactory assurances . . . on certain points" before Britain would participate in the conference.[38] British policy makers were the only ones who could determine if the assurances were satisfactory. Therefore, when the United States agreed to this demand, it placed Britain in control of determining when the Hague Conference would meet. In essence, it gave Britain the deciding voice Grey had desired. The British were primarily interested in restricting German drug exports. Now they could delay the conference until the Germans complied with the British conditions. Ideally, the United States would weigh in against the Germans as well.

This hope was soon realized. In October 1910 Reid informed Grey that the resolutions adopted by the Shanghai Commission in 1909 were evidence that the British conditions on morphine and cocaine had already been "satisfactorily" met. Resolution 5 had called on the delegates to urge drastic measures to deal with the morphine trade. The U.S. opinion was that this resolution, together with the tenor of informal discussions on cocaine during the commission meetings, implied that governments were willing to take drastic steps against cocaine as well.[39] In reply, Grey simply restated the position to which the United States had earlier agreed, that Great Britain's participation in the Hague Conference was conditional, and he asked what "steps have been taken to obtain the assurances desired from the other Powers" that these conditions had been met.[40] Less than two weeks later, Reid informed Grey that the Netherlands government as host to the conference had notified the United States that it was making the British conditions known to the other invited countries. In December 1910 Reid notified Grey that other countries had been informed of the British position.[41]

From December 1910 until October 1911, the United States, the Dutch, the Germans, the Japanese, the Portuguese, the French, and the British attempted to sort out the extent to which other countries had met the British conditions.[42] Frustrated with the delay, American policy makers renewed diplomatic pressure on the British in April, this time by announcing the names of the U.S. delegates to the Hague Conference. Grey responded the following month by noting correspondence from the Netherlands indicating that Germany, Portugal, and Japan, were unable to meet all the conditions prior to the conference. Grey informed Reid that since these countries were going to be absent, it made sense to delay the conference again.[43]

American policy makers then put pressure on Germany, Portugal, and Japan to comply with the British conditions and put pressure on Great Britain to agree that its conditions had been met. On July 29 the German government informed the British government that in response to the inquiries of the United States, Germany agreed "in principle" to the British conditions, although domestic legislation would not permit it to "enter for the present into binding international agreements" on the sale of morphine and cocaine.[44] On August 3 Reid informed Grey that the United States had acquired pledges from France, Germany, and Japan that the British conditions would be met by October 1 and that "Portugal would make every effort to do so."[45] Following efforts to obtain final assurances that the Germans would indeed have the necessary information on the morphine and cocaine trade collected prior to the conference, Grey notified Reid on September 6 that the British government was ready to participate in the Hague Conference as soon as Germany, Japan, Portugal, and France informed the Netherlands government that they were ready.[46] On October 2, having the necessary assurances, the Netherlands government proposed December 1, 1911, as the starting date for the conference. On October 21, the conditions it had first laid out over a year before finally being met, the British government agreed.[47]

In 1909, it is clear, British policy makers misled the United States about the scope and future influence of the Shanghai Opium Commission until it was too late. Ambiguity in the British pledge to participate in the Hague Conference also allowed British policy makers to mislead the United States about the onset, scope, and leadership of the conference. More important from the standpoint of this book, British efforts to drive a wedge between the United States and Germany and Japan over the issue of international drug control were successful. After largely supporting the U.S position in Shanghai, German and Japanese policy makers found themselves faced with an expanding American drug control agenda in the events leading up to Hague Conference.

2

Germany and the
Cocaine Connection

By 1911 German prominence in the international cocaine trade and in the trade of manufactured narcotics such as heroin and morphine had won it the attention of the United States. As we have seen, British machinations over the Hague conference stimulated U.S. pressure for German compliance with the American agenda. This chapter explores German drug control policy, especially regarding cocaine, during the period from 1909 to 1934—that is, from the Shanghai Opium Commission to Germany's withdrawal from the League of Nations. This broader analysis reveals the selective impact of elements of state capacity and raises questions about the actual effects of U.S. drug control strategy on German policy makers.

Transition and Capacity

The "general underpinnings of state capacity" noted by Theda Skocpol were fairly weak in Germany during the early 1900s.[1] After World War I, Germany lost territorial control as well as financial resources. The provisions of the Versailles Treaty and disputes with France left portions of German territory under either foreign control or weak central administration. The Saar region, for example, was under the administration of the League of Nations but its coal mines were under French control. The Rhineland was demilitarized with Allied occupation of the "left bank and bridgeheads."[2] French disputes with Germany over compliance with treaty regulations brought about the temporary occupations of 1920 (Frankfurt, Darmstadt, Homberg, Hanau), 1921 (Dusseldorf, Duisberg, and Rohrort), and 1923 (Ruhr district).[3] These areas, we shall see, contained the primary locations for the German pharmaceutical industry.

Financially, the national debt, reparations, and rampant inflation undermined the resources of the state during the 1920s. By 1922 the German national debt stood at an estimated $58.6 billion, and reparations agreed to under the London Payments Plan amounted to $28.3 billion. Compliance with the plan, Eberhard Kolb estimated, would "require annual payments of 2,000 million gold marks plus 26 percent of the value of [Germany's] exports." By August 1923 inflation had also eroded the mark's value to an exchange rate of one million marks to one dollar.[4] In effect, state leaders appear to have lacked key aspects of state power.

German state structure during the 1920s was in transition from forty-seven years of constitutional monarchy dominated by Prussia to a parliamentary republic. The Weimar constitution of 1919 fragmented authority primarily between the executive and legislative branches and between the national (*Reich*) and state (*Länder*) governments. For example, the president was directly elected and empowered to appoint a chancellor and cabinet ministers and to dissolve the lower house (the Reichstag) for new elections but also needed the cooperation of the Reichstag and its vote of confidence to govern.[5]

Neither was consistently forthcoming. The extensive scholarship on Weimar stresses factors that exacerbated the republic's structural weaknesses, including the proliferation of political parties and power struggles within them, and challenges from the Right as well as the Left played out in the Reichstag and in the streets.[6] As a result, from 1919 to 1925 alone, the Weimar Republic experienced twelve different national governments, only two lasting more than one year, and nine different chancellors.[7] The Weimar constitution increased the Reich's authority relative to that held by the Länder governments through steps including tax, military, and administrative reform as well as a reduced legislative role for the upper house (Reichsrat).[8] Yet, the transition from states' rights to Reich control, especially the consolidation and disarmament of Länder military and paramilitary forces, proved difficult.[9]

The fragmentation also appears to have affected drug control.[10] Prior to the 1920s, the Foreign Office responded to foreign demands concerning regulation of the cocaine trade by turning to the Ministry of the Interior. Interior, however, although in large part able to bypass input from the Ministries of Economics and Finance, faced potential opposition from both houses of the parliament over any regulatory steps that would impinge on the authority of state governments. Beginning in 1921, the Reich Office of Health emerged as the primary agency charged with implementing drug legislation.[11] Despite this shift, Foreign Office requests were still transmitted to the Office of Health through the Interior Ministry. Moreover, the Office of Health was required to consult with each Länder hosting narcotics producers or traders on the issuing of import and export licenses and oversight and regulation of narcotics manufacture.

Prior to 1934, Länder authority to issue licenses independently gradually eroded so that first consultation with the Office of Health was required and then approval. These shifts were codified in the Law Relating to the Traffic in Narcotics Drugs—Opium Act (Gesetz über den Vehrkehr mit Betäubungsmitteln—Opiumgesetz) of 1929 and subsequent amendments in 1930. In 1934 an additional amendment completed the shift in the roles of the Länder and national authorities, with the Health Office assuming authority to issue licenses in consultation with the Länder.[12] Nevertheless, enforcement of regulations remained primarily the province of Länder officials, including police forces focused more on political challenges to the Länder and, until its collapse, the Weimar regime than on illicit narcotic transactions.[13]

The structure of the German pharmaceutical industry, especially in the production of cocaine, illustrates a pattern of limited pyramidal organization. The international cocaine trade in large part originated in Germany. For example, several histories of the drug posit that cocaine was first extracted from Latin American coca by German-Austrian scientists.[14] More important, in 1862 the company E. Merck, located in Darmstadt, began the first commercial production and distribution of the drug.[15]

In addition to Merck, eleven other firms were engaged in cocaine production and export, six located along the Rhine within roughly a fifty-mile radius of Frankfurt. These firms included C. F. Böhringer und Söhne (Mannheim-Wildhof), C. H. Böhringer Sohn (Nieder— Ingelheim), J. D. Riedel (Berlin), Vereinigte Chinin-Fabriken Zimmer und Co. (Frankfurt am Main), Chemische Werke vorm Dr. H. Byk (Berlin-Charlottenberg), Chemische Fabrik Güstrow (Güstrow), Joh. Diedr. Bieber (Hamburg), Chemische Fabrik auf Aktien (Berlin), Gehe und Co. (Dresden), F. Hoffmann La Roche und Co. (Grensach), and Knoll und Co. (Ludwigshafen). Reidel, Merck, the Böhringer companies, and Zimmer were also primary producers of morphine.[16] Merck was the largest through the early 1900s, with over two thousand workers by 1913.[17] By 1910 Merck was also the world's single largest source of cocaine, producing fifty-three hundred kilograms annually and exporting 76 percent of its output (Tables 1 and 2). Germany as a

Table 1. German drug production (kgs), 1906–1931 (selected years)

	Morphine	Heroin	Cocaine
1906	2,400	—	2,600
1907	1,600	—	2,700
1908	1,100	—	4,100
1909	1,600	—	3,500
1910	1,800	—	5,300
1913	12,000	n.a.	9,000
1921	8,600	1,140	6,302
1925	14,000	1,100	3,378
1926	20,700	1,800	2,400
1927	12,800	750	2,500
1928	19,120	1,300	3,590
1929	24,000	n.a.	2,100
1930	11,000	n.a.	1,100
1931	5,000	n.a.	1,000

Sources: Merck Archive (Firmenarchiv Merck), file Opium, Opium Konferenz, "Verkauf von E. Merck, Darmstadt," 1911; Albert Wissler, Die Opiumfrage: Eine Studie zur weltwirtschaftlichen und weltpolitischen Lage der Gegenwart (Kiel: Gustav Fischer, 1931), pp. 136–37; Political Archive, Foreign Office, Division Law I/II, file Opium Reports from Brietfeld, "Material Regarding the Opium Question," Report prepared by the Fachgruppe Opium und Cocain, 1933.
Note: Figures for 1906–10 are for E. Merck only.

Table 2. German drug exports (kgs), 1906–1931 (selected years)

	Morphine	Heroin	Cocaine
1906	1,300	—	2,100
1907	1,000	—	2,000
1908	800	—	3,000
1909	900	—	2,800
1910	800	—	4,000
1913	n.a.	n.a.	n.a.
1921	2,257	907	5,291
1925	4,642	1,498	3,132
1926	4,523	1,587	2,190
1927	2,701	807	2,024
1928	3,031	1,292	1,864
1929	2,900	n.a.	1,400
1930	1,000	n.a.	1,000
1931	400	n.a.	700

Source: See Table 1.
Note: Figures for 1906–10 are for E. Merck only.

whole was producing an estimated nine thousand kilograms annually by 1913.[18]

The German cocaine industry was weakly organized but held control over vital information on drug production and trade which the government lacked. In 1906 five major producers—Merck, Gehe, C. F. Böhringer und Söhne, and Riedel—established the Verein zur Wahrung der Interessen der Chemischen Industrie Deutschland (VCI), the Association to Safeguard the Interests of the German Chemical Industry, headed by Merck, to protect the members' interests from foreign competitors and to counterbalance the larger German chemical firms that would establish IG Farben in 1925.[19] As Germany began to participate in United States–led international efforts to restrict and regulate the cocaine trade, the Interior Ministry turned to the association for information requested by the United States, and at the same time, the association tried to derail regulation. By the early 1920s the Weimar government was seeking the association's compliance while evidence of German participation in the illicit cocaine trade grew.[20]

Beyond the American Premise

These elements of weak state capacity reinforce the prominent assessment of the potential difficulties German policy makers faced in trying to comply with the American agenda. Nevertheless, as the following analysis reveals, such weaknesses had selective impact, as did U.S. pressure on the decisions and actions of German policy makers. From 1909 to 1910 the German government, having relatively limited interest in the opium trade, had backed the United States at Shanghai and in the initial proposals for a second conference on the international drug trade.[21] When Britain drew in morphine and especially cocaine, however, the agenda for the Hague Conference clearly altered Germany's stake in the deliberations. U.S. State Department records and prominent scholarship point to the influence of large chemical manufacturing interests to explain the German government's deception and the resulting delays in the onset and conclusion of the conference.[22] According to this view, societal pressures kept Germany from signing the Hague Convention until it was forced to do so under article 295 of the Versailles Treaty in 1919. Even then, it did not ratify the convention until 1921, under foreign pressure. In fact, however, German actions reflected a convergence of domestic and international concerns.

Before Britain proposed to extend the Hague agenda beyond opium, the German government had already begun to explore domestic problems with morphine and cocaine abuse. Responding to a March 1910 Reichstag resolution for stronger control measures, the Health and Interior Ministries completed a study in June which revealed that the growing problem was due more to limited regulation of the wholesale distribution of such drugs than to imports or violations of existing regulations.[23] In January 1911 VCI rejected the study's proposal for limiting the handling of such drugs to pharmacists, however, on the grounds that such measures would disrupt the wholesale trade and the pharmaceutical industry without solving the problem.[24]

Meanwhile, in mid-November 1910, the Interior Ministry had notified Merck of the proposed Hague Conference. The VCI response the following week expressed support for action against the drug problem and willingness to meet on the issue but noted that the proposed agenda was more likely to "hurt legitimate trade and commerce."[25]

Despite the industry's apparent willingness to discuss the issue by late 1910, the interior minister delayed convening a meeting between industry representatives and government officials until June 1911.[26] More important, at the meeting cocaine was hardly mentioned.

The participants vaguely noted that the British conditions reflected fears of a shift from opium to other drugs, which the German ambassador to London had noted in earlier discussion with the German chancellor.[27] In contrast, industry and government representatives alike focused on morphine and the potential damage nonparticipants in the conference might inflict on the legitimate trade.[28] In the view C. F. Böhringer representatives later expressed to Merck, the British motivation had more to do with "crass monetary interests" than humanitarian concerns. The Böhringer representatives also railed against the hypocrisy of aforementioned Reichstag demands for control of morphine and cocaine: "These are the same people who drink brandy and schnapps [the effects of which are] 1000 times more disastrous than morphine or cocaine use."[29]

Further evidence suggests that it was not undue industry influence that drove the German government delay.[30] During the summer of 1911, U.S. embassy officials in Berlin noted indications from the German Foreign Office that the German government was taking steps, albeit with some reservations, to comply with the British conditions.[31] Yet German archive materials reveal that the Interior Ministry did not begin to request data on the cocaine and morphine industries until October 1911, after three deadlines for the beginning of the Hague Convention had already passed.[32] Industry compliance would be necessary here, for as the State Department noted in early 1911, "No statistics or reliable estimates of production and consumption of morphine and cocaine in Germany can be given, as no data are available for that purpose."[33] The industry response to the October request was mixed: Merck wanted partial compliance, but other members of VCI such as C. H. Böhringer wanted to withhold all information from the German government. Following Merck's lead, VCI submitted data to the government in November but omitted recent trends and demanded that the data be used only for vague international comparisons.[34]

The Hague deliberations during 1911–1912 took only limited steps toward restricting the international drug trade. For example, signato-

ries were required only to "use their best efforts" to control manufacture, distribution, sale, and export of cocaine and morphine.[35] The
weakness of these regulations reflected opposition by the German
delegation to more extensive measures and the willingness of the
United States and Britain to back down from a confrontation with the
Germans, jeopardizing both the conference and broader relations. For
example, British Foreign Office files noted that the Germans were opposed to treaty language implying uniform domestic control measures because they were likely to "encroach upon state [Länder]
autonomy."[36] The resulting compromise included changing language
from "will limit" or "will require" to "will use their best endeavors"
to achieve core treaty provisions.[37]

A greater weakness of the Hague Convention emerged on the question of ratification. German and French reluctance to abide by restrictions while nonsignatories to the convention were unhindered,
and therefore likely to gain at the expense of signatories, prompted
provisions for a special protocol to be signed by countries that had not
participated in the conference. After all countries had signed either
the protocol or the convention, a new conference would be held to discuss ratification.[38] U.S. efforts to facilitate this process led to additional Hague conferences in 1913 and 1914 and partial ratification and
implementation of the convention by sixteen signatories in 1915.
Germany, however, although it had signed the convention in 1913, refused to begin ratification proceedings because Turkey, Austria-
Hungary, Serbia, and other nations continued to withhold their
signatures.[39]

According to the prominent view, Germany was forced to override
its pharmaceutical industries when Britain and the United States required ratification of the Hague Convention from those countries
signing the Versailles Treaty.[40] But it is important to recognize that
the situation, both international and domestic, had changed. Internationally, Germany's primary objection to ratification had ceased to
exist, for the Versailles Treaty had also forced Turkey, Austria, Hungary, and Serbia (as part of the new Yugoslavia) to sign the Hague
Convention and take steps to ratify it. Domestically, the pharmaceutical industry had already come under increased regulation during
the war both to maintain wartime stocks (in the face of trade block-
ades) and to combat a growing problem with drug abuse.[41] For exam-

ple, the Regulation of Trade in Opium and other Narcotics of March 22, 1917, limited access to drug supplies, which were to be distributed through the War Ministry's Health Department. The War Ministry, for its part, relied primarily on the Handellsgesellschaft Deutscher Apotheker (German Pharmacists Trading Corporation) for disbursement of stockpiles. Regulations in November and December 1918 placed limits on the release of war stockpiles and introduced restrictions on allowable drug transactions and penalties (including fines and up to six months' imprisonment) for their violation.[42]

When the war ended, deliberations began in Germany over how to respond to domestic problems while implementing the dictates of Versailles. Despite movement toward greater regulation of cocaine, the pharmaceutical industry played no great part. The Health Office and Interior Ministry played the leadership role in drafting the new provisions in consultation primarily with the Foreign Office, Ministry of Economics, and the Länder governments.[43]

Industry concerns over new regulations and what steps would be taken to implement the Hague Convention began to surface in mid-1920, but government officials appear to have continued to discourage industry participation. For example, in April the Foreign Office suggested to the secretary of the interior (with copies to the Ministries of Economics, Finance, and Post and to the Prussian Ministry for Trade and Industry) that the Hague agreement being put in place by Versailles should not be published, to avoid "evoking a disturbance."[44] In May C. H. Böhringer Sohn asked both the Health Office and the Interior Ministry which meetings representatives aside from Merck would be allowed to attend and was informed that it "was too early to tell."[45] Moreover, the primary meeting held with industry representatives to discuss these steps was not scheduled until December 6, 1920, after the proposed enabling legislation had already been drafted.[46] Three days later, Interior submitted the enabling legislation to the Reichstag, which passed the measures without objection. The new regulations licensing and regulating export and import of narcotics were in place by late February 1921.[47]

The German commitment to the dictates of the Hague Convention during the 1920s appears to have reflected a sense of the domestic drug situation as well as the potential ramifications of noncompliance. With the passage of implementing legislation, attention shifted by mid-1921 to the efforts of German firms (as well as the respective Länder governments lobbying on their behalf) to gain authorization from the Interior Ministry to engage in the drug trade.[48] To facilitate compliance with the dictates of the treaty, the Interior Ministry and the Office of Health had begun to limit the number of authorized producers and traders.[49] Länder governments protested to Interior that these restrictions illustrated a Health Office bias against German firms. The Health Office replied emphatically it was far better to comply with the treaty than to permit unrestricted production and trade, which might lead to domestic and foreign backlash and, in turn, the total prohibition of cocaine production in Germany.[50]

Compliance, by contrast, offered the government a means to protect the German industry's interests relative to foreign producers as well as to shape the broader international debate over the nature and extent of control efforts.[51] These considerations were reflected in the efforts of the Weimar government to gain German representation on the Opium Commission of the League of Nations, to comply with league and foreign government requests for information on aspects of drug production, trade, and control, and to participate in a new round of international negotiations over drug control (the Geneva Conferences).[52]

With the beginning of the Geneva deliberations in 1923, German representatives kept a low profile with regard to the American agenda, extending their support and limiting their opposition where appropriate.[53] For example, in 1923 German negotiators supported in principle U.S. proposals to limit the legitimate uses of narcotics to medical and scientific purposes as well as to decrease domestic drug production to a level commensurate with such use. This support was initially well received by the head of the U.S. delegation, Representative Stephen G. Porter (Republican of Pennsylvania), the chairman of the House Foreign Relations Committee, despite the German proviso that production decreases would have to be carried out by all producing countries and despite German opposition to introducing restrictions on codeine. More important, the United States appears to have accepted the pragmatic German support for a less-restrictive British proposal on the question of Indian opium. Germany gave its support out of reluctance to alienate the British, who were urging severe constraints on the cocaine trade, and because Germany needed British support on the codeine question.[54]

During the second conference in Geneva (1925), the German delegation moved toward greater international control while protecting the interests of the German pharmaceutical industry and trying to avoid entanglement in disputes between the United States and Great Britain. For example, the head of the German delegation, Dr. O. Anselmino, recommended that as in 1923 Germany should "choose the mildest form of disinterested abstention" on regulating the production and trade in prepared (for smoking) opium but should take a strong position with other countries against full-scale suppression of heroin and the reclassification of codeine as a narcotic.[55]

With the Geneva Conference moving toward the regulation of narcotics production as well as greater restriction of trade, German officials did what they could to safeguard German interests by attempting to place a representative on the new Central Board being proposed by the conference for data collection and monitoring.[56] Moreover, the delegation kept to the periphery at the negotiations while selectively supporting the U.S. delegation. It withheld support for the complete ban on heroin which the United States was advocating, however, and for other proposals that "went too far" and lacked the support of other delegations.[57]

Despite some opposition from the pharmeceutical industry, moreover, the German government also signed and took steps to ratify the Geneva Convention. The resultant German Opium Act of 1929 introduced restrictions on the production and trade in narcotics (including morphine, heroin, and following the U.S. designation, cocaine) as well as enforcement provisions consisting of fines and imprisonment for up to three years.[58] Industry opposition to the licensing and monitoring provisions for import and export trade brought about by ratification reflected several concerns. The most prominent were that Germany had acted before other countries, such as Switzerland, had signed the convention and that British morphine based on cheap Indian opium was posing a growing competitive threat. Officials from the Health Office and the Interior Ministry noted ongoing efforts to place a German representative on the Central Board of the League of Nations as a means of safeguarding industry interests and rejected industry demands to link ratification to the morphine issue. Government justifications suggest continued concern about the ramifications of noncompliance. As ministry officials noted, withholding ratification or action against morphine would lead to British retaliation and would "discredit Germany's position in the Opium Question and cause a boycott of German goods."[59]

Although Germany participated in international control efforts, however, recurrent questions surfaced during the 1920s concerning its role in the illicit international drug trade. By early 1923 the United States and Great Britain began to fear that Germany was becoming a major source of illicit trafficking.[60] This time, U.S. State Department officials attributed the German duality primarily to an erosion of state capacity—the "general weakening of political authority" of the Weimar government—rather than to the duplicity with which the German government had been charged a decade before.[61] It is possible that this conclusion was based on the bilateral political considerations of U.S. officials. For example, German authorities had been highly cooperative in meeting American requests for data on drug trafficking and control efforts, and they were introducing new control measures through amendments to the Opium Law and executive ordinances during the 1920s.[62] Nevertheless, the American assessment was an oversimplification at best.

During 1923 illegal shipments of German narcotics were seized by authorities in China, Turkey, and the United States.[63] Although the products seized bore the labels of leading German companies such as Merck and C. H. Böhringer, how complicit these companies were in the illicit transactions was not entirely clear. In general, industry support for control had been mixed. Those firms denied authorization to engage in the drug trade were opposed, of course, and the major German drug producers were only partially supportive of the new restrictions. In early 1923, for example, Merck officials supported proposals for new German regulations requiring that export authorization be linked to formal permission to import by the receiving country, but Merck opposed such regulations in those cases where the receiving country was not a Hague signatory (and thus did not require such certification).[64] In contrast, by mid-1923 top Merck officials were calling for new regulations to restrict transshipment of narcotics (especially opium) through German ports.[65]

Government investigations of foreign allegations of illicit drug trafficking also raise questions about the complicity of German companies and the Weimar government. In April, for example, British officials revealed their discovery of a plan by U.S. and U.K. citizens to purchase drugs illicitly from Merck and C. H. Böhringer Sohn with money routed through the American Express office in Hamburg. The drugs would be exported to Basel, Switzerland, transshipped to Hamburg, and then sent on Japanese freighters to Shanghai, China.[66] By the end of the year, British officials were also accusing firms such as MacDonald and Company (a Dutch firm operating out of Freiburg-Baden) and C. H. Böhringer of colluding with Japanese companies to smuggle drugs into China.[67]

Once these allegations were brought to the attention of the German government, officials of the Interior Ministry and the Health Office pledged to investigate, and they turned to the respective Länder authorities for answers. So was set a common pattern: on receiving a foreign protest, the Foreign Office would transfer the information to the Interior Ministry, which would turn the case over to the Health Office. The Health Office would turn to the Länder containing either the port facilities or the drug company in question.[68] Through 1923 such inquiries recurrently found that German drugs had been legally sold in Germany or legally exported to Japan, Turkey, or some other destination but then had been illegally transshipped to other destinations. German companies, the Interior Ministry insisted, had followed the Hague regulations where applicable, and Germany was not responsible for transshipment.[69]

The MacDonald and Böhringer cases, however, led to German criminal investigations. Inquiries revealed that MacDonald had purchased narcotics from a Swiss company (Hoffmann La Roche in Basel) through Antwerp and had transshipped the products under contract with a British company (Wink and Company) through Hamburg to a Japanese company (Miyagawa and Company), which had in turn transshipped the drugs into China.[70] The Health Office investigation focused on how the narcotics were imported into Germany and reexported to Japan. Health officials found no clear violation of German law. Switzerland was not a signatory of the Hague treaty nor were the goods in question produced by a German firm.[71] The key question of criminality hinged on the issue of transshipment through

Hamburg. Although the Health Office and Hamburg authorities bemoaned it as an interpretation contrary to the spirit of the legislation that implemented the Hague Convention in 1921, a court ruling in November declared that since Hamburg was a free port, the transshipment did not violate German drug laws.[72] In 1924 German authorities tightened the monitoring of transshipments by providing that they would be "permitted only in bond and when accompanied by customs certification."[73]

In the Böhringer case Weimar officials faced the first strong challenge to the government's drug control efforts.[74] In early December 1923 the British government notified the German Foreign Office that the recent arrest of a Japanese drug trafficker named Miyagawa in London had produced information directly implicating the company C. H. Böhringer Sohn in the illicit drug trade into China. The British demanded that the German government suspend Böhringer's authorization to trade licit drugs and declared that until such action was taken, imports from Böhringer would not be allowed into Britain.[75] British authorities had evidence of large-scale purchases of heroin from Böhringer as well as papers taken from Miyagawa noting private codes and plans for additional transactions. Moreover, when seized in Hong Kong, the heroin was found packed in with other goods, and the bills of lading simply labeled the shipment "chemicals."[76] German authorities saw nothing sinister in mislabeling, a practice followed by smugglers and legitimate trading companies alike, as Health Officials noted. Legitimate traders felt that false labeling and packaging would "help to protect against thievery and arbitrary seizure."[77]

The initial Health Office investigations focused on a trading house in Bremen, Export-Gesellschaft, which had placed orders with Böhringer including a single order for five hundred kilograms of diacetylmorphine (heroin).[78] By May the Health Office had decided that Export-Gesellschaft would be prosecuted for illicit transactions and that Böhringer, or at least a corrupt employee at the company, was complicit in supplying the Miyagawa company with shipments of narcotics.[79] The extent of Böhringer's complicity and the nature of the Weimar government's response, however, rapidly became points of dispute.

The British in August 1924 chastised the German government for attempting to shift blame to the export company and a single employee of Böhringer and demanded the suspension of the firm's trading privileges. In response the German Foreign Office notified the Ministry of the Interior, "It is politically necessary" to apologize to the British for the Böhringer actions and "to leave no doubt" that the company, rather than a single employee, was at fault. The Foreign Office recognized that rescinding Böhringer's trade authorization would entail domestic political costs. It would be necessary to take legal action against the firm to prove clear guilt, otherwise the Länder authorities in Hesse and Hamburg would be unlikely to support a suspension of authorization.[80] The Foreign Office informed the British that the German government would be looking further into the case.[81]

In subsequent meetings, officials from both the Health Office and the Interior Ministry cited their past experience with Böhringer as cause for rejecting the British charge that it was an active participant in the illicit trade. Nevertheless, because of persistent questions concerning Germany's support for the Hague convention and to guard the reputation of the German chemical industry, the German government decided to send the head of the Health Office, Dr. Anselmino, to conduct a personal investigation at Böhringer.[82] Anselmino, like the Hamburg police and the government of Hesse, concluded that, despite instances of suspicious transactions in the Miyagawa case, "no offenses against German laws and ordinances" had taken place.[83]

During interministerial deliberations on Anselmino's report, Foreign Office representatives pressed for severe actions against Böhringer to forestall a more extensive international reaction. Interior Ministry and Health officials raised the difficulty of gaining Länder support for such steps in the absence of criminal acts. Ministerial officials were receiving memos from Böhringer claiming a British plot and unfair British action against the German chemical industry, but these apparently had limited influence on the debate.[84] Caught in a dilemma, ministry officials agreed to submit their findings to the Länder government and to hold additional meetings in October following Anselmino's return from the current session of the League of Nations Opium Commission.[85] The subsequent decision on the Böhringer case by the Hamburg Senate Commission for Foreign Affairs rejected the severe steps recommended by the Foreign Office, noting the company's compliance with regulations in place at the time and the absence of protest from the Japanese government concerning the case. As an explicit concession to the British, the Hamburg government announced that it had warned Böhringer that "the slightest slip" in future compliance with German regulations would bring revocation of export authorization.[86]

The reluctance of Länder officials to support action against Böhringer swayed the interministerial debate over how to respond to the British allegations. The Foreign Office notified the British government of its findings in November 1924.[87] As in the MacDonald case, the government maintained that Böhringer's actions of late 1923 did not violate German drug regulations "in place at the time" of the transaction. Böhringer had assumed that Miyagawa would be importing the drugs into Japan and had applied to the Japanese government for import permission. Moreover, officials noted the conclusion of the Hesse government that "there was nothing in the circumstances to make Böhringer conclude that something suspicious was going on."[88] Rejecting these arguments, the British government informed the German government in early 1925 of its intent to retain the import ban against Böhringer.[89] Over the next three years, the German government worked in bilateral discussions and through the League of Nations to have the British ban lifted.[90] Then Böhringer and German drug control once again won the international spotlight with the Naarden case.

Germany had become increasingly concerned about transshipment as declining German exports to East Asia were apparently being offset by rising exports to countries such as Switzerland. For example, Health officials discovered in May that during the first four months of 1925, Germany had exported 1,511 kilograms of morphine, 554 kilograms of heroin, and 516 kilograms of cocaine to Switzerland. The Health Office estimated that these exports "would cover Switzerland's morphine and cocaine needs for 10 years and diacetylmorphine [heroin] needs for 150 years."[91]

Although Switzerland had finally ratified the Hague Convention in 1924, authorities there were moving slowly to implement provisions requiring export and import certificates in the international narcotics trade. Responding to the concerns of Health and Interior Ministry officials, the German Foreign Office appealed to the Swiss government

to tighten its trade regulations.[92] The Swiss reply noted that new regulations passed in October 1924 would not come into force until
August 1925 but that Switzerland would consider earlier implementation in view of the concerns raised by Germany.[93] Although the
German exports to Switzerland were legal under German law in the
absence of Swiss regulations, the extent of exports and their likely
transshipment were violating the spirit of the Hague Convention.

Rather than wait for the Swiss government and without consulting
the industry, the German government took two important steps.
First, in December 1924 German officials completed an agreement
with the Chinese government requiring that a Chinese import license
be attached to the German export permit for all German exports to
China.[94] Second, the German government suspended authorization of
narcotics exports to Switzerland in late May.[95] Faced with the export
ban, German industry representatives put pressure on the Interior
Ministry. By mid-June 1925 ministry officials were requesting that
the Foreign Office accelerate negotiations with Switzerland over the
drug issue. The Swiss government, however, remained committed to
the August 1 date, requesting only that the German government notify it if the export ban was to be withdrawn prior to this date.[96]

The combination of the export ban to Switzerland, regulations for
export to China, and the eventual introduction of Swiss regulations
sent German exporters in search of new outlets for the narcotics
trade.[97] The extent of the illicit German trade was not entirely clear
because of the counterfeit labeling that had proliferated during the
mid-1920s. Traffickers most commonly used false labels bearing the
names of Merck or Böhringer. British and League of Nations authorities recognized the problem.[98] Perhaps the most famous case of questionable trade practices, however, was the transshipments carried
out through the Netherlands firm of Chemische Fabrik Naarden. In
1928, before the Netherlands introduced a certificate system for regulating the narcotics trade, Dutch authorities discovered that Naarden had become the transshipment center of Europe. Over roughly
an eighteen-month period during 1927 and 1928, C. H. Böhringer as
well as Swiss (Hoffmann La Roche) and French firms had exported
850 kilograms of morphine, 3,000 kilograms of heroin, and 90 kilograms of cocaine to Naarden, which had, in turn, engaged in illicit
trade to China.[99]

Although the Netherlands had signed the Geneva Convention on drug control by 1925, implementing legislation and a certificate system were not introduced until the Opium Act of 1928. Dutch authorities therefore maintained that Naarden had not violated Dutch law and could not be prosecuted.[100] Similarly, German authorities condemned the actions of Böhringer but noted the absence of the Dutch certificate system and thus the absence of a specific legal violation. Although German officials had threatened Böhringer in 1924 with "withdrawal of its license" if the company violated the intent of the Hague Convention, in the Naarden case, officials issued only a reprimand in 1930.[101]

The notoriety of the Naarden case contributed to a growing international movement to limit the production of narcotics. German cooperation with these efforts as well as with bilateral control efforts of the United States continued into the early 1930s. Within the League of Nations, Germany participated in, signed, and ratified the 1931 Convention on the Limitation of Manufacture of Narcotic Drugs.[102] In bilateral relations, Germany concluded an information-sharing agreement in 1928, and cooperated with U.S. requests to investigate instances of smuggling (including those involving Naarden).[103] By the early 1930s, German officials were also mirroring the shift in the American agenda by more closely monitoring drug transactions destined for the Far East.[104] Nevertheless, as in the Naarden case, the Interior Ministry held that Germany was responsible only for assuring that goods were exported in line with the regulations of the importing country, not for subsequent transshipment.[105] In addition, German firms (such as Merck) had government approval to join other manufacturers in setting up production subsidiaries in Turkey, ostensibly to be closer to supplies of raw materials. The League of Nations was concerned that these facilities were attempts to evade international drug control agreements.[106] By 1934, however, Germany's transition from adversary to ally in the American drug came to an end as the Weimar regime gave way to Adolf Hitler and Germany withdrew from the League of Nations.

The dynamics of German drug control efforts during the early 1900s are not adequately captured by the U.S. view that German policy makers employed deception or were forced into involuntary defection by weak state capacity. Despite the weaknesses of Weimar, German policy makers do not appear to have been forced into either course.

Policy makers did delay domestic discussion of the Hague provisions and requirements in 1910 and 1911, despite their expressed support, but not, apparently, because of industry pressure. Why the Interior Ministry stalled on the second British condition is not entirely clear. Possibly the government, recognizing certain preconditions of state capacity such as German reliance on the financial proceeds of a competitive pharmaceutical industry, was trying to balance international and domestic considerations. Officials may have hoped that Japan, Portugal, or some other holdout would balk and be blamed for derailing the conference. In such a case, Germany would be free of the conference and free of the blame for preventing it. The actual consequences were quite different. The United States developed all sorts of conspiracy theories—based, in part, on information from the French—on how the Germans and British were colluding to delay the conference.[107]

From 1912 to 1914, German officials pursued neither deception nor involuntary defection. Rather, like officials from other countries, they explicitly cited the issue of nonsignatories as the impediment to ratifying the convention. Finally, Germany ratified the Hague Convention in 1920–1921 despite the tumultuous postwar restructuring of the German state. Far from bowing to industry pressures, policy makers drafted and obtained parliamentary approval for new restrictions in part by closing the pharmaceutical industry out of the deliberations.

It is also difficult to reduce the participation of German firms in the illicit drug trade during the 1920s to a simple relationship between state capacity and involuntary defection. Clearly the government enforced existing German regulations and took steps to close loopholes that permitted German companies to act contrary to the intent of drug control agreements. The Böhringer case comes closest to the U.S. perception of German officials caught between international and domestic pressure. Nevertheless, it is not possible to attribute German defection solely to the fragmentation of authority between the Reich and Länder governments. Weimar authorities were able to introduce, extend, and act on drug control provisions. Essentially, Länder opposition limited the ability of central authorities to respond only to those actions by German companies that were legal in Germany, although contrary to the intent of drug control agreements.

It remains unclear why the major cases of German companies exploiting loopholes were largely discovered by foreign rather than German authorities. Weimar officials may have lacked the capacity to make such discoveries or may have operated under the belief that having legislation in place made such investigations unnecessary.[108] Länder police forces, similarly, may not have made drug control a priority or may have been compromised. Yet Länder authorities did take action against illicit trafficking even in the absence of foreign complaints.[109] A complete understanding would require investigation of the nature of German law and how it was interpreted which is beyond the scope of this analysis.

3

Narcotics Trafficking
and Japan

From the commercial treaty of 1856, which accepted Japan's right to restrict U.S. opium exports severely, to the Philippine Commission's exploration of Japanese drug control policy at home and in Formosa (Taiwan) in 1903–1904, American policy makers looked to Japan as a potential model for U.S. drug control policy abroad.[1] By the 1930s, however, the U.S. relationship with Japan had changed drastically. Despite participating in the Shanghai, Hague, and Geneva conferences, in apparent compliance with the American agenda, Japan had also emerged as a primary trafficker in morphine, heroin, cocaine, and opium.

This chapter explores Japanese drug policy, especially with regard to the trade in manufactured narcotics, from 1906, when allegations of Japanese morphine transshipment into China were first made, to 1938, when Japan withdrew from the Opium Advisory Committee of the League of Nations. This analysis reveals that state capacity had a selective influence on Japanese policy makers different from that found in the German case. Whereas German policy makers faced a well-established narcotics industry before American pressure began, the Japanese narcotics industry developed during the interwar period, in the aftermath of the Hague deliberations. The Japanese state was more fragmented between civil and military authorities than that of

Germany and Japanese policy makers found it difficult to draft and especially to implement drug control measures.

Expansion, Fragmentation, and Capacity

In contrast to Germany, Japan during the early 1900s possessed both territorial integrity and relative financial solvency. Japan's history of internal consolidation since the 1600s, its legacy of strictly limited interaction with foreigners, its island geography, and its victory in the Russo-Japanese War and World War I all contributed to this integrity. Japan's financial status was sound until the U.S. stock market crash in 1929 and the subsequent Great Depression undermined it somewhat. The effects were multiplied by the export reliance of the Japanese textile industry and the reintroduction of the gold standard in early 1930. By late 1931, runs on the yen had cost the Bank of Japan roughly "60 percent of its entire specie reserves," according to Michael A. Barnhart, leading policy makers to drop the gold standard in December.[2] During the 1930s, Japanese officials fought inflationary pressures as they expanded government spending on the military and on subsidies to gold and silver mining. Efforts to increase foreign borrowing to offset rising financial burdens by the late 1930s were challenged more and more often by U.S. opposition in international financial markets. Japanese officials turned to territorial holdings abroad, such as those in China, to meet vital economic needs.[3]

Yet territorial and financial concerns plagued Japanese holdings in China. Moreover, it is in and through these holdings, especially Manchuria, U.S. policy makers charged, that Japan was facilitating the illicit narcotics trade in the Far East and beyond. In 1905, in the aftermath of the Russo-Japanese War, Japan obtained title to the southern portion of Manchuria, the Kwantung Leased Territories. By 1907 Prince Saionji's cabinet's statement of national strategy put South Manchuria within the scope of Japan's territorial interests.[4] An area of contention among Japan, China, and Russia since the 1890s, Manchuria offered a combination of highly arable land (for soy beans and other products), extensive mineral reserves (including coal, iron ore, gold, and silver), and through ports such as Dairen, a gateway into

China.[5] Following 1906 and again after the conclusion of the Sino-Japanese Treaty of 1915, the Japanese presence in the region—in terms of both business operations and population—expanded dramatically. By 1925 over nine hundred Japanese companies with a total annual capital of ¥536 million had joined earlier stalwarts such as the South Manchurian Railway Company, Mitsui Bussan, and Mitsubishi in Manchuria. Moreover, by early 1930 approximately 200,000 Japanese and 800,000 Koreans resided in the area, encouraged by the growing Japanese infrastructure and military presence and by Japanese government loans for land purchases.[6]

Japanese territorial control over South Manchuria and the South Manchurian Railway zone was far from complete, however. To deal with contending Chinese warlords in the region as well as potential threats from the Soviet Union, the Kwantung Army together with its intelligence branch, the Mukden Special Service Agency, was established in 1906 as the primary control mechanism, but its resources were limited. Indeed, until 1931 the Kwantung Army was basically an "army in name only" with a total troop strength of 10,400. Following the Mukden Incident in September 1931 and the establishment of Manchukuo the following year, the size of the Kwantung Army was increased to 64,900 troops by late 1931, to 94,100 by 1932, and to 200,000 by 1937.[7] Nevertheless, insurgency by warlords and bandits (*hunghudze*) persisted, and through 1932, Kwantung Army officials maintained their inability to curtail it. They estimated they would need "about 5 years and 300,000 troops" to solve the problem.[8]

The costs of fielding the Kwantung Army and developing infrastructure and industry strained the resources of Japanese holdings in Manchuria and Japan itself.[9] The downturn in the world agricultural market during the early 1930s depressed production and revenue from soybeans, Manchuria's primary export. Falling world trade also reduced the revenues of the South Manchurian Railway, the primary source of development in the region, at the same time as the company was being asked to help finance a new wave of industrialization in Manchukuo.[10] By the mid-1930s, the operations of the Manchukuo government as well as broader industrialization were financed primarily by borrowing. The Manchukuo Central Bank became the primary purchaser of public bonds issued by the government. In turn,

the bank's purchases as well as Kwantung Army expenses and extensive lending to firms and nongovernmental banks—such as the Industrial Bank and the Agricultural Development Bank—were backed
primarily by Central Bank notes rather than deposits. To balance this
increasingly risky economic juggling, Japan was forced to play a larger
role in Manchukuo's financial operations. By 1939, for example, 71
percent of the capital collected for the Manchukuo Five-Year Investment Plan (roughly 1.1 billion yuan) had come from Japan.[11] Yet
Japanese financial resources by the late 1930s were also strained.[12]

Japanese state structure from the early 1900s through the 1930s was
shifting toward greater centralization and concentration of power under the military.[13] The Meiji Constitution of 1889, in place until the
U.S. occupation, formally centralized sovereignty in the emperor, but
in practice, foreign and domestic policy were the province of the privy
council, prime minister, and cabinet—each appointed "at the direction of the emperor" and the general staff of the military.[14] Policy administration belonged to the most powerful ministries of the national
bureaucracy—the Foreign Ministry, Finance, Army/War, and Navy—
designated the Inner Cabinet in 1933.[15] In contrast to the executive,
the Japanese parliament, consisting of an appointed upper house and
an elected lower house, was relatively weak. The influence of the lower
house was limited by restrictions on "political dissent," the absence of
universal male suffrage until 1925, and contending political parties interested more in "achieving and exploiting power," as Robert E. Ward
notes, than in expanding the role of Diet as a democratic institution.[16]

Although stronger than its Weimar counterpart, the Japanese state
was also fragmented, mainly between the civilian ministries and the
military.[17] The question of civilian control over the military was
shaped by a number of provisions the most important of which was
the concept of the "right of supreme command" (dokudan senko),
which, James B. Crowley explains, placed the internal administrative
affairs of the army and navy as well as "military operations in times
of hostilities" under the military's "complete control." The inherent
vagueness of the concept of hostile conditions as well as the overlap
between these military concerns and the broader economic and political conditions in Japan and its territorial holdings abroad opened a
wide range of policy issues to military influence.[18] Civilian control
was made more problematic by fragmentation within the military it-

self. There was interservice rivalry between the army and navy over budgetary resources, and there were power battles between the general staff and the Army/War Ministry, the general staff in Tokyo and the military field commanders abroad, and the general staff and the intelligence units of the army and navy (the special service agencies) assigned to military forces overseas.[19]

The integration of Manchurian holdings into the structure of the Japanese state reveals similar fragmentation of authority between civilian and military officials, shifting toward increased military control. In 1906 the Japanese cabinet placed the administration of the Kwantung Territories under the command of a military governor-general (the Kwantung Army commander), and it gave control over civilian affairs to the Foreign Ministry. In 1917, however, Alvin D. Coox explains, the governor-general was "made responsible to the Prime Minister," and the influence of the consuls dispatched to Manchuria by the Foreign Ministry was thereby undercut. In 1919 Foreign Ministry authority was further reduced as the cabinet separated the positions of governor-general and Kwantung Army commander, opened the governor-generalship to civilians, and shifted the chain of command for the head of the Kwantung Army directly to the general staff in Tokyo rather than through the governor-general.[20]

Through the 1920s and early 1930s, relative civilian influence over the administration of Japanese interests in southern Manchuria continued to erode as seen in the events culminating in the Mukden Incident and the establishment of Manchukuo.[21] By August 1932 when the Japanese government formally recognized Manchukuo, it named the commander in chief of the Kwantung Army rather than a representative from the Foreign Ministry as ambassador.[22] The establishment of the China Affairs Board by the Japanese government in 1938 to coordinate Japanese political and economic policy abroad signaled a further erosion in the influence of the Foreign Ministry. Presided over by the prime minister, the board placed the foreign and finance ministers as vice-presidents along with the ministers of war and the navy and assigned policy implementation to branch offices abroad.[23]

A similar pattern of fragmentation followed by concentration of state power in the hands of the military appears in drug control policy. As in Germany, so in Japan the Foreign Ministry served as the primary conduit for foreign protests—bilateral and through the League of Nations—and governmental responses, but the actual influence of the ministry in shaping drug policy varied over time. During the early 1900s, formal responsibility for drug policy resided with the Ministry for Home Affairs, Hygiene Bureau.[24] Although Home Office ordinances in 1919, 1928, 1930, and 1934 had introduced provisions of the Hague and Geneva conferences,[25] Japanese positions at international conferences and policy decisions at home reflected the input of several state agencies.[26]

From 1924 to 1931 informal liaison committees chaired by the foreign minister brought together representatives from the Home Affairs, Finance, and Justice Ministries, Board of Colonies, and the governors-general of Taiwan, Korea, and the Kwantung Leased Territories.[27] The erosion of Foreign Ministry influence over drug control policy was exacerbated in 1931 by an imperial ordinance that established a formal Opium Committee to be chaired and supervised by the minister for home affairs.[28] Yet the Home Affairs Ministry's influence over the direction of Japanese drug policy through the 1930s should not be overstated. From 1933 to 1937, the Inner Cabinet excluded the Home Affairs Ministry from the core of the policy-making process.[29] By January 1938, over the ministry's opposition, military pressure had led to the formation of a new Ministry of Welfare, and drug control became the formal responsibility of the new Medical Section of its Public Health Bureau. The chairmanship of the Opium Committee also shifted to the Ministry of Welfare, which by mid-1938 had "become absorbed in military-related work."[30]

Within Japan, the implementation of drug control measures fell to the Finance and Home Affairs Ministries. Although steps such as establishment of the Opium Committee aimed at greater coordination, the Finance Ministry's Customs Bureau remained primarily responsible for supervising customs officials as well as import and export procedures.[31] The responsibility of enforcing laws against illicit traffic within Japan fell to the police. Compared to their counterparts in Weimar Germany, the Japanese police were subject to a greater degree of centralization, through the Police Bureau of the Ministry of Home Affairs, prefectural governors appointed by the ministry, and the Tokyo Metropolitan Police Board.[32] Although Japan lacked a central police agency devoted to drug control, the Tokyo board served as the de facto international liaison on drug enforcement.[33] In Japanese territorial holdings, meanwhile, fragmentation gave way to to greater military control. Initially charged with responsibility for enforcement, the consular police increasingly faced structural challenges from the Japanese military, special service agencies, and, by the late-1930s, China Affairs Board branches as well as from the proliferation of government-backed opium monopolies. With the establishment of Manchukuo, the implementation of drug control policy shifted to key agencies of the Manchukuo government.

The desire to avoid the Chinese legacy of uncontrolled opium imports as well as the country's late industrialization contributed to the slow emergence of the Japanese pharmaceutical industry on the stage of international drug producers. Thus, prior to 1914 Japan relied primarily on Germany for cocaine imports and Great Britain for morphine.[34] With the disruption of German drug exports during World War I, Japanese policy makers sought to compensate for lost supplies and to decrease foreign reliance by licensing a limited number of domestic pharmaceutical companies for narcotics production (Tables 3, 4). By 1924 the government had designated three firms based in Tokyo—Hoshi Pharmaceutical Company (cocaine, heroin, morphine), Sankyo Company (morphine and cocaine), and Koto Seiyaku Kabushi Kaisha (cocaine)—and three based in Osaka—Nippon Seiyaku Kabushi Kaisha (morphine, heroin), Takeda Chobei Shoten (cocaine), and Shionogi Shoten (cocaine).[35]

Because narcotics production in Japan was essentially organized from the top down, the pharmaceutical industry was less likely to become a source of organized opposition to government drug control policy than was the German industry. Producers were required to retain official licensing, moreover, and the import of raw materials and cultivation of opium and coca were regulated by the government.[36] This pattern of regulation also supplied the relevant state ministries (such as Home Affairs and Welfare) with a greater degree of control over information concerning domestic drug production than that enjoyed by their German counterparts. At the same time, however, these ministries had an interest in assuring the continued successful operation of those firms that had been licensed by the government.[37]

Table 3. Japanese drug imports (pounds), 1903–1907, 1910–1924

	Raw opium	Coca	Morphine	Heroin	Cocaine
1903	n.a.	n.a.	—	155	n.a.
1904	n.a.	n.a.	14	94	n.a.
1905	n.a.	n.a.	203	75	n.a.
1906	n.a.	n.a.	0	134	n.a.
1907	n.a.	n.a.	451	380	n.a.
1910	n.a.	n.a.	1,387	n.a.	927
1911	n.a.	n.a.	1,829	n.a.	1,273
1912	n.a.	n.a.	2,013	n.a.	2,704
1913	n.a.	n.a.	5,696	n.a.	3,264
1914	n.a.	n.a.	11,298	n.a.	3,726
1915	n.a.	n.a.	22,409	n.a.	4,273
1916	n.a.	n.a.	34,926	n.a.	4,892
1917	n.a.	n.a.	37,514	n.a.	5,630
1918	n.a.	n.a.	10,318	n.a.	2,852
1919	74,999	n.a.	25,569	n.a.	2,642
1920	68,244	n.a.	48,650	n.a.	7,329
1921	24,662	n.a.	13,087	2,427	4,563
1922	22,250	n.a.	690	850	523
1923	35,529	n.a.	7	—	253
1924	6,332	n.a.	—	—	—

Sources: Calculated from *Control of Opium in Japan: Report of the Japanese Delegates to the International Opium Conference* (Shanghai, 1909), pp. 28–29, Japanese Foreign Ministry Archives, 2.9.9.34 (Shanghai Conference), Diplomatic Records Office; *The Opium Trade,* Volume 5 (Wilmington, Del.: Scholarly Resources, 1974), cited as BRIT5, document F 600/504/10 (British Embassy, Tokyo, to Foreign Office, January 9, 1922), 1621/504/10 (British Embassy, Tokyo, to Foreign Office, March 29, 1922); Japan, Ministries of Home Affairs, Sanitation Bureau, and Finance, Statistics Bureau, cited in State Department Diplomatic Records, 1925 Geneva Conference 511.4A2/256 (December 16, 1924) and State Department Diplomatic Records, Internal Affairs of Japan, 1910–29, 894.114 Narcotics/N16/33 (November 25, 1924).

Note: No statistics were collected by the Japanese government on coca imports through 1924, although an estimated four hundred tons of Java coca were imported in 1924. Figures for 1924 cover only January through June.

Table 4. Japanese domestic drug production (pounds), 1919–1923, 1935–1939

	Raw opium	Morphine	Heroin	Coca	Cocaine
1919	3,735	3,695	894	n.a.	1,838
1920	7,767	8,586	10,459	n.a.	4,011
1921	11,785	9,824	9,602	n.a.	5,117
1922	8,607	5,947	5,007	n.a.	8,178
1923	4,759	6,684	5,278	n.a.	7,632
1935	81,327	7,139	550	294,582	1,980
1936	98,188	8,683	440	208,518	1,980
1937	110,702	10,556	440	311,197	1,971
1938	114,706	10,008	440	144,021	1,980
1939	118,591	11,088	403	306,116	1,980

Sources: Ministry of Home Affairs, cited in *511.4A2/256* (December *16, 1924*); *894.114* Narcotics/N*16/33* (November *25, 1924*), *2-2745* (February *27, 1945*).
Note: Raw opium production figures from *1935* to *1939* include Korea (approximately *50* percent of the total), but production figures from Japanese holdings in China are not included. Coca leaf production figures from *1935* to *1939* include Formosa (approximately *60–100* percent of total).

Cooperation versus Narcotization

Policy makers and scholars have used a variety of state-capacity arguments to explain the Japanese response to the American agenda on drug control. The most prominent view, that of U.S. officials such as Harry Anslinger, prosecutors in the Tokyo War Crimes Trials, and those analysts who draw extensively on the trials for their primary data, holds that Japanese policy makers used deception to bring about the "narcotization" of China. The strategy had two purposes: to generate revenue to finance "aggression" and to provide a means for "debauching the people to keep them subservient to the will and desire of Japan."[38] Thus, although Japan signed international conventions, appeared to cooperate with the League of Nations, and strictly regulated domestic drug production and consumption, according to this argument, Japanese policy makers were actually pursuing a "dual," "cynical" strategy abroad.[39]

The defense at the Tokyo trials gave a different explanation, which was also based on state capacity. It attributed Japanese defection from the U.S. agenda to the lack of territorial integrity in Japan's holdings in China and to the fragmentation within the Japanese state. For example, the official Japanese policy of gradual suppression (through the identification and registration of addicts and monopolization of drug supply) as developed for Formosa, faced extensive challenges in its application on the Chinese mainland. Drug addiction and trafficking predated Japanese involvement and intensified as Nationalist and Communist Chinese forces turned to drug production and trafficking to finance operations against each other as well as against Japan. State fragmentation raises questions for the argument that the Japanese prime minister and his cabinet, working, in part, through the China Affairs Board, the Manchurian government, and the Kwantung Army, pursued a coherent strategy of narcotization in China and elsewhere. When and to what extent were Japanese policy makers aware of the transshipment of narcotics through Japan and the actions of the Kwantung Army in China? If they were aware, did policy makers deliberately deceive or were they forced into involuntary defection from the American agenda by power fragmentation between civilian and military authorities or within the military? The following analysis reveals little support for the arguments of the prosecution at the Tokyo trials during the period prior to Japan's withdrawal from the drug control agencies of the League of Nations (at which point the question of duplicity becomes moot).

In contrast to Germany's, Japan's role in the international drug trade attracted relatively little American attention until after the Hague Conference. U.S. overtures to Japan in 1906 to garner support for the Shanghai Opium Commission had been successful. The United States pursued Japanese support because of the country's "influential position in the Far East" and the prominence of the Formosa model in U.S. deliberations over opium control in the Philippines, not out of concern that Japan might promote the international drug trade.[40] By 1908, however, this image of Japan had begun to shift as the United States and Europe became concerned about the transshipment of morphine through Japan and into China. Although the initial dispute over this issue was resolved before the Shanghai deliberations began, the transshipment question would return as a primary point of contention in relations between Japan and the United States.

Direct shipments of morphine from the United States and Europe into China began to face restrictions in the early 1900s with a series of commercial treaties that allowed Chinese authorities to prohibit nonmedical imports of the drug as well as imports of hypodermic syringes. By 1904, with direct export prohibited from the United States, Britain, France, Germany, and Portugal, transshipment through unrestricted Japan had begun. The Japanese took no action against transshipment despite entreaties by Chinese and U.S. consular authorities until 1908. Apparently, Japan's reluctance was related to its own successful manufacture and export of syringes. Moreover, the Japanese saw no reason to impose restrictions on itself when China had not yet introduced its own domestic regulations against morphine (instituted only in 1909).[41] Following two direct appeals from the U.S. State Department in July and September and faced with the upcoming Shanghai deliberations, Japanese authorities finally agreed to a commercial treaty limiting morphine exports.[42]

Japanese cooperation with the United States continued at the Shanghai Commission deliberations in 1909. Although the two delegations did not always agree, on key issues splitting the United States and Great Britain the Japanese delegation often aligned with the United States.[43] In the events leading up to the Hague Conference, U.S. authorities did not see Japan's delayed compliance with the British conditions (despite earlier statements of support in principle for the conference) as part of broader Japanese opposition to drug control. Instead, authorities accepted Japanese assurances that the delay stemmed more from the slowness of interministerial cooperation and noted among themselves the apparent Japanese desire to wait until the British had committed to attend.[44] Moreover, reports of the U.S. delegation and scholarship on the Hague Conference suggest that in contrast to Germany, Japan kept an extremely low profile in the deliberations.[45]

Nevertheless, questions concerning the extent of Japanese cooperation with the American agenda reemerged during the interwar period. As seen in Table 3, the commercial treaty to limit morphine exports to China had done little to stop the trend of increased Japanese imports from Europe and the United States. From 1910–1912, Japanese morphine imports had averaged 1,743 pounds per year. In

1913, however, imports increased sharply and by 1915–1917, there were foreign reports of annual Japanese imports of about 22,400–37,500 pounds, primarily from Great Britain.[46] More important, press and consular reports from U.S. and British officials suggested that the bulk of these imports were being transshipped into China.[47] By 1917, faced with domestic pressure from Parliament and from antiopium groups concerning this pattern, British authorities began to take steps to curtail the trade. The Foreign Office notified the Japanese foreign minister that Britain would be restricting exports to Japan and Kwantung. Only drugs intended for medical use would be exported, and applications for morphine (and cocaine) export to Japan and Japanese holdings in China would be required to include certified import licenses from Japanese or Kwantung authorities.[48]

When direct transit was restricted, however, British exporters began to transship to Japan, primarily through the United States, as well as through Switzerland, France, and Siberia (especially Vladivostok).[49] In addition, more U.S. producers of morphine began to enter the trade. The combined effect of these changes was extensive. In October 1919, for example, U.S. Embassy reports revealed that seven thousand tons of morphine had been transshipped from the United Sates through Japan into China during the first six months of the year.[50] Moreover, the reports suggested that when queried, Japanese authorities had replied that transshipment was neither logged in customs entries nor subject to Japanese control. The State Department responded that the U.S. government had not been aware of this situation and asked for official confirmation of the Japanese position. Ten days later, the Japanese Foreign Ministry confirmed the absence of regulations covering transshipment but noted that steps were being taken to draft such measures under the Hague Convention accepted through article 295 of the Versailles Treaty.[51]

To what extent was halting drug transshipment into China a point of contention between the United States and Japan? Clearly, the United States was not as ignorant of the situation as the State Department claimed. The Japanese Foreign Ministry had responded to U.S. requests for information on the nature of Japanese drug trade regulations three years earlier. This information had revealed the absence of prohibitions against drug transshipment and also that manufactured narcotics could be freely imported into Japan as medical materials.[52] The growing problem with transshipment had also been suggested during 1918 in press reports—supported by the observations of U.S. consular officials in China—of extensive Japanese involvement in importing an estimated eighteen tons of morphine into Manchuria.[53] By February 1919, faced with foreign and domestic press reports on the transshipment issue, top Japanese officials, including the prime minister and vice-minister for foreign affairs had admitted that the morphine traffic persisted despite "drastic action" by Japanese consular officials abroad and had pledged to take additional steps.[54] This pledge won applause from the U.S. mission in Paris in March and the question of possible U.S. steps to curtail transshipment from Europe through the United States and, in turn, Japan were under considerable discussion by U.S. and British authorities by September.[55] In short, U.S. authorities were neither unaware of the situation nor, apparently, putting much pressure on Japan to rectify it. The U.S. position may have been motivated by the primary concern of maintaining access to China (Open Door policy) in the context of increasing Japanese control in the region (the Wilson administration stance even during the 1915 negotiations between Japan and China over the Twenty-one Demands), or the United States may have been trying to win Japanese support for the Versailles Treaty, including article 295.[56]

The Japanese position is more difficult to decipher. Despite claims of drastic action, the absence of regulatory steps against transshipment and the rapid surge in Japanese morphine imports during the interwar period suggest that the very act of agreeing to the earlier treaty with China on morphine had been important to Japanese authorities more as a means to alleviate foreign pressure than as a way actually to curtail the trade. Japan appears to have interpreted the treaty as covering Japanese exports (limited prior to the rise of the pharmaceutical industry), not foreign goods merely transshipped through Japanese ports. This interpretation is reinforced by Japanese proposals to the United States from 1916 on for a Formosa-style gradual suppression of opium in China (including the phasing out of opium monopolies) as the key to reducing Japanese morphine traffic in China.[57] The aforementioned claims of drastic action taken by consular officials against Japanese nationals involved in the trade appear to have had little to do with transshipment.[58] William O. Walker contends that the statements reflected growing concern about "Japanese honor and prestige" abroad, the efforts to gain racial equality provisions in the League of Nations, and the influence of anglophiles on the Japanese premier.[59]

Japan moved slowly against transshipment from 1919 to 1921, first ratifying the Versailles Treaty and then introducing implementing provisions for the Hague Convention. In the interim both Britain and the United States finally acted to curtail the trade at the source. British authorities began requiring import certificates from the United States and France as well as Japan before approving export. Similarly, in November 1920 the U.S. Department of the Treasury announced that it was "declining to permit" exports of "certain narcotics to Japan" in the absence of regulations on transshipment.[60] In December the Japanese Interior Ministry announced the introduction of new regulations in line with the Hague Convention which would cover the trade (import and export), production, and sale of morphine and cocaine and would apply to Japan as well as to Japanese holdings abroad.[61]

During the 1920s, the United States became increasingly concerned about the role of opium and manufactured narcotics in Japan's expansion into China. By early 1921 Japan had begun to implement its new narcotics regulations and to participate as a member of the Opium Advisory Committee of the League of Nations. In this context Japanese participation in the drug trade in China came under greater scrutiny at home and in international forums. Yet, with formal American participation in the league ruled out by Congress, U.S. officials appear to have been more interested in gaining Japanese support for pushing the league toward stricter controls than in pressuring Japan to reduce the trade in China.

Despite Japanese claims of greater cooperation in international drug control efforts, through the early 1920s British publications in Japan—such as the *Japan Chronicle* and the *Japan Advertiser*—continued to allege duplicity.[62] Similar allegations were made more and more often in domestic debates in the Japanese Diet and in the international deliberations of the League of Nations. Beginning in 1921, for example, representatives of opposition political parties such as the Kenseikai began to use the Diet as a forum to question the Japanese government's commitment to controlling transshipment as well as the nature of the Kwantung government's participation in the drug trade. The initial response by the prime minister emphasized the government's strict control efforts and noted that the organization Kosai Zendo,[63] rather than the Kwantung government, played the primary role in the opium suppression program, which generated no excessive revenue, whether through licensing fees or through opium sales.[64] Opposition representatives in the Diet questioned the credibility of these arguments. They disputed government figures and pointed to the charges of embezzlement and drug smuggling which had been raised in 1920 against Japanese employed in the Dairen civil administration, Kosai Zendo, and Mitsui Bussan.[65]

By 1923 the Diet debate over drug control policy had expanded to include questions, again from Kenseikai officials, concerning the role of the Japanese government in facilitating transshipment. The transaction in question occurred in 1922, when eighty-five hundred pounds of crude morphine were shipped from production facilities in Formosa through Japan (where it was processed into five thousand pounds of morphine) and then, it was charged, into mainland China. The Home Affairs Ministry responded that since late 1921 it had imposed a temporary ban on morphine export licenses for China to curtail smuggling. As for imports into Japan, the ministry spokesman noted that although Japan's annual morphine needs had been set in 1917 at four thousand pounds and annual opium imports of forty thousand pounds had been licensed to meet these needs, a special exception had been made in 1922 for Hoshi Pharmaceutical to import the additional crude morphine.[66] The spokesman admitted that the location of the resulting five thousand pounds of morphine (and potential revenue of ¥1.5 million if it was sold) was unknown, but he assumed it was in storage somewhere in Japan.[67]

This instance overshadowed others that appeared in the press during 1922–1924, which, according to British Embassy officials, the Kenseikai planned to use in the Diet to challenge the government. These included instances of transhipment from Great Britain through Vladivostok and Japan into China and the shipment of two thousand boxes of opium from the United States, which were stored in Kobe without clearing customs and then exported to China, reputedly by Hoshi Pharmaceutical.[68] Although Japanese authorities made some seizures in these and other cases, both British and American authorities in Japan lamented that customs officials lacked "zeal" in their attempts to prevent transshipment.[69] Moreover, as in Germany, company officials and the courts appear to have maintained that these instances of transshipment did not violate Japanese narcotics laws since the drugs were not actually imported into Japan.[70] Inasmuch as the 1921 regulations had been touted when they were introduced in 1920 as a solution to the problem of transshipment (albeit primarily of manufactured narcotics such as morphine), this line of reasoning should have provoked more reaction from the United States.

Despite these cases, however, relations between the United States and Japan with regard to drug control remained largely without incident through the mid-1920s.[71] In the deliberations of the Opium Advisory Committee, the Japanese representative continued to stress his country's commitment to strict enforcement of the 1921 regulations. League inquiries about transshipment and the broader issue of Japanese morphine exports into China focused primarily on statistical discrepancies between Japanese import figures and the export figures of other countries (including the United States). Since these inquiries were primarily based on data from the period prior to 1921, the Japanese delegation simply reemphasized the new regulations and their government's commitment to enforcement.[72] Yet the report sent by Helen H. Moorhead, secretary of the Foreign Policy Association Opium Committee, to the State Department concerning her trip to the Opium Advisory Committee in May 1923, reveals a discussion primarily focused on U.S. relations with Britain and France and no mention of Japan.[73]

In the deliberations over the Geneva Opium Conference in 1924–1925, similarly, the United States appeared less interested in Japanese drug control efforts than in enlisting Japan to help shift the league toward the American agenda.[74] Thus, despite concerns about the transshipment of opium and manufactured narcotics into China, the United States stayed out of a volatile dispute between Japan and Britain over tightening trade through Formosa.[75] Moreover, the U.S. delegation "took special pains" to be "friendly . . . socially" with their Japanese counterparts; the head of the U.S. delegation, Stephen Porter, also intervened on behalf of Japan in communications with the House Foreign Affairs Committee.[76] The Japanese delegation, in return, generally supported the United States until the U.S. delegation withdrew from the deliberations in 1925.[77]

Through the late 1920s and into the early 1930s, Japan continued to participate in the efforts of the League of Nations to control the drug trade and took steps to enhance control efforts at home and to curtail smuggling by Japanese nationals abroad.[78] Yet as the Kwantung Army began to expand and consolidate the Japanese presence in Manchuria during the mid-1920s, Japanese policy makers came under increasing pressure to comply with the American agenda.[79] In effect, the apparent coalescence of Japanese civilian and military authorities around the question of Manchuria and the eventual establishment of Manchukuo suggested to U.S. policy makers that Japanese policy in China—including drug control policy—was being coordinated and directed by a cohesive and duplicitous state.[80]

The Kwantung Army's behind-the-scenes efforts included covert arrangements with Chinese warlords, who were extensively involved in the opium trade as a source of revenue. The liaison had been conducted by the Mukden Special Service Agency through the mid-1920s.[81] When the Kwantung Army assassinated the warlord Chang Tso-lin in 1928, its officers were reproached by the emperor, selected cabinet officials, and elements in the Tokyo General Staff.[82] Nevertheless, subsequent personnel changes in the general staff and the Kwantung Army contributed to greater support within the military in Tokyo for action in China. In 1931 this support culminated in the Kwantung Army's military action in Mukden in response to a reputed Chinese attack on the South Manchurian Railway.[83]

Both the assassination and the Mukden attack were carried out despite last-minute discovery and protests by consular officials abroad and by the Foreign Ministry.[84] Other efforts by civilian authorities in late 1931 to reign in the subsequent military advances were also only partially successful. The compromise agreement between civilian authorities and the general staff left the military's interests largely intact and included a pledge by the government to press for a new treaty with China to extend and protect Japanese interests in Manchuria.[85] The relative weakness of civilian authorities in the Hamaguchi Yuko/Wakatsuki Reijiro cabinet (1929–1931) reflected strong opposition from the military, from parties (such as the Seiyukai) in the Diet, and within the Foreign Ministry itself to Foreign Minister Baron Shidehara Kijūro's policy toward China, which was seen as too conciliatory.[86] Placed in the difficult position of essentially having to defend the fait accompli in Mukden to foreign governments and before the League of Nations, the Foreign Ministry found its influence further eroded by its failure to prevent the covert operations of the Mukden Special Service Agency and the Kwantung Army leading to the establishment of Manchukuo in March 1932.[87]

By late 1931 the Seiyukai-dominated cabinet of Inukai Tsuyoshi had moved more to the right, reducing the differences between military and civilian authorities concerning Japan's role in China.[88] This shift permitted the government to pledge support for Manchukuo in early 1932, but it withheld formal recognition out of concern for foreign reaction, especially in light of the pending visit by the Lytton Commission of the League of Nations to investigate the dispute between Japan and China.[89] After Inukai was assassinated in an attempted military coup in May, Prince Saionji constructed a new cabinet led by former navy minister Admiral Saito Mokoto. Saito appointed former South Manchurian Railway president Uchida Yasuya as foreign minister and pressured the lower house for recognition of Manchukuo.[90] By early 1933 in response to the league's condemnation of Japan's military actions in China, Uchida had joined War Minister Araki Sadao in proposing that Japan withdraw from the League of Nations. In March 1933 the Japanese delegation walked out of the league assembly. Two years later, Japan formally withdrew from the league.[91]

The Japanese consolidation of holdings in China and the apparent concord between military authorities in Tokyo and China and civilian authorities in Japan convinced the United States and other nations that Japan was responsible for local conditions and instances of drug trafficking in China.[92] Yet the extent of this responsibility, especially the charges that Japan deliberately pursued the narcotization of China, is by no means clear. Certainly Japan was not solely responsible for the drug situation in China. Detailed archival research by William O. Walker III has revealed that Chinese authorities, including Nationalist forces under Chiang Kai-shek, were extensively involved in the drug trade during this period as a means to achieve military, political, and economic ends. The U.S. State Department downplayed this involvement, however, and stressed the Japanese role, because of broader U.S. strategic support for the Nationalists.[93]

The U.S. allegation of concerted Japanese encouragement of the drug trade in China is also questionable. Policy makers in Tokyo were clearly aware of drug problems in Japanese holdings in China and that the Japanese abroad were one source of these problems. Yet, the limited control of civilian authorities over the Kwantung Army's covert and military operations in China by the late-1920s and early 1930s and the relative lack of standing of the Home Affairs Ministry in such considerations suggest that these authorities also lacked the capacity to control participation by the army and the Mukden Special Service Agency in the Chinese drug trade. Despite continued steps to strengthen domestic drug control and to curtail transshipment[94] and despite participation in the drug control deliberations of the OAC through this period, it was becoming increasingly difficult for Japanese policy makers to control the drug traffic in China.[95]

For example, in 1930 the United States and Japan concluded agreements for information sharing among their narcotics enforcement officials, but the primary tie established was between the U.S. Federal Bureau of Narcotics and the Tokyo Metropolitan Police, the closest equivalent to a centralized enforcement agency in Japan. Similarly, that same year the United States and Japan agreed to permit their consular officials in China to share information, but the Japanese held out on the key exception of Dairen, the area of greatest concern to the United States. Japanese officials noted that it would be necessary to discuss the issue further with the military authorities in Kwantung.[96] In the spring of 1931, the U.S. consulate in Dairen reported that the new governor and the consular police were taking limited steps against Kwantung officials who had facilitated the narcotics trade.[97] These governors were political appointees through the prime minister, had little authority to influence the Kwantung Army, and were not subject to control by consular authorities dispatched by the Foreign Ministry.[98]

The Mukden Incident, the establishment of Manchukuo, and the military's expansion into Jehol province by 1933 further derailed the ability of civilian authorities to press for greater international cooperation on drug control. While the Inukai government withheld recognition, commercial and security relations between Japan and

Manchukuo were conducted primarily through the military, under the leadership of the commander of the Kwantung Army, rather than the Foreign Ministry.[99] By early September 1932 the consul general's office at Changchun (Hsinking, the new capital) informed the Foreign Ministry that a new opium monopoly system was being established by the Manchukuo government.[100] Since the late 1920s, the Kwantung Army had also been trying to consolidate control over the Jehol opium network (established by T'ang Yu-lin and reputedly linking Chinese postal authorities, South Manchurian Railway employees, and Japanese consular police). With military expansion into Jehol, the army finally succeeded. Its hold over these production and distribution networks, in turn, provided an initial source of supply for Manchukuo's new opium monopoly.[101]

With the Home Affairs Ministry cut out of the policy-making loop by the establishment of the Inner Cabinet in 1933 and the position of prime minister increasingly controlled by (former) military officials, the Foreign Ministry and its consular representatives became the primary constraint on drug operations by Japanese in China, but how willing the ministry was to try to rein in the Kwantung Army is not entirely clear. For example, James Crowley says that the ministers in the Saito cabinet were seen as "little more than spokesmen for their respective ministries."[102] As noted, there were factional disputes in the Foreign Ministry. China experts had seen Shidehara as soft on China. The appointment of Uchida, who, Ian Nish explains, favored recognition of Manchukuo and was in "good books" with the army, suggests support for those factions less likely to oppose the army's consolidation of Manchukuo.[103] This support varied among Uchida's successors, such as Hirota Kōki (1934–1936), General Ugaki Kazushige (1938), and Arita Hachiro (1938–1939).[104]

From 1933 until Japan's full withdrawal from the Opium Advisory Committee (OAC) in 1938, Foreign Ministry officials faced U.S. pressure on Manchukuo and the international drug trade. Opposition to Manchukuo and the new opium monopoly was initially played out in the U.S. refusal to extend diplomatic recognition and in appeals for greater Japanese control efforts. Initial responses by Japanese representatives before the league, however, suggest that the Japanese Foreign Ministry considered these issues to be linked. For example, during the November 1933 meeting of the OAC, British and American officials raised concerns about drug use and trafficking in Manchuria and the need for greater information on these issues. The Japanese delegate, Yokoyama Masayuki, agreed on the need for cooperation but noted the difficulties as long as the league refused to recognize the Manchukuo government with which it wanted to cooperate.[105] By 1934, however, strong U.S. opposition to proposals by the British government and a league advisory committee to recognize import certificates issued by the Manchukuo government, and thus to allow raw and processed opium exports to Manchukuo, persuaded the OAC to refuse to sanction the trade.[106]

U.S. officials found special cause for concern in the new Manchukuo opium monopoly and its apparent absence of gradual-suppression provisions.[107] Negative press reports concerning the monopoly in late 1932 had already prompted the Japanese ambassador to the United States to recommend to Foreign Minister Uchida that the Japanese government declare its support for the prohibition of opium smoking in Manchukuo,[108] but no such statement was forthcoming. Gradual suppression had been a component in principle of earlier opium monopolies in South Manchuria under Dairen Kosai Zendo and its successors, such as the Kwantung Government Monopoly Bureau (1928–1932), since the Japanese cabinet decision of 1919.[109] By 1932, however, the success of these efforts appeared limited. The long history of opium production and use in what had become Manchukuo had created an addict population estimated at one million (in addition to occasional and medical users) and an annual consumption of 2.5 million tons.[110] Thus, questions of the enforceability of prohibition aside, not only would a Japanese declaration for prohibition undermine earlier government positions adopted since the Shanghai deliberations, but the revenue concerns of the Kwantung Army and the new Manchukuo government made it difficult for the Foreign Ministry to gain a commitment even to gradual suppression.

Prompted in part by events in Manchukuo, U.S. officials continued to question the extent of Japanese commitment to drug control. In addition to the Manchukuo opium monopoly, consular reports revealed that Japanese firms had established narcotics production facilities in Manchuria and northern China.[111] Beginning in 1932, officials such as the Federal Bureau of Narcotics chief Harry Anslinger increasingly pointed to seizure of drugs in the United States "which appeared to be of Japanese origin" and the limited cooperation of Japanese police (especially in Osaka) in halting this traffic.[112] Yet, the credibility of these charges was as mixed as the efforts of Japanese authorities to curtail the trade.

Efforts to improve police cooperation in Osaka revealed interministerial competition between the U.S. Departments of Treasury and State. It had been increasingly common practice for Treasury to appeal directly to the consulate at Kobe or the Osaka police or both. In early 1933, however, the U.S. Embassy in Tokyo recommended to the State Department that U.S. narcotics officials route their requests through the embassy, which would then deal directly with the Japanese government.[113] By the fall of 1933 the new approach bore fruit in the form of crackdowns by Osaka authorities against the smuggling trade. Moreover, by October 1934 the consulate in Kobe was reporting the arrest of the smuggling ring deemed primarily responsible for shipments to the United States during 1929–1931.[114] In April 1935 the Department of State formalized and clarified the new procedures in instructions to consular and Treasury officials.[115] Consular and embassy officials, however, were also instructed to continue to monitor Japanese customs procedures at the ports of Kobe and Yokohama to collect data on possible smuggling for the U.S. delegation to use before the OAC.[116]

U.S. officials also considered Japanese holdings in China a likely source of the illicit drug trade. To coincide with the needs of the opium monopoly, the Manchukuo government in Dairen had licensed facilities to produce prepared opium. Moreover, consular reports to the Japanese foreign minister in 1933 revealed that Japanese production of narcotics in China had begun as early as 1931, with facilities established in Tientsin.[117] By 1934 drug companies from Osaka had established the South Manchurian Pharmaceutical Company to produce ether, but according to Yamanouchi Saburō, South Manchurian Railway officials and the Kwantung Army were instead encouraging the firm to produce and distribute heroin with proceeds going to the military.[118] By September 1934 Japanese consular officials had informed Hirota of reports of Japanese drug smuggling from Tientsin facilities and had urged stricter control and punishment measures to avoid the potential that "others might consider we promote the smuggling."[119] Such fears were soon realized; reports by Chinese authorities of opium smuggling out of Tientsin in cooperation with Manchukuo authorities were picked up and reported by the *Japan Chronicle*.[120]

The *Chronicle* reports also noted a crackdown by Japanese military authorities against Japanese and Korean peddlers and provincial Chinese officials for drug smuggling in and through the demilitarized zone in north China.[121] If the Japanese military itself or Manchukuo officials were facilitating the trade, however, there was little the Foreign Ministry could do. Japan's 1934 annual report to the league admitted that authorities in Kwantung were still having limited success in curtailing the illicit traffic and declared that the primary impediments were the long-standing drug abuse in the area and the "cleverness" of Chinese and Manchurian (in fact largely Korean) traffickers.[122] Unsatisfied, U.S. officials continued to press for stronger Japanese action against the illicit trade.

Although Japan withdrew from the League of Nations in 1935, it continued to participate in the activities of the OAC, at the OAC's request.[123] (For patterns of import and export in this period, see Table 5.) In May 1936 the United States explicitly charged the Japanese Home Affairs Ministry with facilitating the illicit trade to North America, maintaining before the OAC that the ministry had approved Japanese narcotics production in China.[124] Given the ministry's exclusion from the inner cabinet until December 1937, the charge was rather overstated. Likewise overstated was the claim by the U.S. Embassy in Tokyo that the new domestic control measures introduced under the ministry's ordinances in June 1936 were formulated in reaction to the charges raised before the OAC.[125] U.S. officials two years earlier had reported concerns among Japanese prefectural authorities over rising domestic problems with drug addiction in Japan and the need for tighter regulations, and the ministry had already acted on these concerns.[126] In addition, the Foreign Ministry noted, the 1936 ordinances were part of the implementation of the 1931 convention, which had been ratified by Japan in 1935. More important, less than a week after the announcement of the ordinances, the Foreign Ministry introduced three new ordinances extending regulations and penalties on opium and narcotics trafficking to cover Japanese nationals in China and Manchuria.[127]

Table 5. Japanese drug imports and exports (pounds), 1935–1939

		Imports			
Opium	Coca	Raw morphine	Morphine	Crude cocaine	Cocaine
1935	21,936	142,116	2,596	51	90	—
1936	48,015	109,116	1,210	59	1,793	—
1937	27,060	43,116	2,530	53	755	—
1938	n.a.	99,662	4,578	84	495	—
1939	n.a.	77,000	6,644	n.a.	466	—

	Exports		
	Morphine	Heroin	Cocaine
1935	86	77	26
1936	44	53	11
1937	44	35	7
1938	75	44	31
1939	86	62	7

Source: 894.114 Narcotics/N16/2-2745 (February 27, 1945).

By 1937 the actions of the Foreign Ministry as well as concerns within the Japanese military about the growing instability of the narcotics situation in China apparently sparked a new wave of control efforts, including antinarcotics work by the Japanese consular police,[128] statements of support for control measures by the Kwantung Army commander Ueda Kenkichi,[129] the introduction of a ten-year gradual suppression plan by the Manchukuo General Monopoly Bureau, and the Manchukuo government's creation of the Central Commission for Opium Suppression in 1938.[130] The Kwantung Army's interest in enhancing stability in Manchukuo, however, appears to have been driven more by revenue considerations than by the influence of the Foreign Ministry or concerns about international pressure.[131] Once the control measures began to reduce the illicit trade and the number of registered addicts grew, Ueda began to notify the Foreign Ministry that Manchukuo would be importing, albeit in a "confidential manner," large quantities of narcotics from Japan and opium from Iran.[132]

The potential of Iran as a supplier of opium to China had been a long-standing concern of the United States. Having earlier pressured the League of Nations to reject the legitimacy of import certificates for opium shipments into Manchukuo, U.S. officials became increasingly concerned by 1934 over reports of clandestine plots by the Japanese army in Formosa to import opium through Amoy and the Formosa opium monopoly, flood southern China with opium and narcotics and use the resulting disarray and possible insurgency as an excuse to move in.[133] Walker found no merit in these charges.[134] Nevertheless, by 1937–1938 it had become clear that Iranian opium was moving into Manchukuo as well as into northern China. U.S. officials in the War Department, State Department, and Federal Bureau of Narcotics viewed this trade as evidence of renewed Japanese narcotization.[135] In fact, it represented not a coordinated Japanese drug policy (of either control or narcotization) but brisk competition between the Mitsui and Mitsubishi companies to ship opium into China, a competition facilitated by turf battles between the Kwantung Army in Manchukuo and the Japanese army (especially the special service agencies) and navy in Shanghai over the quantity and destination of the shipments.[136] Despite appeals from Ueda "to do something" to halt the clandestine opium shipments by the army into north China through 1938, the Foreign Ministry appears to have been unable to control either the corporations or the military elements involved.[137]

By June 1938 the opium shipments into northern China had contributed to a new wave of U.S. charges before the OAC concerning Japanese responsibility.[138] Amau Eiji, minister to Switzerland, responded by reaffirming Japan's commitment to drug control, rejecting the charges of military involvement in the trade, and threatening Japan's withdrawal from the OAC.[139] Through the summer of 1938, the Foreign Ministry circulated the OAC charges (as well as U.S. and Canadian press reports of narcotization) to Japanese consulates in China while it deliberated over how to respond.[140] By September the establishment of the China Affairs Board and Ukagi's subsequent resignation had so eroded the ministry's influence as to make its decision moot.[141] On November 2, 1938, after the League Council voted economic sanctions against Japan over the war in China, Japan announced that it was withdrawing from all league organizations, including the OAC.[142]

Japanese drug control policy during the early 1900s only partly sup-
ports the basic U.S. premise that compliance with the American
agenda was a function of capacity. The inability of policy makers in
the Foreign and Home Affairs Ministries to curtail the Kwantung
Army's role in the Chinese drug trade in the late 1920s does seem to
be an instance of involuntary defection due to weak state capacity. In
this period, however, the prominent view in the State Department
and Federal Bureau of Narcotics was not that Japan was unable to enforce drug control agreements but that Japan was pursuing a coherent
and deliberate strategy of deception coordinated by top civilian and
military authorities.

From 1906 through 1920 Japanese policy makers tended to align
with the United States at drug control conferences. The Japanese attitude toward transshipment appears to have had more to do with
Japan's interpretation of commercial treaties with China than with either deception or involuntary defection. Clearly, the absence of Japanese regulations on transshipment facilitated the trade, but as
suggested by the German case studies, the regulation of transshipment had not been clarified by the Hague deliberations. Nor were the
Hague provisions widely in place before the adoption of article 295 of
the Versailles Treaty in 1919. The transshipment issue was clouded,
moreover, by the apparent reluctance of British and American authorities to curtail the attempts by their own producers to evade restrictions on direct trade with China. By 1919–1920, despite relatively
limited U.S. pressure on this issue, Japanese authorities, in the context of the Versailles Treaty had begun to address transshipment.

From 1921 to 1926 Japanese officials implemented the Hague agreement and continued to work with the OAC and the United States
during the Geneva Conference. The actual extent of Japanese compliance with the American agenda received little attention while the
United States courted Japan's support in the League of Nations. There
were inquiries in the Diet over the morphine trade, but the corrup-
tion cases involving Kosai Zendo and Hoshi Pharmaceutical suggest
an erosion of enforcement. By the late 1920s the opium monopoly in
Manchuria and trading companies such as Mitsui had become major
players, along with the Kwantung Army, in the Chinese drug trade.
The special exception made for Hoshi Pharmaceutical Company also
suggests the willingness of Japanese authorities to make questionable

allowances for those pharmaceutical companies that had been licensed during World War I to participate in the licit trade.

From the late 1920s through the 1930s charges of noncompliance multiplied and pressure to adhere to the American agenda grew. Many top U.S. officials believed the gradual convergence between civilian and military authorities over the importance of Japan's expanding presence in Manchuria had also produced a coordinated strategy of narcotization in China. The Kwantung Army and its Special Service Agency were clearly facilitating the opium and narcotics trade into Manchuria and northern China, both for the revenues it would bring and to enforce the subsequent controls imposed by the Manchukuo opium monopoly. Japanese policy makers did not control the actions of the military during the 1930s, however. Competition between Japanese military forces in China by the late 1930s, evident in the efforts to obtain opium from Iran, suggests, moreover, that the military was unable to control itself fully. The exclusion of the Home Affairs Ministry from the Inner Cabinet and the erosion of the Foreign Ministry's authority over operations in China relative to the military support the argument that shifting patterns of state capacity contributed to Japan's involuntary defection from the U.S. agenda. By late 1938, with the consolidation of state authority over Japanese drug control policy through the military, the China Affairs Board, and the new Welfare Ministry, the defection had become voluntary.

4

Japan and the
Global Partnership

The postwar American perception of Japan's conversion from adversary to ally in the war on drugs largely reflects the legacy of occupation. Persuaded by U.S. officials determined to prevent Japan from reentering the illicit drug trade and eager to establish the country as a "long-term model for antiopium programs in Asia," the Office of the Supreme Commander for the Allied Powers (SCAP) introduced "American-style narcotics control" in occupied Japan.[1] Not only was Japan's drug legislation redrafted along American lines but domestic production and trade in narcotics were severely curtailed. Following the occupation, Japanese policy makers continued to follow the political lead of the United States in international drug control efforts through the United Nations and cooperated in dealing with instances of trafficking by U.S. servicemen stationed in Japan. These actions contributed to the sense that Japan had become an ally in the American war on drugs.

The emergence of Asian, Southeast Asian, and Latin American source countries in the international drug trade shifted U.S. attention away from Japan. During the 1970s, the United States was preoccupied with the heroin trade through the Golden Crescent and Golden Triangle. Japan was important largely because of its geographical proximity to the Asian mainland and the potential, albeit seen as limited, for transshipment through Japan into the American market. By the mid-1980s the war on drugs declared by the Reagan administration shifted the focus to Latin American cocaine. U.S. officials approached other advanced industrial countries, especially in Europe and to a lesser extent Japan, for support of the American agenda through regulatory steps and financial assistance. In September 1989 Japan appeared to reaffirm the alliance when Prime Minister Kaifu Toshiki joined President George Bush in declaring a global partnership in the war against drugs.

This perception of Japan's place in the postwar American agenda is flawed. By comparison to the United States and the European Community, Japan has had little problem with heroin and cocaine and far more trouble with amphetamines and methamphetamines, which have traditionally been seen as minimal threats in the United States and were largely ignored by SCAP.[2] This chapter reveals that although international pressures have led Japanese policy makers to cooperate with the United States despite these differences, the extent of cooperation has been largely determined by domestic factors. Japan's participation in the global partnership reflects the link between drug issues and bilateral economic relations with the United States. Faced with increasing threats of economic retaliation, Japanese policy makers have viewed cooperation on drug issues as a means to defuse broader bilateral tensions. Nevertheless, since the end of the American occupation, Japanese drug policy has been largely determined by the nature of the domestic threat as perceived by Japanese authorities and society and by bureaucratic rivalry among those agencies involved in controlling illicit drug use. Because of such domestic factors, Japanese adherence to the American agenda has not been and is unlikely to be as extensive as the concept of global partnership would suggest.

Capacity and the Legacy of Occupation

Japan's defeat in World War II and the subsequent American occupation altered those aspects of state capacity which U.S. policy makers believed had contributed to Japan's role in the international drug trade. The territorial integrity of outlying possessions and the financial needs of Japanese holdings in China were no longer germane, for

Japan was stripped of "all the territorial gains she had made since 1868."[3] Similarly, the military no longer exerted influence over Japanese politics and policy for the simple reason that Japan was demilitarized.[4] SCAP sidelined the pharmaceutical industry and firms such as Mitsui and Mitsubishi by prohibiting narcotics manufacture in Japan, and the industry was also weakened by the initial fragmentation of the *zaibatsu* (oligopolistic conglomerates) holdings.[5]

Unfortunately, SCAP also instituted measures that at first limited the ability of Japanese authorities to deal with a postwar wave of domestic drug problems. Simply put, SCAP officials undermined Japan's territorial integrity by granting Allied military forces and occupation courts primary authority over those areas falling under the "objectives of the occupation," thereby severely restricting the criminal jurisdiction of the Japanese enforcement and judicial systems.[6] The enforcement ability of the Japanese police was further undercut by SCAP purges, decentralization programs, and limits on the size and armament of police forces.[7] SCAP authorities put drug enforcement in the hands of narcotics agents under the jurisdiction of Japan's Ministry of Health and Welfare, instead of the police, but these agents initially numbered only two hundred and they were not even granted powers of arrest until 1947.[8]

The drug enforcement priorities of SCAP reflected those of the United States rather than domestic conditions in Japan. Specifically, the Narcotics Control Division of SCAP's Public Health and Welfare Section made narcotics (a category under U.S. law including heroin, cocaine, opium, and morphine) and marijuana a priority and largely ignored the stimulant trade. During World War II, the Japanese government, like those in the United States and Europe, had sought to bolster industrial productivity and military effectiveness by distributing stimulant drugs to factory workers and soldiers and encouraging their use.[9] The immediate postwar legacy of this practice was a large portion of the Japanese population addicted to stimulants. As economic dislocation increased during the 1940s, stimulant use increased as well.

Drug demand was initially matched by a readily available supply. SCAP officials seized military stockpiles of narcotics worth approximately ¥10 million ($700,000) during 1945–1946, and they confiscated stockpiles of approximately ¥4 million in manufactured narcotics from private firms and directed them to twelve government storage facilities maintained by the Japanese Ministry of Health and Welfare.[10] Unreported military and private stockpiles of narcotics found their way into the hands of Japanese criminal organizations (the *yakuza*) and the growing black market.[11] SCAP officials as well as the yakuza had also seized military and private stockpiles of stimulants produced during the war. These also entered the black market, through direct diversion from SCAP stockpiles by American servicemen, through indirect diversion by Chinese, Taiwanese, and Korean middlemen contracted by SCAP officials to disperse the drugs along with other medical supplies to the Japanese population, and through the yakuza themselves. Violent competition ensued among organized gangs comprising displaced forced laborers from Korea, Taiwan, and China (termed *sangokujin*) and the yakuza for control of the black market. As SCAP and yakuza stockpiles began to dry up in the face of growing demand, clandestine production of stimulants—especially by displaced Koreans—began.[12]

At first, little effort was made to control the stimulant trade. As noted, SCAP directives had resulted in a Japanese police force that was no match for domestic gang warfare. Drawing on the model of U.S. drug legislation, moreover, SCAP authorities focused on narcotics. In September 1945 SCAP directive 2 called on Japanese authorities to provide information concerning all existing stockpiles of drugs and medical supplies. By October 12 SCAP narrowed its focus to narcotics control. General Douglas MacArthur, acting through the Public Health and Welfare Section, called for the declaration of narcotics stockpiles and production facilities; prohibited further cultivation, production, and export of narcotics; and prohibited imports without SCAP authorization. He made no mention of stimulants.[13] Acting on SCAP orders, during 1946 and 1947 the Japanese Ministry of Health and Welfare introduced drug control measures based on the two major pieces of U.S. drug legislation—the 1914 Harrison Narcotics Act and the 1937 Marijuana Tax Act. The resulting ordinances, eventually consolidated in the 1948 Narcotics Control Law and Hemp Control Law, prohibited opium cultivation and import, increased penalties for trafficking in opium and heroin, and introduced restrictions on marijuana cultivation, sale, possession, and use. Again stimulant drugs were not mentioned.[14]

Japanese authorities began to take steps against stimulant drug abuse during the late 1940s, but as new restrictions emerged, the trade in such drugs increasingly fell under the control of organized crime. Moreover, loopholes in the new regulations and the weakness of the Japanese police force undermined government efforts to crack down on clandestine production and trafficking. For example, the 1948 Drug, Cosmetics, and Medical Instruments Law, only required purchasers of stimulants to sign for the drug. A 1949 Ministry of Health ordinance prohibited the production of stimulants in powder or tablet form but not liquid form and failed to restrict possession or use.[15] Similarly, the 1951 Stimulant Control Law criminalized the "import, manufacture, trafficking, receipt, possession and use" of stimulant drugs but imposed a maximum penalty of only three years' imprisonment (in contrast to five years' for heroin) and lacked the police power for enforcement.[16] Once the occupation ended and the police force was reorganized and centralized on a national level in 1953, however, the Japanese government slowly began to make headway.

Among advanced industrialized democracies, Japan has the least fragmentation of authority across state institutions. In contrast to the United States and to a lesser extent Germany, the primary nexus of fragmentation lies within the executive ministries rather than between the executive and legislative branches.[17] The pattern is similar in the area of drug control policy. It is Japanese ministries rather than the Diet which have been the primary source of legislative proposals on drug control and enforcement and on money laundering generated by the international drug trade. Nevertheless, unity on drug control has been the exception rather than the rule within the executive. In 1970 the Japanese government established the Headquarters for Countermeasures against Drug Abuse as a new agency under the Office of the Prime Minister to develop a coordinated antidrug program.[18] Despite this agency's success in winning amendments to existing drug legislation during 1972–1973, subsequent coordination has tended to rely more on informal interministerial negotiations.

Several executive departments are involved in Japanese drug control policy making and enforcement.[19] The Ministry of Health and Welfare is the primary source for bills and ordinances that determine which drugs are subject to prohibition and regulation; restrictions on the production (with the Ministry of International Trade and Industry and the Ministry of Agriculture, Forestry, and Fisheries), sale, and distribution of licit drugs; and treatment and education programs. Drug enforcement provisions—the scope and nature of penalties as well as investigatory procedures—reflect deliberations among representatives from the Ministries of Health and Welfare, Justice (including the Public Prosecutors' Office), Finance (including the Customs Bureau), and Post and Telecommunications and the National Police Agency (NPA). More recent money-laundering provisions have been the product of negotiations among the NPA and the Ministries of Finance (banking system), Post and Telecommunications (postal savings system), Justice, and International Trade and Industry.

Enforcement lies primarily with the NPA and the narcotics agents of the Ministry of Health and Welfare, but resources are limited. By the early 1990s Health and Welfare had roughly 280 narcotics agents, divided between the national and prefectural levels, and the NPA was questioning their effectiveness. The police were investigating 98 percent of Japan's drug cases. The NPA fields a combined police force of 250,000 personnel at the national and prefectural levels, of which roughly 12 percent are civilians. Few officers are devoted solely to drug investigations.[20] For example, the national network of Cocaine Information Centers established by the NPA in 1990 to monitor cocaine trafficking has been severely understaffed and underfunded.[21] In addition, NPA proposals for controlled deliveries (allowing the initial import of drugs in order to catch the major traffickers) were not enacted until 1991 and have been resisted in practice by customs officials.[22]

Finally, the Japanese have participated in bilateral and multilateral drug control efforts through a wide range of different ministries whose objectives often compete. For example, representatives of the Ministry of Foreign Affairs have participated in United Nations efforts, bilateral relations with source and importing countries, and development-assistance programs. The ministry's goal has been to maintain or improve the overall tenor of foreign perceptions of Japan, often at the expense of other ministries and their constituencies. Finance officials representing Japan in forums such as the Financial Action Task Force of the Group of Seven (G-7) have tended to be less conciliatory. Similarly, whereas Foreign Affairs officials have at times shied away from steps that might antagonize source and other countries, Health and Welfare and NPA officials have relied on overtures to their counterparts abroad—through direct appeals, foreign missions, training programs, and the like—to attempt to curtail the trade.

U.S. occupation of Japan largely determined the sources of societal opposition Japanese policy makers would subsequently face. SCAP curtailed the growth of the Japanese narcotics industry and prevented the emergence of a broad population of narcotics users (and organized crime groups attempting to meet the needs of such users) as societal forces. Other SCAP policies, however, including its laissez-faire attitude toward the stimulant trade, helped to foster societal opposition to its control.

In 1947 the initial SCAP prohibition of domestic narcotics production was slightly relaxed, allowing the Ministry of Health and Welfare to license four companies to manufacture codeine for domestic needs.[23] In 1954, over the opposition of the United States and the Narcotics Section of the Ministry of Health and Welfare, the Japanese government turned to the domestic cultivation of opium (estimated at thirty tons) to facilitate production of its estimated annual needs of codeine and morphine.[24] Domestic heroin production remained prohibited.

In 1949 the United States estimated that there were fewer than fifty-six hundred narcotics addicts in Japan, concentrated in the Tokyo-Yokohama and Kobe-Osaka areas.[25] As Table 6 shows, narcotics arrests were also relatively limited. The narcotics feeding the trade were obtained primarily from unconfiscated military stockpiles in Japan and abroad during the 1940s and early 1950s.[26] By the early 1960s the sources supplying a brief resurgence of the heroin trade in Japan (Table 7) were primarily Hong Kong and China.[27] In 1953 the Narcotics Control Law increased the penalties for heroin trafficking to ten years' imprisonment and a ¥500,000 fine.[28] Ten years later, during a slight upsurge in heroin trafficking, these penalties increased to include life imprisonment, a ¥5 million fine, and compulsory hospitalization for addicts possessing or purchasing the drug.[29]

The occupation forestalled the development of societal opposition to narcotics control but fostered it in the case of stimulants. The relative uninterest of SCAP in the stimulant trade, the police purges,

Table 6. Arrests for drug offenses in Japan, 1951–1957

Year	Stimulants	Narcotics
1951	17,528	2,208
1952	18,521	1,642
1953	38,514	1,462
1954	55,664	2,092
1955	32,140	1,753
1956	5,047	1,103
1957	781	1,188

Sources: National Police Agency, *Anti-Drug Activities in Japan in 1989,* (Tokyo: Police Association, 1990), pp. 85, 110; Research and Training Institute, *Summary of the White Paper on Crime 1983* (Tokyo: Ministry of Justice, 1984), p. 41.
Note: During this period, the category of narcotics referred primarily to opium. Specific figures on heroin-related arrests became available in 1960.

Table 7. Arrests for drug offenses in Japan, 1957–1969

Year	Stimulants	Narcotics	Heroin
1957	781	1,188	n.a.
1958	271	1,667	n.a.
1959	372	1,525	n.a.
1960	476	2,081	1,387
1961	477	1,954	1,897
1962	546	2,349	2,139
1963	971	2,288	1,750
1964	860	847	597
1965	735	859	288
1966	694	692	33
1967	675	476	70
1968	775	227	22
1969	704	130	37

Sources: See Table 6.

and lax SCAP policies toward the yakuza and especially the sangokujin permitted Japan's addict population to grow and organized crime with it.[30] Yakuza and sangokujin street warfare during the 1940s had slowly given way by the early 1950s to the consolidation of larger crime organizations such as the Yamaguchi-gumi and Honda-kai in the Osaka-Kobe area and the Kinsei-kai, Tosei-kai, and Sumiyoshi-kai in the Tokyo-Yokohama area.[31] By 1955 the black market in stimulants was meeting the needs of an estimated 550,000 addicts. The reorganized police cracked down from 1954 to 1957 temporarily disrupting the trade and decreasing the influence of the sangokujin,[32] but the yakuza continued to expand.

Together with the police crackdown, Japanese authorities instituted tougher regulations under the Stimulant Control Law in 1954 and began a nationwide public education campaign. Stricter penalties, including threats of hospitalization for "cold-turkey" withdrawal, education campaigns, and the indirect effects of improving economic and social conditions helped to reduce domestic demand.[33] On the supply side, coordinated police action against clandestine domestic laboratories and distributors, deportation of sangokujin who were running such factories, and longer prison sentences of up to ten years temporarily undercut the role of organized crime in promoting the stimulant trade.[34]

Through the late 1950s and early 1960s, the yakuza underwent a period of transition, increasing membership and centralizing territorial organization. By 1963 NPA officials were reporting an estimated 5,107 organized groups with a membership of 184,000, dominated by seven major syndicates.[35] Although they briefly experimented with the heroin trade during this period, the primary yakuza organizations placed greater emphasis on territorial expansion.[36] For example, the Yamaguchi-gumi wanted to expand into the Tokyo-Yokohama area, the domain of the rival Inagawa-kai (the old Kinsei-kai). To deflect public criticism the Yamaguchi-gumi sent representatives into Yokohama and Tokyo on the pretext of waging an antidrug campaign.[37] The resulting gang warfare prompted an active police and media campaign highlighting the antisocial nature of gang violence.[38] Police crackdowns against what became termed the *boryokudan* (literally, the violent groups) disrupted drug trafficking and other yakuza operations through the remainder of the decade. By the early 1970s, however, the gang disputes had been resolved through new alliances, and the yakuza had returned to promoting the stimulant trade.[39]

According to the NPA, a wave of societal affluence during the 1970s broadened the pool of stimulant users in Japan from yakuza, laborers, and truck drivers to housewives, students, and others who wanted maximum enjoyment of leisure time. Feeding this demand were yakuza leaders and dealers who had been arrested in the earlier drug campaigns but had completed their sentences and were released during the early 1970s.[40] This time, in contrast to the 1950s, the yakuza relied on external sources of supply rather than domestic laboratories. Drawing on links with the leadership of Korean yakuza based in Japan, the Yamaguchi-gumi and Inagawa-kai developed a transnational, vertically integrated network for stimulant production and distribution between South Korea and Japan. By the mid-1970s the yakuza were deriving an estimated 44 percent of their income from stimulant trafficking.[41] As Table 8 shows, despite increased domestic penalties (including life imprisonment) and cooperation with authorities in source countries such as Korea and more recently Taiwan and China, the trade has continued.[42] The yakuza continue to meet the needs of a Japanese addict population conservatively estimated at 400,000 and millions of occasional users.[43]

Table 8. Stimulant drug seizures (kilograms) and arrests in Japan, 1970–1991

Year	Seizures	Arrests	Year	Seizures	Arrests
1970	5.9	1,682	1981	140.6	22,024
1971	25.8	2,634	1982	106.9	23,301
1972	29.4	4,709	1983	99.0	23,365
1973	34.0	8,301	1984	197.6	24,022
1974	23.2	5,919	1985	294.1	22,980
1975	34.4	8,218	1986	396.7	21,052
1976	31.7	10,678	1987	620.5	20,643
1977	65.0	14,447	1988	214.1	20,399
1978	99.6	17,740	1989	217.6	16,613
1979	119.3	18,297	1990	275.8	15,038
1980	152.3	19,291	1991	121.0	16,093

Sources: National Police Agency, White Paper on Police 1984 (Excerpt) (Tokyo: Police Association, 1985) pp. 109, 112; National Police Agency, White Paper on Police 1988 (Excerpt) (Tokyo: Japan Times, 1989), pp. 66, 69; National Police Agency, White Paper on Police 1990 (Excerpt) (Tokyo: Police Association, 1991), p. 69; National Police Agency, White Paper on Police 1992 (Excerpt) (Tokyo: Police Association, 1993), p. 75.

The Limits of Partnership

From the end of the American occupation until the mid-1980s, U.S. pressure on Japanese policy makers to adhere to the American agenda on the war against drugs was limited. By the 1950s, after having been forced to accept American narcotics laws during the occupation, Japan was essentially seen by the United States as a supporter of the American agenda. This view was reinforced during the early 1960s with the participation of Japanese representatives in the United Nations Commission on Narcotic Drugs in 1961 and Japan's ratification of the 1961 Single Convention on Narcotic Drugs in 1964.[44] By the onset of President Richard Nixon's high-profile and high-priority war on drugs during the late 1960s, the United States paid little attention to Japan.

The U.S. problems were heroin abuse and rising consumption of marijuana, and policy makers focused primarily on source countries including Turkey, Thailand, and Mexico. Since Japan served as a transit point for American troops stationed in Southeast Asia, both U.S. and Japanese authorities were concerned about potential heroin trafficking through Japan. Rather than pressure Japan for increased enforcement, the Nixon administration expanded the presence of the U.S. Drug Enforcement Agency (to six agents).[45] Japan continued to appear supportive of U.S. efforts under the auspices of the UN to strengthen international regulations and to expand the types of drugs covered by such regulations and signed the UN Convention on Narcotics and Psychotropic Substances in 1971.[46] Moreover, in 1973 Japan began to make annual contributions to the newly established United Nations Fund for Drug Abuse Control.[47]

Although Japan participated in multilateral efforts, its compliance with the American agenda was far from complete; for example, Japan did not ratify the 1971 convention until 1990. There was domestic opposition from doctors, researchers, and pharmaceutical producers as well as the Ministry of Health and Welfare to measures concerning the production, sale, and distribution of psychotropic substances, which made Health and Welfare officials reluctant to bring Japanese regulations in line with the international agreement. On the enforcement side, postal, customs, and Ministry of Justice officials were reluctant to bring the Japanese criminal code in line with the penal provisions of the 1971 convention. For example, they opposed the changes that would be necessary to comply with article 22, section 2:a:ii, on the pursuit and punishment of conspiracy, such as allowing the controlled delivery of drugs, although the NPA favored it.[48] Through the remainder of the 1970s, however, the drug issue ceased to be an American policy priority. Instead, the U.S. pressure on Japan turned to international trade disputes.

President Reagan's declaration of a war on drugs in 1984 returned the issue to high priority in American foreign policy. At the same time as the United States began the new campaign to pressure other advanced industrial countries for cooperation on drugs, however, American trade and monetary officials were also demanding cooperation on what had become volatile international economic issues. Rising protectionist pressures, American trade deficits, European and Japanese trade surpluses, and the related issue of the strength of the dollar relative to the yen and the deutsche mark preoccupied those concerned with international economic relations during the mid-1980s. Beginning in 1985, the United States began to link these issues implicitly with the American war against drugs. Reagan broadened the focus of the May 1985 economic summit of the G-7 by calling for more extensive international cooperation against the drug problem. The president's proposal had followed a First Ladies Summit on the drug problem organized by Nancy Reagan in April 1985. The proposal led to the establishment of a group of experts to prepare a report on the issue for distribution at the next G-7 summit scheduled for Tokyo in 1986.[49]

In contrast to the American agenda of the late 1960s and 1970s, the Reagan war focused more on the threat of Latin American cocaine than on Southeast Asian heroin. As seen in Table 9, however, the relevance of the new American agenda to Japanese drug problems was questionable at best. Simply put, the largest total annual seizure in Japan was less than most single seizures in an average U.S. city. Through the 1980s, NPA officials contended that the rise in cocaine use in Japan stemmed, in large part, from the country's growing internationalization. More Japanese traveling to the United States, young Japanese eager to emulate the "Western lifestyle and values," and the rising wealth and leisure time of the whole population suggested a growing demand pool for the drug.[50] When two Colombians holding over a kilogram of cocaine were arrested in 1983, police con-

Table 9. Cocaine seizures (kilograms) and arrests, 1980–1991

Year	Seizures	Arrests
1980	0.117	12
1981	0.020	11
1982	0.029	2
1983	1.028	17
1984	0.012	14
1985	0.129	26
1986	0.460	26
1987	1.608	35
1988	0.208	37
1989	13.679	88
1990	68.785	93
1991	22.467	110

Source: National Police Agency, *White Paper on Police 1990 (Excerpt)* (Tokyo: Police Association, 1991), pp. 72–73; National Police Agency, *White Paper on Police 1992 (Excerpt)* (Tokyo: Police Association, 1993), pp. 77–78.

Note: The English-language versions of the NPA White Papers have mistakenly reversed the figures for heroin and cocaine arrests since the early 1990s. The correct figures are used here.

cluded that Colombian drug syndicates were viewing Japan as a potential market.[51] Yet, citing the reluctance of yakuza to deal with South Americans, the prohibitively high wholesale price of cocaine in Japan, and the absence of extensive crack use, NPA officials initially downplayed the cocaine threat.[52]

Despite such considerations, opposing U.S. calls for international cooperation on the drug issue in 1985 would have risked further disruption of an already problematic economic relationship. During the summer of 1985, the United States began to threaten tariff retaliation against what were designated as unfair European trading practices. Moreover, by the end of September the Reagan administration had initiated proceedings against the unfair trade practices of Japan, the European Community, and other countries and had pressured the Germans and the Japanese into the Plaza Accord (aimed at reversing the rise of the American dollar).[53]

In this context, both the draft report on drugs released by the G-7 expert group in October 1985 and the final report released in May

1986 called for greater international cooperation to deal with illicit production, trafficking, smuggling, and drug abuse, especially involving cocaine. The pledge of the G-7 countries at the Tokyo Economic Summit in 1986 to achieve this end in turn facilitated the 1987 UN world conference on drug problems and an accord to conclude a new international treaty against drug trafficking.[54] At the Toronto Economic Summit in June 1988, representatives from the G-7 countries endorsed the U.S. proposal of a special task force on drug issues. The task force at its first meeting in September issued recommendations backed by the United States calling for coordinated action against money laundering and to facilitate the seizure of profits from the illicit drug trade. Two months later, representatives from the G-7 countries turned to incorporating these recommendations into what would become the 1988 United Nations Convention against Illicit Traffic in Narcotic Drugs and Psychotropic Substances.[55]

Japan, despite its low profile in past relations with the United States over drug issues and its freedom from the kind of drug threats facing the United States and Europe, found itself forced by the implicit linkage between cooperation on drugs and international economic relations to take a more active role. In February 1985 Prime Minister Nakesone Yasuhiro had urged his wife to attend the April drug summit coordinated by Nancy Reagan. In May 1985 the G-7 Summit selected Japan's Foreign Minister Abe Shintaro to direct the expert committee charged with drafting the drug report.[56]

Following the discussion of the report at the Tokyo Economic Summit and the resulting Tokyo Declaration calling for increased international drug control efforts in May 1986, the NPA and Japan International Cooperation Agency announced a new international role. Specifically, participation in their annual Conference on the Control of Narcotics Offenses was to be expanded for the first time to include director-level central government officials from twenty-four countries, including the United States, who would be "authorized to speak on behalf of drug control officers in their respective nations."[57] In addition to conferences sponsored by Japan, through 1987 and 1988 Japanese representatives participated in the UN conferences on a new drug treaty as well as the special task force created during the Toronto Economic Summit. At the September 1988 meeting of the task force in Washington, D.C., the chief Japanese delegate stressed "Japan's readiness to cooperate" despite a drug problem in Japan that, while "changing, . . . [was] not as acute as in other industrial countries."[58]

While Japan was making these well-publicized overtures abroad, attempts to implement the American agenda at home had run into difficulty. Japanese law enforcement officials continued to work against the methamphetamine trade. Similarly, during 1985 and 1986, NPA and Health and Welfare officials were emphasizing discussions with Taiwan (despite the opposition of the Ministry of Foreign Affairs) over curtailing the stimulant trade; they were giving little attention to Latin America.[59] During the summer of 1987, an advisory group in the Ministry of Justice had recommended that Japanese authorities be allowed to use surveillance, wiretaps, and access to bank records to facilitate the investigation of suspected drug traffickers, as U.S. Drug Enforcement Agency officials stationed in Japan and the NPA had long advocated.[60] The ministry declared itself unwilling to introduce measures that infringed on privacy, however, and it chose not to act on these recommendations.[61]

The Bush administration, which took office in early 1989, differed from its predecessor in its approach to Japan on international economic and drug issues and in the extent to which these were linked. For example, economic conflicts had culminated in the U.S. threat of Super 301 action against Japanese trade practices and the onset of negotiations between the two countries over structural impediments to trade. In addition to concessions on trade issues, American officials sought greater Japanese participation in the war on drugs.

Japanese compliance with the American agenda had remained limited through the summer of 1989. Following the completion of the UN convention in January 1989, press reports began to indicate that the Ministry of Justice and the NPA were taking steps to amend the penal code to allow seizure of funds generated by drug transactions. Such steps were touted as necessary to bring Japanese laws in line with the UN convention.[62] Yet, by the summer of 1989 Japan had neither signed the convention nor made progress in modifying the penal code. In July 1989 at the Paris G-7 Summit the United States put direct pressure on Japan over drug policy. The U.S. proposal for a new special task force (the Financial Action Task Force) to deal with the issue of money laundering included a direct appeal by Secretary of State James Baker to the Japanese representatives that Japan take "more aggressive steps" on this issue. Although Japanese officials had expressed their support for action against money laundering at the G-7 conference in September 1988, little progress on this issue had been made in Japan by the summer of 1989.[63]

By September 1989 Japanese policy makers were attempting to achieve some degree of domestic political stability after a summer of scandals that rocked the ruling Liberal Democratic party and brought the resignations of two prime ministers. Three weeks into his term, to help solidify his position as Japan's newest prime minister, Kaifu Toshiki met with President Bush in the United States. Both leaders emerged from this meeting with calls for easing trade tensions between the two countries as a step toward establishing a new "global partnership."[64]

Although initial press reports described an economic partnership and spoke of the ongoing Structural Impediments Initiative talks on competition and trade issues, the discussions between Bush and Kaifu had been more far-reaching.[65] Responding to Bush's general expressions of concern, Kaifu had expressed Japan's willingness to explore potential areas of cooperation on the drug issue and suggested the convening of an experts' meeting later in the year. During the next few weeks, the two leaders also exchanged letters in which they laid out a rough division of labor in the war against drugs. Since Japan's constitution prohibited military involvement abroad (and, therefore, direct participation in foreign eradication and interdiction efforts) the leaders agreed that Japan would focus on economic assistance to drug-exporting countries, especially those in Asia and Southeast Asia.[66] In late September the broader global partnership was made public. During a visit to Japan, Vice-President Dan Quayle announced that in addition to trade, the global partnership would cooperate on three new areas: the war on drugs, space exploration, and the promotion of democracy. Quayle also revealed that Bush and Kaifu had been corresponding on the drug issue and that Kaifu was drafting proposals for an increased Japanese role.[67]

American and Japanese officials alike noted that Kaifu's actions appeared to be motivated less by actual drug problems in Japan than by the need to find an area where cooperation with the United States could be expanded.[68] For example, the global partnership apparently placed little emphasis on coordinated action against stimulant exports from Taiwan and South Korea. Similarly, providing economic assistance to heroin-exporting countries in Asia and Southeast Asia to reduce their dependence on drug exports, would not solve Japan's major drug problems. In late August 1989 Japanese authorities were alarmed by a seizure of twelve kilograms of Colombian cocaine at the port of Kobe.[69] Yet, if the cocaine threat was increasing, it would not be eased by Japanese economic assistance to Asia and Southeast Asia. Moreover, the amount of cocaine seized in 1989 was still minuscule compared to stimulant drugs seized.[70]

Thus, from September 1989 through the early 1990s, the American agenda called for Japanese cooperation in aid programs to Asia and Southeast Asia, steps against the cocaine trade, and measures to prevent money laundering. By November 1989 the U.S. special trade representative had also begun outlining to the G-7 the U.S. interest in an economic-assistance package for the Andean countries. Japanese compliance with these aspects of the American agenda was far from complete.

First, international cooperation on the drug issue beyond the level of law enforcement and work within the United Nations was a relatively new issue for the Japanese bureaucracy. The ministers were especially unfamiliar with how to tailor development-assistance programs to drug-exporting countries.[71] Japanese economic measures capable of reducing the reliance of countries on drugs were inhibited by this lack of experience. For example, economic assistance to Thailand in 1989 on the drug issue consisted primarily of providing vehicles to help with crop substitution. Aid programs to Peru (1990–1992) also included provisions aimed at crop substitution. Yet Japanese officials had done relatively little to create new markets for proposed exports such as coffee necessary to support such programs.[72] Antidrug aid programs to Colombia (1989–1990) included loans of ¥8.38 billion, grants of ¥48 million, and untied loans of $100 million. The tied loans and grants, however, appear to have had little relevance to the drug issue. The loans were to be used for a new sewage system for Bogota, and the grants were to be used to purchase audiovisual equipment for the government music archive. The untied loans were granted by the Export-Import Bank of Japan to purchase goods from Japan.[73]

At a broader level, Japanese assistance programs were constrained by poor coordination and divided financial responsibility among the Ministries of Finance, Foreign Affairs, Health and Welfare, Justice, Transportation, Trade and Industry, and Agriculture, Forestry, and Fisheries.[74] In addition, drug-related violence in Latin America raised concerns among policy makers over the possible ramifications of expanding Japan's role in the region. More than fifty Japanese companies had direct investments in Colombia, Peru, and Bolivia; roughly nine thousand Japanese natives were working and studying in these countries; and about seventy-three thousand individuals of Japanese descent lived there, including the activist president of Peru, Alberto Fujimori.[75] During 1989, Japanese in Colombia and Peru, fearing retaliation, had appealed to the Japanese government to avoid high-profile action against drugs. By 1990 Kaifu had reportedly received death threats from Colombian drug lords who wanted Colombians arrested on drug charges released.[76]

Japanese steps against the cocaine trade began to increase during the early 1990s. By early 1990, NPA officials were acknowledging a potential threat from cocaine but still maintaining that the "situation [was] not out of control."[77] High-profile incidents related to cocaine had primarily been limited to Nancy Reagan's visit in late 1989 to establish Japan's first Just Say No Club and the early 1990 arrest of the popular Japanese actor Katsu Shintaro (Okimura Toshio) on possession charges.[78] In 1990, however, 62.3 kilograms of cocaine were seized in two major arrests of Colombian nationals, the largest confiscation ever in Japan.[79] By 1991 officials were afraid that the Japanese proclivity for stimulant drugs and the U.S. crackdown on the cocaine trade might lead to a wave of cocaine abuse and trafficking.[80] NPA officials were also warning that seizures of Latin American cocaine for 1991 would easily break the hundred-kilogram mark.[81]

As Table 9 illustrates, this prediction did not come to pass. The primary government response to these concerns had been twofold. In 1990 the NPA established a national network of cocaine information centers to monitor cocaine trafficking, and the revised Narcotics Control Act passed by the Diet in October 1991 permitted new law enforcement procedures such as controlled deliveries to monitor and track drug shipments.[82] The impetus for the new enforcement measures stemmed less from internal dynamics than from obligations incurred from signing the 1988 UN Convention in December 1989 and subsequent U.S. pressure to implement it.

Nevertheless, as I have noted, the information centers were severely understaffed and underfunded, and the new enforcement procedures—although a major step for Japan, given past opposition to such measures—continued to face resistance in implementation from immigration and customs officials.[83] Ironically, the primary constraint on the cocaine trade appears to have been the yakuza. Since the 1970s the stimulant trade had been a well-established and lucrative enterprise for organized crime.[84] The cocaine trade might disrupt the market for the established yakuza, but it offered newer or splinter organized crime groups the means to gain financial resources. Such groups faced two constraints. First, in contrast to the successful methamphetamine trade, cocaine operations in Japan tended to lack an external source of supply vertically integrated into a yakuza-controlled distribution network.[85] During the early 1990s those arrested for offenses involving cocaine were mainly Colombian prostitutes and Colombian and Bolivian nationals of Japanese, Taiwanese, or Korean descent rather than yakuza members.[86] Second, the context within which the yakuza operated in Japan changed during the early 1990s, in part because of a rash of financial scandals involving organized crime. The Boryokudan Countermeasures Law passed in 1991 and implemented in 1992 allowed the NPA to "designate certain organizations as organized crime groups" and to restrict their assembly, recruiting, and other activities.[87] A large-scale shift into cocaine, especially sales to young Japanese, risked more intensive government monitoring of the yakuza and even more severe legislation against them. The announcement by the Yamaguchi-gumi in late 1991 that it would be establishing a new antidrug organization, credibility aside, suggests that the yakuza recognized this connection.[88]

Against money laundering, Japan was the last of the G-7 countries to take steps.[89] The yakuza had been making use of bank secrecy regulations and business and political ties to launder funds—including an estimated annual $3.7 billion in stimulant drug revenue—through a wide array of banks, businesses, and political organizations.[90] In the early 1990s U.S. and Japanese drug enforcement officials began to report negotiations between Latin American cocaine cartels and the yakuza over money laundering.[91] Prior to 1989 opposition by the Ministry of Justice had limited government action to informal measures such as notices from the Ministry of Finance to banks "warning them against money laundering."[92]

By 1989 new U.S. money-laundering provisions empowered the president to withhold access to U.S. financial markets in cases of noncooperation.[93] In addition, the 1988 UN Convention required signatories to introduce legislation criminalizing money laundering, allowing seizure of funds, and waiving aspects of bank secrecy.[94] Thus, one month after the Bush-Kaifu declaration of global partnership, Finance Minister Hashimoto Ryutaro pledged to participate in bilateral consultations with the United States on the money-laundering issue. By the end of the year Japan had signed the UN convention and Finance officials had announced plans to draft money-laundering measures.[95] In January 1990 the Finance Ministry announced its intent to submit money-laundering legislation to the Diet by the end of the year and to have legislation in place by fiscal year 1991. Japanese officials renewed this pledge at a spring UN drug summit and following the Financial Action Task Force report in April.[96]

Yet, although external pressure helps to explain why the Japanese government adopted more formal regulations, the details of the pending Japanese provisions were still under negotiation at home. Despite the minister's statements, Finance officials were concerned with the structural ramifications of action against money laundering. In October 1989, noting Japan's limited problems with heroin and cocaine compared to those in the United States, these officials initially questioned the necessity of burdening Japanese financial institutions.[97] By February 1990, however, the Ministry of Finance was publicly supporting broad proposals such as those that allowed banks to waive confidentiality to report suspicious cases, but it explicitly rejected the U.S. practice of monitoring all cash transactions over $10,000 as too restrictive. Citing the cash orientation and large cash turnover in Japanese business, Finance officials proposed a higher ceiling of ¥50–100 million ($385,000–770,000).[98]

The Japanese banking industry was not totally opposed to the idea of money-laundering regulations. If properly drafted, such steps could offer the industry a means to increase oversight of its primary competitor, the postal savings system. Beginning in 1979 the banking industry and the Ministry of Finance had attempted to increase regulatory control over postal savings, citing the need for vigilance against tax evasion. Yet, by 1985 the resulting deliberations as played out in the Diet among the Ministry of Finance, the Ministry of Post and Telecommunications, the banking industry, and the postal savings system produced only a self-check system to be carried out by the respective ministries.[99] Five years later, the debate over money-laundering regulations appears to have followed a similar path. Although rejecting the idea of the ten-thousand-dollar breakpoint for monitoring cash transactions, the Japanese Federation of Bankers' Associations raised only general concerns about the potential cost and inconvenience of identification procedures and reporting requirements. Banking industry officials explicitly noted, however, that to minimize the adverse impact of such steps, regulations would have to be extended to other Japanese financial institutions, including the postal savings system.[100]

In May 1990 the press began to report on deliberations among the Ministries of Finance, Justice, and Health and Welfare on money laundering. By June these reports were also noting new identification measures under consideration by the Ministry of Finance.[101] In early September Finance officials announced that beginning October 1, 1990, all financial institutions were to require proof of identification from individual and corporate customers opening new accounts, making domestic cash transactions over ¥30 million ($230,000), or conducting international cash transactions over ¥5 million ($38,000).[102] This was an interim step timed to coincide with the U.S. attorney general's September visit to Japan.[103] With the exception of the threshold requirements, these new regulations appear to have been little more than a slight extension of the tax evasion compromise reached in 1985.

In April 1991 two bills prepared by the Ministries of Finance, Justice, and Health and Welfare were endorsed by the Social Affairs Division of the Liberal Democratic party and the cabinet and presented to the Diet.[104] In early October the Diet passed the Law Controlling the Encouragement of Illegal Acts Relating to Controlled Drugs with International Cooperation and the Law Amending the Narcotic Drugs and Psychotropic Substances Control Law.[105] The laws empowered authorities to confiscate the proceeds from drug-related offenses and impose criminal penalties for false identification and illegal transactions.[106] In addition, the laws imposed reporting requirements on financial institutions.

Yet, from the standpoint of compliance with the American agenda, these requirements were extremely limited. Financial institutions were required to report only suspicious (defined as drug-related) transactions.[107] Banks were to report to the Ministry of Finance; post offices to the Ministry of Post and Telecommunications; and nonbanks to the Ministry of International Trade and Industry. Suspected cases of money laundering were to be investigated by the NPA, but only following notification by the relevant ministry.[108] In short, although committing Japan to greater steps against money laundering, the new provisions appear to have emphasized the protection of ministerial influence more than compliance with the American agenda.

Although the U.S. occupation contributed to the perception that Japan had been transformed from adversary to ally in the American war on drugs, the extent of Japanese adherence to the American agenda has been overstated. Japanese policy makers repeatedly declared their support in bilateral and multilateral forums but took few concrete steps during the Reagan drug war. Japan was more active during the Bush war on drugs, enacting new provisions in enforcement (controlled delivery, and steps against cocaine), foreign aid (to Asian and Latin American source countries), and against money laundering. Yet the impetus for such steps was largely external—veiled and at times explicit threats of U.S. trade and financial retaliation.

One irony of Japan's response to the American agenda is that SCAP policies with regard to organized crime and the stimulant drug trade during the 1940s helped to shape the very issues that have diverted Japanese resources and support away from greater cooperation with the United States during the 1980s and 1990s. Specifically, the proliferation of the yakuza and the postwar breadth of the stimulant trade partially reflect SCAP's application of American drug and political agendas during the occupation. Moreover, subsequent U.S. policy has tended to ignore problems faced by Japan. For example, the United States took international steps against methamphetamines only during the 1980s, in response to a growing U.S. problem with domestic production of the drug (under the street name of Crank) and an apparent wave of trafficking (under the street name of Ice) in Hawaii and on the West Coast.[109]

A second irony is that the American premise—linking state capacity to foreign compliance—has rarely been applied to advanced industrial countries such as Japan. Growing numbers of policy analysts and scholars find little utility in the common assumption of Japanese governmental cohesion in foreign economic policy. This chapter suggest a similar finding for Japanese drug control policy. Specifically, the extent of Japanese compliance with the American agenda has to some degree been shaped by the fragmentation of authority among key ministries and their implementation agencies and bureaus. Although the Japanese may respond to international pressures, the key to the details lies in the domestic bargain.

5

Germany and the
American Agenda

The U.S. perception from the 1920s that Germany had become
an ally rather than an adversary with regard to drugs remained
largely intact during the postwar years. For example, whereas the
Treasury Department Bureau of Narcotics dispatched five agents to
aid MacArthur's staff in Japan during the 1940s, only one agent was
sent to Germany "to assist in reestablishing the drug control
system."[1] Although U.S. authorities altered the administrative
structure of German drug control efforts during the 1940s, with few
exceptions they left the substantive provisions of the country's
Opium Act of 1929, as amended, in place. Following the occupation
and through the 1950s and 1960s, the United States sought German
cooperation in curtailing drug abuse within the U.S. military and in
facilitating the broader American agenda under the auspices of the
United Nations. During the Nixon drug wars, German drug policy
expanded to include efforts against the Turkish and Southeast Asian
heroin trade. In the mid-1980s during the Reagan-Bush drug war,
German authorities took steps against the drug and financial
activities of the Latin American cocaine cartels. In 1989, following
the lead of the Bush administration, Prime Minister Helmut Kohl
not only pledged a substantial support package for Colombia but
began to institute a new National Drug Control Program.

As in the case of Japan, however, this perception of Germany's place in the postwar American agenda is flawed. This chapter reveals that the division of Germany in 1945 and its position on the front line of the Cold War helped to create a domestic drug situation similar to that in the United States—that is, a substantial rise in the heroin trade but only a limited stimulant problem. Domestic drug use patterns thus encouraged Germany to support the U.S. line. When the U.S. bias shifted toward cocaine and Latin America during the 1980s, however, German policy makers remained more focused on heroin. In addition, German concessions to the American agenda on cocaine enforcement and assistance to Latin American countries, have been counterbalanced by disputes through the early 1990s over the pace of German action against money laundering and exports of precursor chemicals in cocaine production. In addition, since the 1970s, domestic debates at the federal and Länder levels have slowly shifted the country away from the enforcement approach adopted by the United States.[2] More than either the United States or Japan, Germany has placed growing emphasis on rehabilitation, treatment, and partial decriminalization.

Capacity and Division

During the 1920s, U.S. policy makers attributed apparent German participation in the illicit drug trade to the weak state capacity of the Weimar regime. By the mid-1930s the Nazi regime had changed these conditions. In addition to consolidating and expanding territorial integrity, the Third Reich had recentralized the German state. The Reich Office of Health was given authority over drug control policy vis-à-vis the Länder as well as the German pharmaceutical industry. Once Germany was defeated in World War II, divided, and occupied, German policy makers once again found drug control curtailed by weak territorial integrity and power fragmentation.

Directives of the Supreme Headquarters Allied European Forces (SHAEF) from autumn 1945 called for the victors to "reestablish prewar [drug] control measures" in Germany.[3] From the standpoint of U.S. authorities, however, it seemed that narcotics control had collapsed.[4] The "rigid control" practiced during the late 1930s and early

1940s had degenerated into "complete confusion."[5] Records concerning drug enforcement, military and medical stockpiles, and production facilities had either been destroyed in the war or transferred from Berlin to Silesia, in what had become the Soviet occupation zone, to avoid Allied bombing raids.[6] In the absence of such records, drug stockpiles discovered by Allied forces were initially "handed over more or less indiscriminately to wholesalers, pharmacies, and even unauthorized persons."[7] By 1946 U.S. authorities were estimating that roughly 90 percent of military stockpiles had been "recovered and restored to legitimate channels."[8] Through 1947, however, the illicit trafficking from unconfiscated wartime medical and military depots, and from the rubble of wholesale, retail, and production facilities continued.[9]

Drug control was initially hampered by the Allied division of Germany into American, French, British, and Soviet sectors and by the broader dismantling of the centralized German state. Within the occupation zones, Allied authorities all reintroduced the control measures in place under the Opium Act.[10] In the absence of a central health ministry and police coordination, however, administrative schemes and the degree of enforcement were far from consistent across the zones. For example, British and French authorities relied on single Opium Offices for their respective zones, but U.S. officials in 1946 turned to new Opium Offices established on a Länder basis and coordinated by the Office of Military Government, United States (OMGUS).[11] Staffing problems as well as growing concern about drug abuse within Germany prompted OMGUS officials to seek updating of the 1929 Opium Act and uniform administration across the Allied sectors. Although the Allied Health Committee established a working party in September 1946 to explore the issue, the matter was tabled indefinitely after the Soviet Union blocked it.[12]

Derailed within the working party, OMGUS officials turned to consolidating control over the American zone. German external trade in narcotics had been suspended in 1946. In 1948, although imports remained prohibited, exports resumed under permits issued by OMGUS authorities.[13] Intra and interzonal transactions were allowed to take place but were administered by a three-tiered structure linking the opium offices, a new Länder Narcotics Subcommittee, and the OMGUS Public Health Branch.[14] To strengthen enforcement of the Opium Act, OMGUS officials also introduced police-training programs on narcotics, established criminal identification and data collection offices, and pressured the German courts to impose the maximum penalties for drug infractions allowed under the law (three years' imprisonment and a fine of two hundred reichsmarks).[15]

As in Japan, U.S. efforts focused on narcotics. OMGUS authorities emphasized the need to identify and control narcotics stockpiles, curtail the German role in the international narcotics trade, and limit or, in the case of heroin, ban narcotics production. Despite this focus on narcotics, Germany avoided the postwar wave of stimulant abuse found in Japan. Two characteristics of the occupation helped to prevent it. First, through the early stages of the war, Germany had relied extensively on the use of amphetamines and methaphetamines (especially Pervatin) among the military, but in June 1941 German policy makers, concerned about the adverse physical effects of such drugs, had added Pervatin and other selected stimulants to the list of restricted substances under 1929 Opium Act, over the opposition of domestic producers.[16] By reinstituting the Opium Act during the occupation, therefore, Allied authorities reintroduced formal restrictions on many stimulants as well as narcotics.[17]

Second, the occupation disrupted domestic production of stimulant drugs. By the late 1930s, the primary German producer of Pervatin was the Temmler-Werke of the Vereinigte Chemische Fabriken located in Berlin-Joachimstahl. This area became a part of the Soviet occupation zone in late 1945, and the Soviet authorities expropriated the factory. American pharmaceutical producers with strong interest in the commercial potential of stimulant drugs (especially in what would become the diet pill industry) began purchasing German production facilities in the western zones. Although Temmler relocated to Marburg and gradually reestablished production, by the early 1960s as the use of amphetamines in diet preparations became popular in Germany, U.S. companies dominated the market.[18]

If the occupation helped to prevent the development of a stimulant problem in Germany, its territorial legacy facilitated the rise of the illicit heroin trade. In 1949 the intensifying Cold War resulted in the formal division of Germany along the lines of the Western and Soviet occupation zones. The split had two main ramifications for drug control policy in the new West Germany. First, drug abuse problems among more than 200,000 American soldiers stationed there by the 1960s and 1970s would turn U.S. military bases into both a conduit and a draw for heroin trafficking.[19] German control efforts were limited by the extent of cooperation with the U.S. military investigative divisions, how much priority the military gave the drug issue, and during the early 1970s, turf disputes between the military and the DEA.[20]

Second, despite strict border controls between East and West Germany, Berlin's division offered a gateway for the heroin trade. The West German, and in turn U.S., refusal to recognize East Germany as a separate country meant an absence of extensive customs provisions in dealing with border traffic from the East, especially through Berlin. By the 1970s DEA officials had identified Shönfeld Airport in East Berlin as the primary air transport point for heroin into Germany. Once the drugs were in East Berlin, traffickers would simply take the subway into West Berlin, disappearing in a volume of common traffic that easily overwhelmed the police and customs officials at the stations.[21]

Germany's ability to comply with the American agenda has also been shaped by more power fragmentation than that found in Japan. Although the legislature is also involved in policy making, the primary fragmentation occurs within the executive and especially in policy implementation, between the federal and Länder governments. Moreover, secondary fragmentation has developed between the German government and the supranational institutions of the European Union.

German federal ministries rather than the Bundestag or Bundesrat (lower and upper houses of the legislature) have been the primary source for drug control bills, including enforcement and money-laundering measures.[22] For decades few changes were made. The Opium Act remained the centerpiece of German drug control policy until 1971, when it was replaced by the Narcotics Act. Adoption of the new law and subsequent amendments in the early 1980s were driven by government action plans drafted by the executive ministries, in part to implement provisions of the 1971 UN drug convention.[23] In 1992 similar dynamics brought additional provisions under the Law against Illegal Drug Trade and Other Manifestations of Organized Crime.[24]

In general, there has been more centralization within the executive on drug control policy than in Japan. For example, the federal government Program of Action on Drug Abuse Control in 1980 designated the Family Ministry—that is, the Federal Ministry for Youth, Family, Women, and Health as the coordinating agency for national drug strategy. Working groups and committees established under the program helped coordinate the efforts of the Family, Health, Justice, Interior, Finance, Foreign, and Economic Cooperation Ministries.[25] Prior to 1980, however, centralization focused either on linking specific federal and Länder ministries or on organizing a broad array of officials into working groups to implement U.S. drug control strategy. For example, beginning in the early 1970s, a standing working party within the federal and Länder health ministries was responsible for drug issues, and a standing conference of federal and Länder interior ministers coordinated police activities, including drug control.[26] By the late 1970s bilateral agreements on drug control with the United States had prompted the formation of groups such as the Central Working Group. Although chaired by the Family Ministry, the working group and its subcommittees provided an annual forum more for linking U.S. (State Department, embassy, and military) and German (such as Interior, Finance, Defense, Foreign, and Justice) officials than as a mechanism for centralizing German efforts.[27]

Despite the large number of executive ministries involved, domestic conflict has tended to arise along the lines of the relative emphasis placed on repressive (enforcement) versus preventative (education and information, therapy, and rehabilitation) approaches. In deliberations at the federal level repression tends to be advocated by the Ministries of the Interior and Finance and their enforcement arms (police and customs), whereas the Ministries of Health and Family tend to favor prevention.[28] These biases reflect the institutionalized responsibilities of the respective ministries over organized and drug crime (Interior), border traffic and financial transactions (Finance), alterations to the German criminal code (Justice), and prevention (Family). Health and Family officials are also empowered under the Narcotics Act to supervise and regulate the licit production, sale, and domestic and international trade of narcotics and other drugs.[29]

In all these areas, federal officials rely heavily on their Länder counterparts, especially in policy implementation and drafting of measures that fall within Länder jurisdiction—such as police, health, and social issues—under the German constitution (Basic Law).[30] As at the federal level, ministries contend over repression and prevention. Generally, the northern Länder lean more toward prevention than do the southern Länder.

Since the 1970s, enforcement has rested primarily with the narcotics agents of the Federal Criminal Office, established in 1951, and its Länder counterparts. Additional enforcement agencies include the Investigative Section of the Customs Bureau and the Federal Border Police.[31] Until the 1970s the Federal Criminal Office served as a limited coordinating agency and information repository while investigations were largely carried out by the Länder police. Growing concerns about terrorism during the 1970s, combined with U.S. pressure for greater centralization, led to legislation that gave the federal office original jurisdiction in drug cases and established it as the primary contact office for all foreign contacts in such cases. By the mid-1980s, the Länder had established their own "elite criminal investigative units" based on the federal model.[32]

Germany devotes more police to drug enforcement than does Japan, but their numbers remain limited. For example, in the late 1970s the narcotics police division in West Berlin consisted of only forty full-time officers even though the city was a gateway for the illicit trade.[33] By the mid-1980s, total Länder police forces stood at an estimated 100,000,[34] of which only a small portion was devoted exclusively to narcotics matters. At the federal level, the antidrug division of the Criminal Office was established in 1986 with a membership of 260 officers, out of a total force of 3,400.[35] By 1990 this division employed approximately 300 officers with an additional 2,700 officials indirectly working on drug issues.[36] In addition to the Länder and federal police forces, approximately 10,000 customs border guards, and 340 drug investigators (of the 1,300 in the Customs Investigative Service) are working in drug control.[37] Coordination among federal and land police forces takes place through an array of working groups, including the Narcotics Commission, as well as through a national drug data base (PIOS).[38] As in Japan, there are disputes between police and customs officials, especially over the practice of controlled deliveries. The disputes, however, are less over the procedure itself, in place in Germany since the 1980s, than over who has jurisdiction once the drugs pass the border.[39]

Overlapping jurisdiction is also a problem in bilateral and multilateral efforts. For example, although the regional and coordination bureaus of the Foreign Office have formal responsibility for international cooperation in drug issues,[40] the primacy of the Foreign Office has been the exception rather than the rule. Since the early 1980s the Federal Criminal Office has increasingly relied on police liaison officials stationed in German embassies in producer and transit countries as a form of long-range or extended defense strategy.[41] Broader foreign assistance has been directed by the Ministry for Economic Cooperation, with the help of the Interior, Health, and Family Ministries as well as the Foreign Office.[42] The proliferation of European Community drug control efforts since the early 1970s—through the Pompidou Group, the European Council's ad hoc Committee for a People's Europe (Adonnino Committee), the European Committee for the Fight against Drugs (CELAD), the TREVI Groups (Terrorism, Radicalism, Extremism, Violence, International), and the Schengen Subgroups (especially those on narcotics, and police and customs cooperation)—has also increased the number of German ministries and enforcement agencies directly involved in multilateral control activities and, in turn, the difficulties in coordinating German drug policy.[43] Such difficulties have been exacerbated by the cross-cutting regional working groups for police, customs, and border officials established or encouraged by the United States, including STAR (Standing Working Group on Narcotics) and the north, southeast, and southwest working groups.[44]

In Germany, unlike Japan, the U.S. occupation had relatively little influence on postwar sources of opposition to German drug control efforts. Although curtailed under the provisions of the Opium Act, the German narcotics industry reemerged during the 1940s with the same players that had influenced the Hague deliberations and control problems during the 1920s. Narcotics control measures introduced by the occupation authorities included prohibitions on heroin production, but specific firms were licensed to produce morphine and cocaine, including Merck and C. F. Böhringer und Söhne in the U.S. zone; C. H. Böhringer Sohn, Knoll, and Hoffman La Roche in the French zone; and C. H. Böhringer Sohn, Chinafabrik Buchler, and Chemishe Werke Mindern (a Knoll subsidiary) in the British zone.[45] Merck was the sole licensed cocaine producer in the U.S. zone and, by agreement of the German narcotics industry, the coordinating agency for the collection of domestic opium throughout the Allied zone. Through the 1940s companies such as Merck and Knoll also established "branch offices and depots" to facilitate trade among the zones.[46]

Yet, despite the resurgence of the German narcotics industry during the 1940s, it was narcotics from abroad which would become the source of domestic drug problems, partly because of addiction patterns and partly because of changes in the focus of the pharmaceutical industry. As OMGUS authorities noted, despite illicit trafficking from old stockpiles, strict controls under the Opium Act initially mitigated postwar problems with addiction. Within the U.S. zone, for example, the estimated addict population in 1947 stood at only 408 persons, of which over 50 percent were addicted to morphine and none to heroin or cocaine.[47] Strict controls on domestic narcotics production, as well as the relative absence of "clandestine manufacture," kept the numbers from rising.[48] By the late 1950s and early 1960s, moreover, the German pharmaceutical industry was no longer interested in producing narcotics. Companies such as Höchst, BASF, Merck, and Schering had shifted into production of a wide array of synthetic drugs.[49]

Germany's addict population began to expand during the late 1960s and early 1970s, its growth fed by youth unemployment, limited educational opportunities, and emulation of the U.S. drug culture and by a growing drug trade from the Middle East and Southeast Asia. By 1976 West Germany's estimated addict population was 40,000.[50] By the early 1980s, West German authorities were estimating between 68,000 and 80,000 (primarily heroin) addicts; in the early 1990s they estimated between 80,000 and 120,000 heroin and cocaine addicts and 200,000 to 2.5 million users of hashish and marijuana out of a total population of 56 million.[51] Because of the difficulties in obtaining accurate assessments of addiction as an indicator of drug problems, German authorities have focused on drug arrest and seizure data (Tables 10 and 11).[52] They have also given much credence to what they consider a more concrete indicator of drug problems—the number of drug-related (usually heroin) deaths (Table 12).[53]

As noted, drug use in Japan has facilitated the rise and influence of indigenous organized crime groups. Although German authorities have increasingly acknowledged the role of organized crime in the German drug trade, these groups have been seen as primarily foreign. During the late 1970s Chinese gangs linking Southeast Asian heroin to operations in Amsterdam had emerged to fill the gap created by the

Table 10. German drug seizures (kilograms), 1962–1991

Year	Heroin	Cocaine	Stimulants	Hashish and Marijuana
1962	—	—	—	5.5
1963	—	0.098	—	38.2
1964	—	0.016	—	40.2
1965	—	—	—	45.4
1966	—	—	—	135.0
1967	—	0.001	—	167.2
1968	1.8	0.016	—	381.0
1969	0.6	0.087	—	2,278.2
1970	0.5	—	—	4,332.0
1971	2.9	9.2	—	6,669.0
1972	3.7	1.7	6.6	6,114.0
1973	15.4	4.3	9.0	4,731.9
1974	33.0	5.4	6.1	3,910.6
1975	31.0	1.4	3.6	6,627.8
1976	167.2	2.4	17.5	5,325.9
1977	61.1	7.7	16.2	9,821.6
1978	187.3	4.3	2.7	4,723.5
1979	207.3	19.0	0.1	6,407.3
1980	267.1	22.2	3.8	3,200.2
1981	93.1	24.0	5.6	6,696.0
1982	202.3	32.7	16.5	3,189.6
1983	260.0	106.3	24.8	4,605.5
1984	263.8	171.1	14.4	5,646.0
1985	208.0	165.0	28.2	11,498.0
1986	157.2	186.0	84.5	2,675.0
1987	319.9	296.0	61.7	2,997.0
1988	537.2	496.1	91.4	11,350.2
1989	727.4	1,405.6	66.8	12,073.2
1990	846.8	2,473.8	85.5	13,640.7
1991	1,594.9	964.0	n.a.	12,344.0

Sources: BKA, *Rauschgift Jahresbericht, 1990* (Wiesbaden: BKA, 1991),
table 13; Hans-Dieter Schwind, *Kriminologie: Eine Praxisorientierte Einführung
mit Beispeilen* (Heidelberg: Kriminalistik Verlag, 1993), p. 374; Christine Bauer,
Heroin Freigabe: Möglichkeiten und Grenzen einer anderen Drogenpolitik
(Hamburg: Rowohlt, 1992), p. 37.

Table 11. Arrests for drug offenses in Germany, 1962–1990

Year	Total	Heroin	Cocaine	Cannabis	Stimulants
1962	852	n.a.	n.a.	n.a.	n.a.
1963	820	n.a.	n.a.	n.a.	n.a.
1964	992	n.a.	n.a.	n.a.	n.a.
1965	1,003	n.a.	n.a.	n.a.	n.a.
1966	1,080	n.a.	n.a.	n.a.	n.a.
1967	1,349	n.a.	n.a.	n.a.	n.a.
1968	1,891	n.a.	n.a.	n.a.	n.a.
1969	4,761	n.a.	n.a.	n.a.	n.a.
1970	16,104	n.a.	n.a.	n.a.	n.a.
1971	25,287	n.a.	n.a.	n.a.	n.a.
1972	25,679	n.a.	n.a.	n.a.	n.a.
1973	27,027	n.a.	n.a.	n.a.	n.a.
1974	26,909	n.a.	n.a.	n.a.	n.a.
1975	29,805	n.a.	n.a.	n.a.	n.a.
1976	35,122	n.a.	n.a.	n.a.	n.a.
1977	39,089	n.a.	n.a.	n.a.	n.a.
1978	42,878	n.a.	n.a.	n.a.	n.a.
1979	51,445	n.a.	n.a.	n.a.	n.a.
1980	62,395	n.a.	n.a.	n.a.	n.a.
1981	61,802	18,190	1,224	36,889	n.a.
1982	63,002	15,457	1,049	40,792	n.a.
1983	63,742	16,030	1,443	41,698	n.a.
1984	60,588	15,335	1,973	39,515	n.a.
1985	60,941	14,462	2,343	39,936	n.a.
1986	68,694	14,868	2,464	44,901	n.a.
1987	74,894	18,966	2,857	45,015	n.a.
1988	84,998	24,906	4,016	47,055	2,604
1989	94,000	31,067	5,112	48,977	2,812
1990	103,629	38,179	6,265	52,633	3,045

Sources: BKA, *Rauschgift Jahresbericht, 1990* (Wiesbaden: BKA, 1991), tables
1, 2; Horst Schramm, "Die Rauschgiftkriminalität in der Bundesrepublik
Deutschland einschleisslich Berlin (West)," *Werkbericht 5: Drogen—eine
tödliche Gefahr*, Konrad Adenauer Stiftung, (Melle: Ernst Knoth, 1980), p. 104.
Note: Prior to *1988*, arrests for amphetamine and methamphetamine were included in the category of drugs other than heroin, cocaine, cannabis (marijuana
and hashish), and LSD.

Table 12. Drug-related deaths in
Germany, 1970, 1979–1993

Year	Deaths
1970	29
1979	623
1980	494
1981	360
1982	383
1983	472
1984	361
1985	324
1986	348
1987	442
1988	670
1989	991
1990	1,491
1991	2,125
1992	2,096
1993	1,738

Sources: Butz Peters, *Die Absahner:
Organisierte Kriminalität in der Bun-
desrepublik* (Hamburg: Rowohlt, 1990),
pp. 214–15; Schwind, *Kriminologie*
(1993), p. 374; BKA, *Rauschgift Jahres-
bericht*, 1990 (Wiesbaden: BKA, *1991*),
tables 26–27; Laura M. Wiconski,
"Europe Awash with Heroin," *Drug
Enforcement* (Summer 1981): 14–16;
Hubert Meyer and Klaus Wolf,
Kriminalistisches Lehrbuch der Polizei
(Hilden: Deutsche Polizeiliteratur,
1994), p. 401; Heiner Gatzemeier,
*Heroin vom Staat: Für eine kontrol-
lierte Freigabe harter Drogen* (Munich:
Knaur, 1993), p. 182.

disruption of the French Connection, which had linked Turkish
opium supplies to Corsican heroin processors and traders in Marseilles.[54] By the early 1990s German officials believed that Italian organizations such as the Camorra, the 'Ndrangheta, and the Sacra
Corona Unita, Russian crime groups, Colombian cartels, and the
yakuza were all involved in a wide range of illicit activities in Ger-

many.[55] In drug control efforts, however, authorities have tended to focus more on the large population of guest workers. Those from Turkey have attracted most attention, in view of Turkey's location (as a potential transit point), its earlier role as source country in the international heroin trade, and the tendency for such workers to enter Germany through the limited customs facilities in Berlin. By the late 1970s an estimated 500,000 Turkish workers and their families were living in West Germany with between 65,000 and 100,000 in Berlin alone.[56]

Finally, the size and urban concentration of the German addict population have also contributed to the emergence of societal constituencies that favor prevention over enforcement as well as decriminalization and legalization. By the mid-1980s West Germany had over 4,000 self-help groups, 450 walk-in treatment centers, and 400 hospitals and psychiatric centers dedicated to addiction therapy for drugs and alcohol.[57] The centralization of these and other organizations and institutions active in drug and alcohol rehabilitation has been facilitated since 1947 by the German Center against the Danger of Addiction. [58] In contrast, the extent and organization of the German legalization/decriminalization movement has ebbed and flowed since the 1960s. Popular proposals during the 1970s for the legalization of marijuana and hashish and the introduction of extensive methadone programs were replaced by calls for decriminalization of white (cannabis) drugs during the mid-1980s.[59] By the late 1980s and early 1990s scholars, organizations, and political officials in the northern Länder and within the Social Democratic party's Narcotics Working Group in the Bundestag had begun to urge a greater emphasis on prevention programs; certain scholars and Länder officials advocated government distribution of hard drugs (heroin and cocaine) to addicts.[60]

Drug Waves and Wars

Whereas Japan attracted relatively little attention in postwar American drug control efforts until the 1980s, German policy makers began to face U.S. pressure two decades earlier, when the Nixon war on drugs focused on Europe. Because of U.S. concerns about the French Connection and about troops deployed in Germany, the United States was eager to gain German cooperation. In the 1980s citing a cocaine wave that had blanketed the United States and would soon envelop Europe and the need for participation by advanced industrial countries against this threat, Reagan and Bush administration officials again turned to Germany. In this war, however, the American agenda had expanded from questions of drug cultivation and trafficking to include the issues of precursor chemicals and money laundering.

In the late 1960s, in the context of a growing domestic problem with drug abuse, Nixon administration officials turned to the drug issue as a means of implementing broader law-and-order promises made in the presidential campaign. Administration officials took steps that, according to John C. McWilliams, generated "widespread hysteria" over the drug problem and public support for new federal enforcement measures and administrative agencies such as the Bureau of Narcotics and Dangerous Drugs (BNDD) and in 1973 its successor, the DEA.[61] Internationally, beginning in mid-1971, the Nixon administration made the heroin trade a priority.[62]

By the late 1960s heroin importation into the United States was dominated by what had become known as the French Connection, a Corsican network that linked Turkish opium growers and suppliers of morphine base, heroin processors in Marseilles, and traffickers in the United States. American officials responded to the connection by targeting both the source and the processing point. By mid-1971 the combination of U.S. threats and financial assistance persuaded Turkish officials to curtail the cultivation of opium poppies.[63] Meetings between French and U.S. officials during 1970 and 1971, public charges by top Nixon administration officials that the French were "turning a blind eye" to Marseilles's role in the international drug trade, and growing French concerns with domestic drug problems also brought several steps by French authorities. There were police crackdowns in Marseilles, and senior officials including President Georges Pompidou and Foreign Minister Maurice Shumann called for a "united front against drugs" within the European Community. These efforts led to the formation of the Pompidou Group.[64]

At first, Germany received less attention in the Nixon war on drugs. Through the 1960s West Germany experienced a growing trade in hashish, marijuana, and to a lesser extent LSD.[65] The sources of these drugs appeared to be external. In the Bundestag the interior minister noted the opinion of the Federal Criminal Office that responsibility lay with the "increasing number of foreigners" entering Germany from countries where such drugs were cultivated. Among the foreigners the Hesse police blamed, however, were minorities in the U.S. military. The police estimated that 20 percent of them smoked marijuana, and they had spread the practice into the broader population through friendships with German women. By late 1964, these concerns as well as broader U.S. efforts to curtail drug abuse in the military had led to joint raids by the German police, U.S. military police, and U.S. CID officials in cities including Kaiserslauten, Munich, Stuttgart, Hamburg, and Hanau.[66]

Despite these efforts, drug access and usage continued to increase especially among German youth.[67] In addition to cannabis and LSD, consumption began to spread in heroin and, to a lesser extent, cocaine.[68] In 1969 drug offenses under the Opium Act increased by almost 152 percent over the previous year.[69] To stop this trend, German officials established a series of expert, support, and advisory groups, including special working parties of federal and Länder health officials.[70] These efforts resulted in the cabinet's adoption of a national Action Program against drug abuse in November 1970.[71]

Under the Action Program West Germany created a standing conference of federal and Länder interior ministry officials, a national information campaign by the Federal Criminal Office and Länder police to educate the public about dealers and smugglers, and most important, legislation to replace the Opium Act.[72] Passed by the Bundestag in October, the new Narcotics Act incorporated the Action Program's recommendations for increased penalties and stricter enforcement as well as the obligations to be incurred when West Germany signed the UN Convention on Psychotropic Substances.[73] Penalties were increased to a minimum of one year's imprisonment and in severe cases a maximum of ten years'. Although it emphasized enforcement, however, the Narcotics Act also signaled a small shift toward a preventative approach. Specifically, the law allowed prosecutors to dismiss or suspend penalties for addicts in cases of minimum sentences if the addict would agree to participate in a licensed treatment program.[74] This shift failed to satisfy societal organizations that had favored more commitment to prevention.[75]

During 1971 the United States also started to shift its attention to Germany. U.S. drug enforcement efforts in Europe by the early 1970s increasingly relied on the combination of a "global presence of U.S. agents" and an active role by local law enforcement officials.[76] Yet by 1969 Germany was home to only one U.S. Bureau of Narcotics and Dangerous Drugs office (based in Frankfurt) staffed by two officers, out of the total of ten offices and fourteen agents located in Europe.[77] During 1971 the bureau moved to establish additional offices in Munich and Bonn and added three agents to operate in Germany.[78] By November 1971 a special U.S. task force under General McCarthy (assistant deputy chief of staff, U.S. Army, Europe) had also begun meetings with an interministerial group of German officials on drug questions.[79]

German policy makers were more inclined than the Japanese to follow the American agenda because of the extent of the U.S. military and economic presence in Germany, though the overlap of U.S. and German interests was not complete. The U.S. task force, for example, was mainly interested in better coordination of U.S. and German efforts (through designating the Federal Criminal Office in Wiesbaden as the "centralized point [for] . . . information exchange"), in limiting the amphetamine traffic to U.S. troops (through prescriptions filled at German pharmacies), and in preventing former U.S. servicemen from returning to Germany to engage in drug trafficking.[80] These suggestions were geared to the concerns of the U.S. military, but centralization through the Federal Criminal Office would also serve the interests of the Interior Ministry (and the Criminal Office itself) and would facilitate the move toward enforcement proposed in the Action Program. Thus, German policy makers expressed their intent to follow the organizational proposal and began discussing other substantive issues raised by the task force.[81]

The following year U.S. embassy personnel pushed for the establishment of a new German-American Working Group based in Bavaria. The group was to address not German drug problems or those affecting the U.S. military in Germany but the role of southern Germany in facilitating the French Connection. By the early 1970s the U.S. BNDD and Bavarian authorities believed Munich had become a transit point for shipments of morphine base from Turkey to Marseilles.[82] When the working group found no evidence of clandestine heroin production, the United States criticized it strongly, attributing the finding largely to poor investigative work by the Bavarian officials.[83] This experience combined with earlier U.S. task force proposal on centralization, led German and U.S. authorities to establish STAR as a centralized, standing working group at the national level under the direction of the Federal Criminal Office in December 1972.[84] Yet, these efforts would be far from sufficient to solve the drug problems in Germany.

By the mid-1970s U.S. officials were claiming that the collapse of the French Connection had reduced European drug traffic and that drug problems had declined among military personnel in the European theater. Both claims, however, were overstated. Southeast Asian opium and Chinese organized crime groups quickly filled the empty market niche in Europe, and a second pipeline developed to ship heroin from sources in Turkey, Afghanistan, and Iran through the Balkans into Berlin.[85] In 1974 German officials were estimating that over 70 percent of the heroin seized was destined for consumption outside of Germany. By 1978 the percentages had reversed in favor of domestic consumption.[86] According to DEA officials, German officials were at a loss how to respond to "a huge drug problem."[87] Although press reports suggested that officials in Berlin were taking steps against the growing heroin problem,[88] by mid-1978 the United States had again intervened in German drug control policy.

In June 1978 the United States and Germany signed the U.S. -F.R.G. Narcotics Control Agreement, which reaffirmed past cooperation and called for the establishment of a new central working group and related subgroups linking German officials and American embassy representatives (including DEA and military) to develop enforcement and prevention measures.[89] The U.S. efforts reflected growing skepticism in Congress over the military's claims of declining drug problems among U.S. forces in Europe. Following the formation of a congressional task force on drug abuse and seeking to forestall a planned congressional fact-finding mission to Germany, the Pentagon had established its own Special Berlin Task Force and had pushed for the new agreement with Germany. These efforts failed to prevent the congressional mission or the finding that actual drug abuse rates among the military in Europe were two to three times higher than officially reported.[90] In addition, the head of the congressional mission, in meetings with East and West German authorities during November 1978, maintained that West Germany was being especially lax about the heroin traffic through Berlin.[91] By 1980 U.S. military authorities, in response to congressional pressure, were conducting extensive drug sweeps of military bases in Germany. Reports suggested that heroin consumption was falling, although marijuana and cocaine use appeared to be on the rise.[92]

Drawing, in part, on the framework of the central working group, German officials at the federal and Länder levels developed a new action program against domestic drug abuse during 1979. The program, introduced in 1980, reaffirmed the Family Ministry's role as the coordinating agency for drug policy and called for increased penalties for violations of the Narcotics Act (to a maximum of fifteen years' imprisonment).[93] Yet the ministry emphasized that "health-oriented prevention and treatment measures are just as important as repressive ones." Preventative measures included health education, counseling, and treatment programs. More important, the July 1981 revisions to the Narcotics Act explicitly recognized drug addiction as a "disease" and included the principle of "therapy instead of penalty" (Therepie statt Strafe), allowing reduced or deferred sentences for those addicts facing minimum charges (one to two years) if they voluntarily submitted to licensed drug abuse programs.[94]

By the early 1980s Germans were becoming concerned about increases in drug seizures, arrests, deaths, and particularly youth addiction, brought to notoriety by the film Christine F. about teenage drug use and prostitution in Berlin.[95] Although one response was the emphasis on prevention, especially in the northern Länder, another was the introduction of more intrusive criminal procedures along the lines of those practiced in the United States. Despite some controversy among criminal justice officials and scholars, Germany gave the courts more discretion, allowing them to reduce sentences in exchange for cooperation by defendants in drug trafficking cases, and worked toward detailed guidelines for controlled deliveries.[96] Then, in the context of this battle against the heroin trade, German policy makers began to face a new drug threat and a renewed American drug war.

The Reagan administration's declaration of war on drugs in the mid-1980s and subsequent calls for cooperation on the drug issue at the G-7 Summits did not create the quandary for German policy mak-

Table 13. Cocaine seizures (pounds) in selected EC countries, 1984–1988

	1984	1985	1986	1987	1988
Spain	328	667	1,472	2,493	11,682
Italy	153	229	279	708	2,332
France	263	211	568	1,733	458
Britain	121	187	222	924	845
Portugal	132	156	363	484	999
Germany	376	363	396	638	1,302

Source: DEA statistics reprinted in "The Coming Cocaine Plague in Europe," U.S. News and World Report, February 20, 1989, p. 35.

ers that their Japanese counterparts faced. Market shifts by the Colombian cartels during the early 1980s had made the anticocaine focus of the new American agenda increasingly relevant to Germany. As seen in Table 13, direct cocaine shipments to Europe, especially through Spain (and later through Italy), had increased through the 1980s. Faced with overproduction and the increasing saturation of the U.S. market, Latin American cocaine producers had taken advantage of Spain's geography, relatively lax enforcement, and Colombian communities in cities such as Madrid to gain access to Europe.[97]

Within Germany cocaine consumption appeared to be spreading from artists and the jet set into the broader population. Yet, the actual extent of addiction and consumption was unclear. For example, heroin continued to be the main cause of drug-related deaths.[98] Other indicators, however, such as increases in arrests (Table 11) and seizures (Table 10) and the large scale of the seizures, suggested that the drug problem was growing. In 1989, for example, German authorities seized a total of a thousand kilograms of cocaine in two incidents alone (one in Munich and one in Stuttgart). Seizures of crack cocaine also increased to fifty-three grams in 1989. Although these numbers fell far short of the crack wave predicted by drug analysts, they suggested the potential convergence between German concerns and the American agenda.[99]

German cooperation with the United States was also facilitated by the European Community, through its response to domestic drug problems and the demands of the United States during the G-7 summits of the mid-1980s. In June 1985, for example, the European Council adopted the recommendations of the Adonnino Committee for greater cooperation within the EC on drug issues. The committee was established to explore such issues the previous year; its recommendations followed similar calls by the United States at the G-7 summit. In June 1986 the European Council's repeated call for greater international cooperation also followed similar recommendations by the G-7 expert group at the 1986 summit.[100] Although coinciding with the summit declarations, European efforts primarily aimed at greater coordination within the community. Recommendations of the European Parliament, EC interior ministers, and the European Commission during 1986 included such steps as uniform drug regulations, the exchange of drug liaison officers among the member states, and active participation in the 1987 UN deliberations over the new drug convention.[101] By 1989, these EC efforts had culminated in the signing of the 1988 convention and the formation of CELAD to play a centralizing role in drug control policy.[102]

By the onset of the Bush administration's drug war, however, the focus of German policy had diverged from the American agenda. As noted, Bush had pursued foreign compliance through foreign aid, the prioritization of cocaine, and steps against money laundering. In the German case export of precursor chemicals was a high-profile area of dispute. Yet, while German policy makers were moving toward partial cooperation in each of these areas, German drug control policy was apparently shifting farther away from the broader enforcement bias of the American agenda.

First, in contrast to Japan, Germany had expanded assistance programs to drug-exporting countries well beyond UNFDAC contributions since the early 1970s.[103] In addition to enforcement, training, and equipment assistance offered through the Federal Criminal Office, aid programs were introduced through the Ministry of Economic Cooperation. By 1984, the ministry was earmarking 56 to 68 percent of its drug assistance funds for bilateral aid programs to source countries in Asia and Southeast Asia, directed primarily at rural development rather than law enforcement. By 1987 ministry officials wanted a strict separation of enforcement from development programs.[104] Moreover, unlike the United States, Germany did not make these programs conditional on the certification of antidrug programs (such as domestic eradication campaigns) by the recipients.[105]

Thus, by the time the Bush administration was calling for burden sharing in aid to the Andean countries at the 1989 Paris Summit, the German bureaucracy had the experience to join in. Nevertheless, German assistance would be directed less at supplementing enforcement budgets and would also be less conditional than those offered by the United States. Chancellor Helmut Kohl responded to the U.S. request by pledging an aid package worth more than DM 100 million for Colombia as well as funds for Bolivia and Peru in 1989. Approximately DM 80 million was earmarked for Colombia in the form of credits, support for crop substitution, and other employment. Another DM 13 million went to a special program for Medellín, including social services for youth and support for small business. The final component of the Colombian package included DM 18 million in grants for a forensics lab and police and customs equipment. The German package for Bolivia consisted of DM 15 million in soft loans to enhance counternarcotics efforts such as crop substitution and DM 1 million to assist the Bolivian police. An additional DM 10 million were proposed for an aerial observation and cartography program, but it was delayed by a feasibility study. Finally, the Peruvian aid package consisted of DM 50 million in soft loans for counternarcotics efforts, conditional on Peruvian efforts to improve the country's overall debt situation.[106]

German officials made it plain in 1990, however, that this aid package was likely to be a one-shot deal.[107] By 1991 this prediction had proved accurate, and funds pledged by Germany in support of the American agenda in Latin America dropped markedly. Proposed German aid for Colombia consisted of DM 27 million in credits and DM 2.5 million in equipment to be disbursed over a three-year period. There were similar reductions for Bolivia (DM 7 million in soft loans for alternative employment and DM 1.5 million for police agency assistance over three years) and Peru (DM 1.5 million for police equipment).[108] Part of the reason for this shift was the German reaction to the second component of the American agenda—the prioritization of cocaine.[109]

Despite the rise in cocaine seizures and arrests by the early 1990s, German policy makers had also become increasingly disturbed by patterns in the heroin trade.[110] The growing availability of higher-quality, lower-priced heroin from the Middle and Far East as well as

Southeast Asia had translated into bigger seizures, more arrests, and more drug-related deaths. As Table 10 shows, seizure rates began to surge during the late 1980s and early 1990s (Turkey being the single largest source and transit country in 1990 at 54.9 percent).[111] Heroin arrests also began to surge in 1989, particularly arrests of first-time users, twenty-one to thirty years old. These arrests outpaced those for cocaine.[112] More disturbing, however, was the pattern in drug-related (primarily heroin) deaths. As revealed in Table 12, these increased more than 50 percent from 1988 to 1989 and then more than doubled, from 991 in 1989 to over 2,100 by 1991. Faced with this surge in the heroin trade, German policy makers were less likely to devote development aid to the Andean states. As resources were being spread more thinly to cover both cocaine and heroin, moreover, German policy was shifting even farther from penalties to prevention.

German domestic concerns together with the lobbying of the Bush administration and the 1988 UN Convention prompted Länder policy makers to begin to work on the country's third postwar action program against drugs in December 1989.[113] The National Program on Drug Abuse Control released in June 1990 was largely a discussion paper for shaping the future direction of German drug policy. It reflected a compromise among the Länder and federal ministries (as well as the input of twenty-seven private organizations) which balanced different visions of drug prevention and repression.[114] Although offering proposals for enhanced enforcement and international cooperation, the plan stressed the view that drug addiction was a sickness, best addressed through prevention and therapy, not punishment.[115]

These recommendations appeared in subsequent proposed legislation including revisions to the Narcotics Act (as expressed in the draft Law against Illegal Drug Trade and Other Manifestations of Organized Crime proposed by the Bundersrat in 1990) and to the German Criminal Code. Proposed amendments would increase minimum sentences to five years for offenses related to trafficking, but others held out the possibility of suspending sentences in favor of therapy and increasing exemptions from punishment "in cases involving small quantities for personal use."[116] In July 1992 the passage of the additions to the Narcotics Act strengthened its enforcement provisions in a number of areas consistent with the American agenda.[117] By September it was clear that the prevention emphasis had resulted in increased variation in enforcement across the Länder. In Schleswig-Holstein, for example, prosecutors were waiving sentences for possession of up to five grams of cocaine, one gram of heroin, or thirty grams of cannabis for personal use.[118]

The U.S. reaction was relatively favorable, perhaps because the changes also included increased enforcement provisions and concurrent steps in the areas of money laundering and precursor chemicals. Like Japan, Germany did little to curtail money laundering until the American agenda expanded in the late 1980s. Revisions in the 1970s to German financial regulations on data collection and monitoring had been directed mainly toward credit checking.[119] Thus, by the early 1980s, analysts were estimating that DM 4–6 billion in drug money had been washed through German financial institutions, primarily by Turkish traffickers. By 1989 Colombian cartels had laundered money through branches of Comerzbank ($6.5 million), BFG-Bank (DM 4.3 million), Bayerischen Vereinsbank (DM 5 million), and the Deutsch-Südamerikanische Bank ($20 million) among others located in major cities throughout Germany.[120]

For years DEA officials in Germany had been expressing concern, but not until U.S. overtures in 1988, the 1988 UN Convention, the 1989 Paris Summit, and the deliberations of the Financial Action Task Force did Germany take action against money laundering. Despite indications of British and French provisions and steps by the European Commission toward the development of provisions at the community level by early 1990, the proposed easing of border controls in 1992 raised the potential of laundering through those countries lacking regulations, such as Germany.[121] U.S. pressure in this case was minimal, apparently because of growing support for control measures among German policy makers.[122]

By October 1989 the Interior and Justice Ministries (as well as the Federal Criminal Office) were advocating criminal penalties, asset forfeiture, and other provisions, and money laundering had become one area of deliberations in what would become the National Drug Program.[123] In March 1990 Länder interior and justice officials involved in these deliberations were asking for more extensive action than that proposed in federal initiatives scheduled for consideration by Bundesrat subcommittees in April.[124] These initiatives were noted in the National Program released in June. Specifically, the criminalization of money laundering and seizure of assets were already under

consideration by the Bundesrat and a new law on "tracing profits de-
rived from serious crimes" was scheduled for submission to the Bundesrat the following month.[125] All three measures were introduced
with the amendments to the Narcotics Act and the criminal code in
July 1992 and included penalties of fines and imprisonment from six
months to twelve years.[126]

The new legislation, however, failed to set threshold levels for identification of cash transactions. As noted in the National Program,
identification and recording provisions would apply to "cash payments of a size to be determined."[127] Through 1991, deliberations
among the Ministries of Finance, Justice, and Interior as well as the
Federal Association of German Banks led to proposals ranging from
DM 30,000 to DM 100,000.[128] By early 1992 cabinet proposals called
for a threefold scheme requiring identification at DM 20,000, bank
records of transactions at DM 30,000–50,000, and reports to authorities of transactions over DM 100,000. The banking industry supported the criminalization of money laundering but remained
concerned about the financial burden of monitoring the roughly
seven million transactions that would fall under the DM 50,000
threshold.[129] These deliberations were concluded in September 1993
with the introduction of a new law covering all German financial institutions, which set a threshold of DM20,000 ($11,650) for identifi-
cation and required notification of the police when there was
suspicion that a transaction was linked to the drug trade or other
criminal activities.[130]

If the United States was largely content with German money-laundering measures, it was decidedly unhappy with German policy toward precursor chemicals used in the manufacture of cocaine. The
1988 UN Convention urged trade controls and the G-7 established
the Chemical Action Task Force (CATF) in July 1990 to deal with the
issue.[131] In August 1990 President César Gaviria Trujillo of Colombia
demanded that the United States bear some of the costs of curtailing
the international drug trade by halting its own exports of precursor
chemicals.[132] Most of these chemicals, such as acetone, had many
uses in addition to the manufacture of cocaine; it was estimated that
about 20 percent of the total production was diverted to illegal purposes. Constraining the trade would clearly hurt the U.S. chemical in-

dustry, particularly because as the United States turned to control measures, German exports appeared to be filling the gap.[133]

In this context, U.S. officials began to accuse Germany of being the primary exporter of cocaine precursors into Latin America. In charges reminiscent of those first made in the early 1900s, U.S. officials accused Germany of knuckling under to its chemical industry.[134] Tensions increased when Germany asked for evidence to back these accusations and the United States replied that five weeks would be necessary to assemble the evidence.[135] DEA figures eventually released for 1989 revealed German exports to Colombia of 14,315 tons of precursor chemicals (out of a total 17,000 tons exported by the EC) such as acetone and ethyl ether.[136]

During the early 1980s, analysts and the UN had charged German involvement in the export of precursor chemicals for heroin.[137] Growing concern about this trade led the Federal Criminal Office, in cooperation with the Interior Ministry and chemical industry associations, to introduce a voluntary monitoring system for trade patterns in precursor chemicals in 1985 and an expanded national system in 1988.[138] In 1990 the National Program called for amendments to this system and the Narcotics Act to provide an updated "system of export controls" but stressed the need for a uniform standard at the EC level.[139] In December 1990 the EC Council of Ministers introduced new regulations covering trade in precursor chemicals with third countries.[140] In July 1992, these EC provisions became the basis for new German restrictions incorporated into the Narcotics Act, and bilateral relations between Germany and the United States eased.[141]

When both U.S. and German authorities speak of the excellent relationship between the two countries, the underlying suggestion is that Germany has become a staunch ally in the American war on drugs. This description, however, oversimplifies the nature of the bilateral relationship as well as its sources. As in Japan so in Germany, the occupation interacted with preconditions of state capacity (especially territorial integrity) to shape the drug problems faced by German policy makers. In Germany's case, these dynamics led to an antinarcotics bias that initially complemented the American agenda.

By the early 1970s power fragmentation between federal and Länder institutions began to shift Germany away from full compliance.

During the Nixon drug war and its aftermath, U.S. authorities intervened in German drug policy to curtail drug problems within the U.S. military (1960s, late 1970s) and in pursuit of the French Connection (early 1970s). German responses to the American agenda included efforts to centralize drug policy making and implementation and adoption of the U.S. enforcement model. Thus, greater penalties for drug offenses were incorporated into the Narcotics Act in 1971 and 1981. These steps reflected the importance of the U.S. presence in Germany in the context of the Cold War as well as growing problems with narcotics and support for U.S. proposals, especially within the Federal Criminal Office and the Ministry of the Interior. Interministerial and federal-Länder dynamics, however, had also begun to shift the focus of German drug policy away from enforcement and toward prevention. In 1971 this shift was evident in allowances for suspending the new increased minimum penalties in favor of therapy. By 1981 the principle of therapy instead of punishment had become an explicit component of drug control.

This pattern of stricter enforcement accompanied by greater emphasis on prevention continued during the Reagan-Bush drug war. Federal and Länder support for stronger enforcement provisions by the late 1980s and early 1990s reflected growing problems with the cocaine and heroin trades and associated organized crime, as well as commitments through the European Community to enact the provisions of the 1988 UN Convention. Subsequent German compliance with the American agenda, albeit not always a smooth process, included increased drug penalties in addition to the Narcotics Act as well as steps against money laundering and precursor chemicals. The 1990 Action Program and its resulting legislation represented the third stage in deliberations and compromise between and among federal ministries and the Länder over the place of enforcement and prevention in German drug control policy.

6

Capacity and Compliance

German and Japanese compliance with the American agenda has been far from complete, though both countries have participated in international control agreements from the Shanghai Commission in 1909 to the UN Convention of 1988. The United States has taken it as a basic premise that this pattern of partial compliance is directly related to the domestic capacity of each country's policy makers. Clearly, however, this explanation, applied for the past ninety or so years to bilateral and multilateral relations, has failed to read German and Japanese responses accurately. This final chapter briefly summarizes the findings of the preceding analysis before turning to their implications for the future of U.S. drug control.

Capacity and Response

Prominent scholarship suggests that weak state capacity, stemming from preconditions such as limited territorial integrity and financial resources or from dynamics generated by state and societal structure, can lead to involuntary or voluntary defection from agreements. The United States has taken this hypothesis as its basic premise in attempting to account for noncompliance with the

American agenda. The difficult task is to determine which pattern of defection is taking place and which aspects of capacity are at issue.

From the standpoint of U.S. officials it appeared that societal structure drove German policy makers to deception during the Hague deliberations, and state fragmentation forced them into involuntary defection from the American agenda during the Weimar years. U.S. officials believed Japanese policy makers were using deception in the 1920s, initially generated by state fragmentation and then by rapid state centralization. All these interpretations oversimplified the situations.

The German pharmaceutical industry was the world's single largest production source of cocaine. Although the industry was weakly organized but retained control over information, societal structure was less important in shaping the responses of German policy makers than the basic financial preconditions of capacity during the Hague deliberations. By the 1920s, despite Weimar fragmentation, German authorities at the national and Länder levels enforced German drug laws and extended their coverage as loopholes became apparent. In contrast, state fragmentation did come into play in Japan, but it led not to deception but to involuntary defection prior to the late 1930s. Japanese civilian authorities had difficulty controlling elements of the military at home and abroad, and the military proved unable to control itself during the 1920s and early 1930s.

The U.S. occupation of Germany and Japan contributed to the assessment that both countries had changed from adversaries to allies in the post-1945 campaigns against drugs. As U.S. attention shifted to source countries in Asia and Latin America, however, the analysis of the details of German and Japanese drug control policy based on capacity faded. The irony of this shift is that capacity considerations influenced drug policy in both countries during the Nixon and Reagan-Bush campaigns. Japanese compliance with the American agenda was consistently impeded by the fragmentation of state power among key ministries and their implementation agencies and bureaus. Divisions among the German federal ministries, Länder ministries, and between the two levels have also contributed to a gradual shift away from the enforcement core of the American agenda.

Capacity has certainly affected foreign compliance, but other factors have clearly come into play. Not the least is the domestic drug situation facing policy makers in adversary and allied countries alike. Rather than article 295 of the Versailles Treaty, it was domestic drug problems that pushed Germany toward control. Japan's strict domestic regulations on narcotics traffic into the country reflected a determination beginning in the nineteenth century to avoid the experience of China, while the American agenda was supporting the opium trade. Postwar Germany and Japan have also faced domestic drug problems different from those in the United States. The German heroin problem and especially the waves of Japanese stimulant abuse have decreased the willingness of policy makers to toe the American line. The common argument of U.S. officials abroad that foreign cooperation is necessary now because the wave is coming, because Europe and Japan are but a few years (anywhere from two to ten) behind the drug situation faced by the United States, lacks persuasiveness.[1] The Japanese case in particular suggests that it is not always clear that the big wave comes. More important, the very image of a coming wave suggests that the current situations are different in different countries. In this context, policy makers abroad are not likely to be willing to divert resources from current threats to forestall potential future problems.

The Limits of Enhancing Capacity

U.S. operations in Latin America, including support for aerial herbicide spraying and direct intervention in eradication and interdiction campaigns, have led to suggestions that the United States ought to do more to shore up the weak capacity of source and transit countries.[2] These arguments also surface in deliberations over alternative roles for the military in the aftermath of the Cold War.[3] Although clearly not fully comparable, the experience of the U.S. occupation of Germany and Japan suggests a note of caution. In both countries occupation led to changes in the scope and administration of domestic drug laws. These changes, however, also led to unintended results that eroded support for subsequent U.S. drug control efforts.

Direct intervention can create the potential for future drug problems and responses that may or may not coincide with the American agenda. In the Japanese case, for example, occupation policies emphasizing narcotics control, democratization, and anticommunism permitted the growth of an illicit methamphetamine trade conducted by organized crime groups; these, of necessity, have been the focus of Japanese drug control efforts ever since. In Germany occupation policies and Germany's position on the front line of the Cold War contributed to the rise of the heroin trade as well as a long-standing heroin bias in drug control efforts at home and abroad.

Direct intervention can also replace one capacity problem with another. For example, the occupation solved Japan's problem with territorial integrity abroad by removing colonial holdings in China, but it undermined domestic integrity by imposing the priorities of the U.S. occupation authorities. Similarly, German policy makers traded Allied occupation of the Ruhr during the early interwar years for the occupation and division of the country into Allied zones after World War II. The attempt to alter state or societal structure can also backfire. The initial emphasis of SCAP and OMGUS authorities on democratization (prior to the reverse course suspending decentralization in the late 1940s out of fear of communist expansion) extended to the areas of drug control as well. The subsequent fragmentation of the Japanese executive ministries and the decentralization of the German state between the federal and Länder levels made it less possible for these countries to comply fully with the American agenda.

If the occupation of Germany and Japan failed to bring about compliance, the prospects for remaking Latin American or Southeast Asian source and transit countries from adversaries into allies is even more problematic. For example, the bases of Colombia's cocaine cartels have been located since the late 1970s and early 1980s in the eastern plains (Meta, Vaupes, Guainia) and southeastern jungle regions (Caqueta, Amazonas), which are relatively inaccessible.[4] Accounting for roughly 60 percent of Colombia's land mass but only 3 percent of its population, these areas are distinguished by limited infrastructure in transportation and communication.[5] Preconditions have also been shaped by financial considerations. During the mid-1980s, for example, Colombia's debt, even partially offset by the cocaine trade, stood at an estimated $17.7 billion and the country was committed to annual payments of $3.2 billion (roughly 7 percent of annual gross domestic product).[6] By comparison, it was estimated that the annual revenues generated by the contending Medellín and Cali cartels during the 1980s were $5–14 billion.[7]

Two factors—the massive wealth generated by the trade and the use of violence as a historically grounded means of dispute resolution in Colombian politics—have worked against opponents of the trade. Cartels have had the financial resources to bribe police and judicial officials, make political contributions, finance the campaigns of cartel members for political office, and purchase informants in the executive ministries.[8] Where bribes have not been successful, the cartels, especially Medellín, have turned to threats, bombings, murder of police and judicial officials, and political assassination.[9] When the Medellín cartel collapsed under pressure from government crackdowns and intercartel violence in the early 1990s, an entrenched lower-profile Cali organization took its place, and the government debated alternatives to a war along American lines. By the mid-1990s U.S. pressure had contributed to a renewed Colombian campaign against the Cali organization and the subsequent capture of the cartel's leadership. Nevertheless, at the time of this writing, Colombian compliance remains far from complete. Charges linking the cartel to President Ernesto Samper's 1994 electoral campaign are currently under investigation and questions remain concerning the actual penalties the Cali leaders will face, the status of the remaining organization, and potential Colombian successors to the cartel.[10]

Clearly, the full-scale U.S. occupation of source countries such as Colombia would be a daunting task with little guarantee of success in either the short run or, judging from the lessons of the German and Japanese cases, the long run. Steps to enhance capacity short of occupation can bring greater cooperation but do not necessarily lead to full compliance. Despite these considerations and although the priority of the drug war was reduced as a foreign and domestic policy issue by the Clinton administration, U.S. drug control policy continues to act on the basic premise that capacity brings compliance as it seeks allies in the war on drugs. German and Japanese responses to the American agenda suggest the limits of this approach as well as the complexity of the war.

NOTES

Preface

1. The distinction between voluntary and involuntary defection is drawn from Robert Putnam, "Diplomacy and Domestic Politics: The Logic of Two-Level Games," *International Organization* 42 (Summer 1988): 427–60.

Chapter 1. The Dynamics of Defection

1. Theda Skocpol, "Bringing the State Back In: Strategies of Analysis in Current Research," in Peter B. Evans, Dietrich Rueschemeyer, and Theda Skocpol, eds., *Bringing the State Back In* (Cambridge: Cambridge University Press, 1985), pp. 3–43, esp. 9.
2. Renewed interest in the state since the late 1970s has prompted extensive debate. The definition used here is discussed in greater detail in H. Richard Friman, *Patchwork Protectionism: Textile Trade Policy in the United States, Japan, and West Germany* (Ithaca: Cornell University Press, 1990), p. 21.
3. Skocpol, "Bringing the State Back In," pp. 16–17.
4. Stephen D. Krasner, *Defending the National Interest* (Princeton: Princeton University Press, 1978).
5. Skocpol, "Bringing the State Back In," pp. 17–18; Peter J. Katzenstein, ed., *Between Power and Plenty: The Foreign Economic Policies of Advanced Industrial States* (Madison: University of Wisconsin Press, 1978); G. John Ikenberry, David Lake, and Michael Mastanduno, "Introduction: Approaches

to Explaining American Foreign Policy," *International Organization* 42, 1 (1988): 1–14.

6. Joel S. Migdal, *Strong Societies and Weak States: State-Society Relations and State Capabilities in the Third World* (Princeton: Princeton University Press, 1988). See also Katzenstein, *Between Power and Plenty;* Peter J. Katzenstein, *Corporatism and Change* (Ithaca: Cornell University Press, 1985); Peter Gourevitch, *Politics in Hard Times* (Ithaca: Cornell University Press, 1986).

7. Migdal, *Strong Societies and Weak States,* pp. xiii, 33–35, 261. Migdal does not indicate clearly whether the apex of this social pyramid is located in the state or society (pp. 34–35). The latter interpretation is followed here.

8. Ibid., p. 33.

9. Katzenstein, *Corporatism and Change,* and other scholarship on corporatism suggest, on the contrary, that strong societal organization (especially pyramidal) tends to increase state capacity. For a broader argument on the structural power of societal groups—especially business/capital—see, for example, Charles E. Lindblom, *Politics and Markets: The World's Political-Economic Systems* (New York: Basic Books, 1977); Stephen Gill, *American Hegemony and the Trilateral Commission* (Cambridge: Cambridge University Press, 1990).

10. See Robert Putnam, "Diplomacy and Domestic Politics: The Logic of Two-Level Games," *International Organization* 42 (Summer 1988): 427–60; Peter B. Evans, Harold K. Jacobson, and Robert D. Putnam, eds., *Double-Edged Diplomacy: International Bargaining and Domestic Politics* (Berkeley: University of California Press, 1993).

11. For example, Migdal, *Strong Societies and Weak States,* p. 26; G. John Ikenberry, "Conclusion: An Institutional Approach to American Foreign Economic Policy," *International Organization* 42 (Winter 1988): 236–41; H. Richard Friman, "Side-Payments versus Security Cards: Domestic Bargaining in International Economic Negotiations," *International Organization* 47 (Summer 1993): 387–410.

12. Unlike journalists, scholars have tended to ignore deception as a deliberate strategy. Yet, a systematic analysis of deception has the potential to provide insights into what James Scott has termed the "hidden transcript," the actual preferences and behavior of actors beyond their official public stance, and the effects of this transcript on foreign policy. See John Orman, *Presidential Secrecy and Deception: Beyond the Power to Persuade* (Westport, Conn.: Greenwood Press, 1980); James Scott, *Domination and the Arts of Resistance* (New Haven: Yale University Press, 1990).

13. David Yoffie, *Power and Protectionism: Strategies of the Newly Industrializing Countries* (New York: Columbia University Press, 1983), pp. 26–28, 31–34.

14. Jon Elster, *Sour Grapes: Studies in the Subversion of Rationality* (Cambridge: Cambridge University Press, 1985); pp. 7–8.

15. An exception in the study of Japan is William O. Walker III, *Opium and Foreign Policy: The Anglo-American Search for Order in Asia, 1912–1954.* (Chapel Hill: University of North Carolina Press, 1991).

16. David Owen, *British Opium Policy in China and India* (New Haven: Yale University Press, 1934); Charles C. Stelle, *Americans and the Chinese Opium Trade in the 19th Century* (Chicago: University of Chicago Libraries, 1941); Peter D. Lowes, *The Genesis of International Narcotics Control* (Geneva: Droz, 1966); S. D. Stein, *International Diplomacy, State Administration, and Narcotics Control: The Origins of a Social Problem* (Aldershot, U.K.: Gower, 1985).

17. Arnold H. Taylor, *American Diplomacy and the Narcotics Traffic, 1900–1939: A Study in International Humanitarian Reform* (Durham, N.C.: Duke University Press, 1969), pp. 28–30. See also David F. Musto, *The American Disease: Origins of Narcotics Control* (New Haven: Yale University Press, 1987), pp. 24–29; Stein, *International Diplomacy,* pp. 29–48.

18. Taylor, *American Diplomacy and the Narcotics Traffic,* pp. 24–25; Musto, *The American Disease,* p. 29; Stein, *International Diplomacy,* p. 50.

19. Stein, *International Diplomacy,* pp. 9–16; Bruce Johnson, "Righteousness before Revenue: The Forgotten Moral Crusade against the Indo-Chinese Opium Trade," *Journal of Drug Issues* 5 (1975): 307–16; Owen, *British Opium Policy,* pp. 311–17, 328–29.

20. Resolution quoted in Johnson, "Righteousness before Revenue," p. 322, and see pp. 316–17; Owen, *British Opium Policy,* pp. 333–35; Taylor, *American Diplomacy and the Narcotics Traffic,* p. 25.

21. Morely quoted in Johnson, "Righteousness before Revenue," p. 317; and see Owen, *British Opium Policy,* p. 330; Stein, *International Diplomacy,* pp. 20–22.

22. Stein, *International Diplomacy,* p. 22.

23. Taylor, *American Diplomacy and the Narcotics Traffic,* p. 22.

24. This analysis is based on reprints of British Foreign Office files on opium and related drug issues in *The Opium Trade, 1910–1941,* vol. 1 (Wilmington, Del.: Scholarly Resources, 1974), cited as BRIT1, document 15996 (Max Mueller to Sir Edward Grey, April 20, 1910), 20712 (India Office to Foreign Office, June 9, 1910), 21517 (Grey to Mueller, June 17, 1910).

25. Taylor, *American Diplomacy and the Narcotics Traffic,* p. 25.

26. Lowes, *The Genesis of International Narcotics Control,* pp. 112–14; Taylor, *American Diplomacy and the Narcotics Traffic,* pp. 49–52; Musto, *The American Disease,* p. 5.

27. Taylor, *American Diplomacy and the Narcotics Traffic,* pp. 64–65.

28. Ibid., pp. 64–65.

29. Ibid., pp. 67, 69–74; Stein, *International Diplomacy,* p. 54.

30. Stein, *International Diplomacy,* pp. 61–63; BRIT1, 10346 (India Office to Foreign Office, March 24, 1910), 11818 (India Office to Foreign Office, April 6, 1910), 15369 (Colonial Office to Foreign Office, May 3, 1910), 17527 (Colonial Office to Foreign Office, May 14, 1910).

31. Grey quoted in Stein, *International Diplomacy*, pp. 62–63; BRIT1, 23734 (India Office to Foreign Office, July 1, 1910). Domestic pressure for British attendance was rather limited, with antiopium forces focusing more on the status of the Ten Year Agreement. For example, see BRIT1, 5267 (London and Edinburgh Anti-Opium Organizations to Foreign Office, February 12, 1910), 4824 (Professor Caldecott to Grey, February 10, 1910), 5267 (Foreign Office to India Office, February 21, 1910), 9956 (question asked in the House of Commons, March 10, 1910), 7503 (Foreign Office to Caldecott, March 11, 1910), 9922 (Caldecott to Foreign Office, March 21, 1910), 8942 (question asked in the House of Commons, March 10, 1910), 12293 (question asked, March 28, 1911), 22028 (question asked, June 1, 1911), 32783 (question asked, August 17, 1911).

32. BRIT1, 20713 (Foreign Office to India Office, June 14, 1910), 23734 (Foreign Office to India Office, July 6, 1910), 23734 (India Office to Foreign Office, July 1, 1910), 24450 (India Office to Foreign Office, July 6, 1910), 25196 (India Office to Foreign Office, July 11, 1910), 24066 (Board of Trade to Foreign Office, July 2, 1910, Foreign Office to Board of Trade, July 6, 1910), 23734 (Foreign Office to Colonial Office, July 6, 1910).

33. BRIT1, 26971 (Foreign Office to India Office, July 27, 1910), 28253 (India Office to Foreign Office, August 3, 1910), 30202 (Board of Trade to Foreign Office, August 18, 1910), 31841 (Board of Trade to Foreign Office, August 31, 1910), 32477 (Colonial Office to Foreign Office, September 5, 1910).

34. BRIT1, 29030 (Whitelaw Reid to Sir F. Campbell, August 8, 1910).

35. BRIT1, 33412 (Grey to Reid, September 17, 1910); also Stein, *International Diplomacy*, pp. 62, 65–66.

36. Taylor, *American Diplomacy and the Narcotics Traffic*, pp. 90–91; Stein, *International Diplomacy*, pp. 64–65.

37. BRIT1, 290 (Colonial Office to Foreign Office, January 1, 1910), 4645 (Colonial Office to Foreign Office, February 8, 1910), 1563 (Colonial Office to Foreign Office, May 3, 1910), 17527 (Colonial Office to Foreign Office, May 14, 1910), 17147 (Board of Trade to Foreign Office, May 12, 1910).

38. BRIT1, 33412 (Grey to Reid, September 17, 1910).

39. BRIT1, 36069 (Reid to Grey, October 4, 1910).

40. BRIT1, 38869 (Grey to Reid, November 3, 1910); Stein, *International Diplomacy*, pp. 66–67.

41. BRIT1, 41776 (Reid to Grey, November 15, 1910), 46341 (December 22, 1910).

42. BRIT1, 42866 (Grey to M. van der Goes, December 1, 1910), 1993 (Foreign Office to Board of Trade, January 23, 1911; Foreign Office to India Office, January 23, 1911), 3034 (India Office to Foreign Office, January 25, 1911), 3034 (Grey to Baron Gericke, January 31, 1911; Grey to M. Cambon, January 31, 1911; Campbell to M. Manoel, January 31, 1911), 9313 (Grey to H. von Kühlmann, March 22, 1911).

43. BRIT1, 14685 (Reid to Grey, April 18, 1911), 16412 (Grey to Reid, May 4, 1911).

44. BRIT1, 29888 (Note communicated by Count Metternich, July 29, 1911).

45. BRIT1, 30763 (Reid to Grey, August 3, 1911).

46. BRIT1, 30763 (Foreign Office to Board of Trade, August 9, 1911), 32199 (Colonial Office to Foreign Office, August 14, 1911), 32413 (India Office to Foreign Office, August 16, 1911), 32348 (Grey to Reid, August 19, 1911), 34424 (Grey to Reid, September 6, 1911), 33013 (Reid to Grey, August 20, 1911), 33013 (Foreign Office to India Office, August 23, 1911), 34424 (Grey to Gericke, September 5, 1911).

47. BRIT1, 38685 (van der Goes to Grey, October 2, 1911), 39958 (Board of Trade to Foreign Office, October 10, 1911), 40711 (India Office to Foreign Office, October 14, 1911), 41000 (Colonial Office to Foreign Office, October 17, 1911), 40711 (Grey to van der Goes, October 21, 1911).

Chapter 2. Germany and the Cocaine Connection

1. Theda Skocpol, "Bringing the State Back In: Strategies of Analysis in Current Research," in Peter B. Evans, Dietrich Rueschemeyer, and Theda Skocpol, eds., *Bringing the State Back In* (Cambridge: Cambridge University Press, 1985), p. 16.

2. Eberhard Kolb, *The Weimar Republic*, trans. P. S. Falla (London: Unwin Hyman, 1988), p. 28.

3. Ibid., pp. 41, 46; Erich Eyck, *A History of the Weimar Republic*, trans. Harlan P. Hanson and Robert G. L. Waite (Cambridge: Harvard University Press, 1962), pp. 155–56.

4. Kolb, *The Weimar Republic*, pp. 40–41; Eyck, *A History of the Weimar Republic*, p. 131.

5. The one exception was set forth in article 48, which allowed the president to "proclaim a state of emergency to preserve public security and order." Kolb, *The Weimar Republic*, pp. 18–19.

6. See the extensive literature review and bibliography in Kolb, *The Weimar Republic*, pp. 129–231. See also David Abraham, *The Collapse of the Weimar Republic: Political Economy and Crisis* (Princeton: Princeton University Press, 1981).

7. Eyck, *A History of the Weimar Republic*, pp. 341–42.

8. Dietrich Orlow, *Weimar Prussia, 1918–1925: The Unlikely Rock of Democracy* (Pittsburgh: Pittsburgh University Press, 1986), p. 92; Kolb, *The Weimar Republic*, pp. 18–19.

9. Examples are the Freikorps support of the Kapp putsch in Berlin in 1920 and the resistance of Bavaria to the dismantling of the Bavarian Home Guards (320,000 strong) in 1920–21. Kolb, *The Weimar Republic*, pp. 36–37; Eyck, *A History of the Weimar Republic*, pp. 147–56, 176–77, 179, 188; Orlow, *Weimar Prussia*, p. 148.

10. The following account is based primarily on information drawn from German public and private archival files.

11. In addition to relying on the health ministry, in 1934 the Nazi government also introduced an antidrug working group under the Committee for Public Health Service to deal with what was seen as a growing domestic narcotics problem. Berndt Georg Thamm, *Drogen Report: Und nun auch noch Crack?* (Bergisch Gladbach: Gustav Lübbe, 1988), pp. 93–96.

12. Armin Linz, *German Opium Legislation* (Control Commission for Germany, Printing and Stationery Office, 1947), pp. 2–4, 8–9, 17, 19–21. In February 1925 the Ministry of Finance called for expanding Ministry of Health oversight to domestic as well as international transactions—to increase control over smuggling. See Political Archive, German Foreign Office, Division III, file Opium from January 1925–on, cited as III R, document 270 (Finance to Interior, February 28, 1925).

13. For example, see the discussions of the role of the Kriminalpolizei (Kripo) and the Sicherheitspolizei (Sipo) in Hsi-Huey Liang, *The Berlin Police Force in the Weimar Republic* (Berkeley: University of California Press, 1970); Orlow, *Weimar Prussia*, pp. 142–50.

14. Hermann P. Voight, *Zum Thema: Kokain* (Basel: Sphinx, 1982), p. 20; Ernst Joel and F. Fränkel, *Der Cocainismus: Ein Beitrag zur Geschichte und Psychopathologie der Rauschgifte* (Berlin: Julius Springer, 1924), p. 11.

15. Thamm, *Drogen Report*, pp. 37–42, 75–76. Cocaine was primarily used by injection until the 1920s, when inhalation became the dominant method. Berndt Georg Thamm, *Andenschnee: Die lange Linie des Kokain* (Basel: Sphinx, 1986), pp. 85, 122.

16. State Department Diplomatic Records, International Conferences, Narcotics, 1910–29, 511.4A1/962 (consul general, Berlin, to secretary of state, January 7, 1911).

17. L. F. Haber, *The Chemical Industry, 1990–1930: International Growth and Technological Change* (Oxford: Clarendon Press, 1971), p. 133.

18. The single largest market was China (21 percent) followed by Russia and Austria-Hungary. By comparison, British, Swiss, and French exports of cocaine during the 1920s averaged 300, 270, and 580 kilograms, respectively. Merck Archives (Firmenarchiv Merck), file Opium, Opium Konferenz, "Verkauf von E. Merck, Darmstadt, 1911"; Political Archive, German Foreign Office, Division Law I/II, file Opium Reports from Brietfeld, "Material Regarding the Opium Question," report prepared by the Fachgruppe Opium und Cocain, 1933; Albert Wissler, *Die Opiumfrage: Eine Studie zur weltwirtschaftlichen und weltpolitischen Lage der Gegenwart* (Kiel: Gustav Fischer, 1931), pp. 132, 137, 142.

19. Interviews (Germany, 1991); and see entries in Merck Archives, file Opium, Opium Konferenz. On the role and impact of IG Farben during Weimar, see Abraham, *The Collapse of the Weimar Republic*, pp. 129–33.

20. After 1921 the importance of VCI appears to have faded. Merck and C. H. Böhringer emerged in the German archival files as spokesmen for a new Fachgruppe Opium und Cocaine (Expert Group on Opium and Cocaine).

21. See, for example, Arnold H. Taylor, *American Diplomacy and the Narcotics Traffic, 1900–1939: A Study in International Humanitarian Reform*

(Durham, N.C.: Duke University Press, 1969), pp. 48, 71; Political Archive, German Foreign Office, Division II, file The Hague Embassy: Opium, 1907–11, cited as II U, document 1665 (U.S. acknowledgment, March 16, 1910), 3750 (Health Ministry to Interior, May 23, 1910; Interior to Foreign Office, June 27, 1910); 511.4A1/703 (U.S. Embassy, Berlin to secretary of state, February 21, 1910); German Central State Archive, Interior Ministry Records, Division II 5A, file Distribution of Opium and Morphine, cited as II 5A with volume # and document # where available or page # beginning in 1919, 10393, n.a. (Foreign Office to Interior Ministry, February 17, 1910), n.a. (Justice Ministry to Foreign Office, February 25, 1910), n.a. (Post Office to Foreign Office, February 25, 1910).

22. For example, see Taylor, *American Diplomacy and the Narcotics Traffic*, pp. 93–95, 102–3; S. D. Stein, *International Diplomacy, State Administration, and Narcotics Control: The Origins of a Social Problem* (Aldershot, U.K.: Gower, 1985), p. 74; 511.4A1/1238 (Division of Far Eastern Affairs to Huntington Wilson, July 18, 24, 1911), 1195 (Arthur Beaupre, the Hague, to secretary of state, September 7, 1911).

23. German Central Archive, Foreign Office Records, Division IIm, file Drug and Medical Conferences, cited as IIm, document n.a. (Interior Ministry to Foreign Office, June 15, 1910).

24. IIm 4090 (Interior Ministry to Foreign Office, May 18, 1911).

25. Merck Archive, file Opium, Opium Konferenz (Merck to Interior Ministry, November 21, 1910, and see Gehe to Merck, November 18, 1910).

26. These issues included those raised by the Reichstag, the ministerial reports, and those "in light of the upcoming international opium conference." IIm 4090 (Interior Ministry to Foreign Office, May 18, 1911).

27. See II U 385 (Metternich to Dr. von Bethmann Hollweg, January 20, 1911).

28. Merck Archive, file Opium, Opium Konferenz (Notes from the October 24 Interior Ministry Meeting, October 27, 1911); IIm 5251 (Interior Ministry to Foreign Office, June 26, 1911).

29. Merck Archive, file Opium, Opium Konferenz (C. F. Böhringer und Söhne to Merck, October 21, 1911).

30. In addition to the example cited in text, undue industry influence was seen as only a "slight possibility" by the Committee of the German Evangelical Missionary Societies which itself was urging the government to participate. *The Opium Trade, 1910–1941*, vol. 2 (Wilmington, Del.: Scholarly Resources, 1971), cited as BRIT2, document 137 (Society for the Suppression of the Opium Trade to McKinnon Wood, October 4, 1911; Dr. Richter to Dr. Maxwell, September 20, 1911).

31. 511.4A1/1114 (U.S. Embassy, Berlin, to Department of State, May 19, 1911), 1133 (Embassy, Berlin, to Department of State, May 24, 1911), 1160 (Embassy, Berlin, to Department of State, July 14, 1911) 1162 (German Embassy to Department of State, July 26, 1911), and 1163 (U.S. Embassy, Berlin, to Department of State, July 27, 1911).

32. Merck Archive, file Opium, Opium Konferenz (Interior Ministry to Merck, October 25, 1911).

33. 511.4A1/962 (consul general, Berlin, to secretary of state, January 7, 1911).
34. See Merck Archive, file Opium, Opium Konferenz (Merck to Interior Ministry, November 21, 1910, Gehe to Merck, November 18, 1910, C. H. Böhringer Sohn to Merck, November 3, 1911, Merck to Interior Ministry, November 3, 1911, Zimmer to Merck, November 2, 1911, and Merck to VCI members, November 1, 1911).
35. Export restriction would rely on licensing provisions including authorization from the importing country. Taylor, *American Diplomacy and the Narcotics Traffic*, pp. 101–3; Stein, *International Diplomacy*, pp. 72–73.
36. Quoted in Stein, *International Diplomacy*, p. 74.
37. BRIT2, 1286 (British delegates to Grey, January 9, 1912), and see 1460 (delegates to Grey, January 10, 1912), 16201 (delegates to Grey, April 18, 1912). For detail on U.S. and British reluctance to challenge Germany, see Taylor, *American Diplomacy and the Narcotics Traffic*, p. 102; Stein, *International Diplomacy*, pp. 73, 77; 511.4A1/1283 ("The International Opium Conference at the Hague," Frederic Huidekoper, secretary, American delegation, February 12, 1912).
38. Taylor, *American Diplomacy and the Narcotics Traffic*, p. 107; BRIT2, 1700 (British delegates to Grey, January 11, 1912), 1713 (Board of Trade to Foreign Office, January 12, 1912), 1858 (Board of Trade to Foreign Office, January 13, 1912), 16201 (British delegates to Grey, April 18, 1912); 511.4A1/1283 (Huidekoper report, February 12, 1912).
39. Taylor, *American Diplomacy and the Narcotics Traffic*, pp. 113, 116, 120; 511.4A1/1477 (Henry Van Dyke to secretary of state, June 17, 1914).
40. Taylor, *American Diplomacy and the Narcotics Traffic*, pp. 141–43, Stein, *International Diplomacy*, pp. 114–22; 511.4A1/1535 (Department of State to U.S. Embassy, London, January 25, 1919), 1539 (Department of State to U.S. Embassy, London, February 8, 1919), 1545 (U.S. Mission, Paris, to Department of State, March 31, 1919).
41. See Sebastian Scheerer, "Rauschmittelmiβbrauch: Juristischkriminologischer Beitrag," in Rudolf Sieverts and Hans Joachim Schneider, eds., *Handwörterbuch der Kriminologies* (Berlin: Walter De Gruyter, 1977), p. 481; Wissler, *Die Opiumfrage*, pp. 139; Joel and Fränkel, *Der Cocainismus*, pp. 13–23; Thamm, *Andenschnee*, p. 106; and Voight, *Zum Thema Kokain*, p. 23.
42. Sebastian Scheerer, *Die Genese der Betäubungsmittelgesetze in der Bundesrepublik Deutschland und in den Niederlanden* (Göttingen: Otto Schwartz, 1982), pp. 41–47, 53–56; II 5A 10394, n.a. (Health Office to Interior Ministry, July 23, 1918), n.a. (Interior Ministry to chancellor, August 8, 1918); and II 5A 10395, pp. 323–32 (Interior Ministry to chancellor, November 12, 1920).
43. For detail on the ministerial deliberations, see II 5A 10395, pp. 26 (Economics Ministry to Interior Ministry, May 8, 1919), 28 (brief by Dr. Bourwig, Interior Ministry, May 19, 1919), 30–32 (records of interministerial meeting regarding drug management/rationing, May 20, 1919), 39–41 (Health Office to Interior Ministry, July 19, 1919), 48–49 (Health Office to Interior Ministry,

July 31, 1919), 53–56 (Economics Ministry to Interior Ministry, November 12, 1919), 105–9 (Economics Ministry to Interior Ministry, December 9, 1919), 229 (Interior Ministry to Foreign Office, June 7, 1920), 230 (Health Office to Interior Ministry, June 28, 1920), 237–47 (new German regulations on distribution, July 1920), 296–303 (Interior Ministry to Foreign Office, October 30, 1920), 310 (Interior Ministry to Länder governments and Reichsrat committees, November 10, 1920).

44. II 5A 10395, pp. 194–215 (Foreign Office to Interior Ministry, April 30, 1920).

45. II 5A 10395, pp. 217 (C. H. Böhringer to Interior Ministry, May 27, 1920), and see 219 (Health Office to Interior Ministry, May 15, 1920).

46. II 5A 10395, pp. 358–71 (reprint of the enabling legislation, 1920), 377 (Interior Ministry to Economics, Finance, Statistical Office, Commissioner for Import and Export, and selected Prussian ministers, November 20, 1920).

47. II 5A 10395, pp. 406 (Interior Ministry to Reichstag, December 9, 1920), 421–35 (copy of Interior Ministry bill, 1920), 444 (Reichstag, 49th session, December 17, 1920), 447 (president, Reichstag, to Interior Ministry, December 17, 1920).

48. II 5A 10395, pp. 463–500 (Interior Ministry to and from Länder governments and drug companies, December 1920), 10396, pp. 152–53 (Health Office to Interior Ministry, March 17, 1921, Interior Ministry to Länder governments, March 23, 1921).

49. As of May 1923, 71 firms were authorized to import narcotics and 256 were allowed to export. II 5A 10401, pp. 327–34 (Health Office to Interior Ministry, May 14, 1923).

50. The demands of individual firms rather than industry or trade associations seem to have been behind the protests, which came primarily from the Prussian and Baden governments. The Health Office feared a domestic backlash because concern about drug abuse was growing in Germany. See II 5A 10397, pp. 404–6 (Health Office to Interior Ministry, July 18, 1921), 10401, pp. 120–23 (Interior Ministry to Foreign Ministry, February 18, 1923); Thamm, *Drogen Report*, pp. 84–91.

51. For example, see II 5A R10396, pp. 297–306 (British minister of foreign affairs to German Foreign Office, March 21, 1921), 562–63 (Health Office to Interior Ministry, May 11, 1921), 572–78 (Fachgruppe Opium und Cocain to Interior Ministry, May 23, 1921), 10401, pp. 165–67 (Interior Ministry to Foreign Office, March 16, 1923).

52. For example, II 5A 10401, pp. 20–21 (Health Office to Interior Ministry, December 24, 1922), 22 (Interior Ministry to Foreign Office, January 8, 1929), 45–46 (Health Office to Interior Ministry, January 9, 1923), 67 (Interior Ministry to Länder governments, January 25, 1923), 91–92 (Health Office to Interior Ministry, January 27, 1923), 120–23 (Interior Ministry to Foreign Office, February 18, 1923), 294–307 (Foreign Office to Interior Ministry, April 20, 1923).

53. II 5A 10401, pp. 498–502 (German Consulate, Geneva, to Foreign Office, May 26, 1923).

54. See II 5A 10401, pp. 611–24 (German Consulate, Geneva, to Foreign Office, June 7, 1923), 10402, pp. 39–51 (Dr. O. Anselmino, Health Office supplementary report on Geneva, August 17, 1923).

55. II 5A 10406, pp. 422–27 (Foreign Office to Interior Ministry, December 13, 1924).

56. For details on other German proposals at the conference, see III R 232/25 (German Consulate, Geneva, to Foreign Office, February 9, 1925), 233/25 (German Consulate, Geneva, to Foreign Office, February 10, 1925), 230/25 (notes regarding the opium conference, February 26, 1925). For extensive detail on the two Geneva Conferences, see Westel W. Willoughby, *Opium as an International Problem: The Geneva Conferences* (New York: Arno Press, 1976).

57. III R 233/25 (German Consulate, Geneva, to Foreign Office, February 10, 1925).

58. Scheerer, "Rauschmittelmißbrauch," p. 481; Ralf Beke-Bramkamp, *Die Drogenpolitik der USA, 1969–1990* (Baden-Baden: Nomos Verlagsgesellschaft, 1992), p. 80; Linz, *German Opium Legislation*, pp. 7–11 (in 862.53/2-2750).

59. III R n.a. [document partially coded II 2623 but in III R file] (Interior Ministry to Economics Ministry, March 31, 1925), 297 (Merck to Foreign Office, March 18, 1925), 301 (Health Office Memo, March 17, 1925), 388/25 (Brietfeld, Foreign Office, re: notes to Geneva Conference, April 21, 1925).

60. For example, see 511.4A1/1672 (League of Nations, "Traffic in Opium: Summary of Answers to the Opium Questionnaire, 1921," June 1, 1922), 1720 (Division of Far Eastern Affairs to William Phillips, October 16, 1922); II 5A 10401, pp. 76–77 (German consul general, British India and Ceylon, to Foreign Office, December 6, 1922). For press reports claiming German complicity in the illicit drug trade into China, see *Peking and Tientsin Times* March 14, 1923; *Peking Leader*, March 23, 1923.

61. For example, see 511.4A1/1720 (Division of Far Eastern Affairs to Phillips, October 16, 1922).

62. See II 5A 10402, pp. 233–37 (Interior Ministry to chancellor, November 10, 1923), 325–40 (Interior Ministry, draft bill, October 10, December 19, 1923), 10403, pp. 49–57 (Senate Commission to Interior Ministry, July 4, 1924), 10404, pp. 201 (Health Office to Interior Ministry, July 1, 1924), 202 (Interior Ministry to Foreign Office, July 17, 1924), 10407, p. 3 (press reports, December 25, 1924).

63. In addition to the cases I discuss, see II 5A 10401, pp. 154 (German Embassy, Peking, to Foreign Office, January 8, 1923), 311 (Health Office to Interior Ministry, May 2, 1923); Political Archive, German Foreign Office, Division III, file Opium, Case of Böhringer und Sohn [file misnamed], cited as III E, document 3184 (British Embassy, Berlin, to German Foreign Office, November 5, 1923), 3420 (Interior Ministry to Foreign Office, December 3, 1923); State Department Diplomatic Records, Records Relating to the Internal Affairs of Germany, 1910–29, 862.114/5 (Dr. Robert A.

Valentine to U.S. ambassador, France, forwarded to secretary of state, March 14, 1923).

64. For example, see Merck's views in II 5A 10401, pp. 354–56 (Hesse minister, Reichsrat, to Interior Ministry, May 22, 1923). For additional discussions of the chemical industry's concerns with the costs of the German drug regulations, see II 5A 10401, pp. 535–38 (Health Office to Interior Ministry, June 7, 1923), 10402, pp. 140–41 (Health Office to Interior Ministry, September 17, 1923).

65. II 5A 10401, pp. 544–49 (Health Office to Interior Ministry, June 26, 1923).

66. II 5A 10401, pp. 294–307 (Foreign Office to Interior Ministry, April 20, 1923).

67. For example, see II 5A R10402, pp. 105–18 (Foreign Office to Interior Ministry, September 6, 1923); III E 3184 (British Embassy, Berlin, to German Foreign Office, November 5, 1923), 2471 (British Embassy, Berlin, to German Foreign Office, August 24, 1923), 3286 (Interior Ministry to Foreign Office, November 16, 1923).

68. For example, see II 5A R10401, p. 529 (Health Office to Interior Ministry, June 15, 1923).

69. III E 3420 (Interior Ministry to Foreign Office, December 3, 1923); II 5A R10401, pp. 440–41 (Health Office to Interior Ministry, May 19, 1923).

70. III E 3286 (Interior Ministry to Foreign Office, November 16, 1923); II 5A 10402, pp. 264–66 (Health Office to Interior Ministry, October 29, 1923).

71. Later reports suggested that the British company—Wink and Company (actually Whiffen and Company)—had falsely labeled the products as German to shift attention to Germany. II 5A R10402, pp. 105–18 (Foreign Office to Interior Ministry, September 6, 1923), 264–66 (Health Office to Interior Ministry, October 29, 1923), 281–83 (Health Office to Interior Ministry, November 7, 1923); III E 3286 (Interior Ministry to Foreign Office, November 16, 1923). The case is further complicated by questions concerning when Switzerland finally signed and ratified the Hague treaty and the fact that Hoffmann La Roche, though Swiss based, had a facility in Grensach, Germany.

72. II 5A R10402, n.a. (Health Office to Interior Ministry, November 19, 1923), n.a. (Interior Ministry to Hamburg Senate Commission, November 27, 1923).

73. 862.114/13 ("New Executive Regulations . . . ," June 1924). See also Günther Bauer, *Rauschgift: Ein Handbuch über die Rauschgiftsucht, den Rauschgifthandel, die Bekämpfungsmaßnehmen, und die Hilfen für die Gefährdete* (Lübeck: Max Schmidt-Römhild, 1972), p. 293. For detail on efforts during 1924 to close this loophole in Hamburg, see II 5A R10403, pp. 17–21 (Interior Ministry to Finance Ministry, February 6, 1924), 184–85 (Interior Ministry to Hamburg Senate Commission, March 31, 1924), 193–94 (Foreign Office to Interior Ministry, March 31, 1924).

74. Lesser challenges had come from smaller firms such as Max L. Tornow of Frankfurt, which was authorized to export to Russia but had illegally shipped narcotics to the United States in early 1923. Following an investigation, the German government withdrew permission for Tornow to make any

further exports. See II 5A R10401, pp. 311–13 (Health Office to Interior Ministry, May 2, 1923), R10403, p. 7 (Interior Ministry, Karlsruhe, to Regional Authority, Lörrach, October 1, 1924).

75. II 5A R10402, pp. 404–19 (Foreign Office to Interior Ministry, January 16, 1924).

76. III E n.a. [coded as II A 2700/22.7 but in III E file], (Eric E. Ekstrand, League of Nations, to Dr. Kahler, Interior Ministry, passed on to Foreign Office, July 22, 1932).

77. II 5A 10404, pp. 161–62 (Health Office to Interior Ministry, August 1, 1924).

78. Chinese authorities in early January had also confiscated 509 kilograms of heroin in an illicit shipment with falsified labels on a Japanese freighter. Gehe, which had produced the heroin, maintained that it had properly shipped the goods to the same Bremen trading house. II 5A R10402, pp. 428–29 (Health Office to Interior Ministry, January 15, 1924).

79. II 5A R10403, pp. 458–61 (Health Office to Interior Ministry, May 29, 1924). Acting on the suggestion of the Health Office, the German Foreign Office also approached the Japanese government about what steps it might take against excessive Japanese purchases of German narcotics. II 5A R10403, pp. 223–25 (Health Office to Interior Ministry, April 9, 1924), 312 (Foreign Office to Japanese Embassy, Berlin, May 7, 1924).

80. II 5A R10404, pp. 177 (Foreign Office to Interior Ministry, August 17, 1924); III R 749 [but located in III E file] (meeting regarding Böhringer-Miyagawa case, August 21, 1924).

81. In an attempt to protect other German companies, the Foreign Office also explained that C. H. Böhringer Sohn of Hamburg and Nieder-Ingelheim was not the same as C. F. Böhringer und Söhne of Mannheim. The British replied that they were already aware of the distinction and sent additional data for the Böhringer Sohn case. III E Aug III (Foreign Office to British Embassy, Berlin, August 23, 1924); III R 749 (British Embassy, Berlin, to German Foreign Office, August 11, 1924), 749 (meeting regarding Böhringer-Miyagawa case, August 21, 1924), 839 (British Embassy, Berlin, to German Foreign Office, September 13, 1924). [All these III R document entries were located in the III E file.]

82. III R 749 (meeting regarding Böhringer-Miyagawa case, August 21, 1924); II 5A R10404, pp. 238–40 (Health Office to Interior Ministry, August 29, 1924), 255 (Anselmino to Interior Ministry, September 15, 1924). In September the British Government had also raised the case before the League of Nations. III R 878/24 (Interior Ministry to Foreign Office, September 20, 1924). [All of the III R entries were located in the III E file.]

83. III R 852/24 (Anselmino report and police reports to Interior Ministry, September 9, 11, 1924, forwarded to Foreign Office, September 16, 1924). [This entry was located in the III E file.]

84. See for example, II 5A R10405, pp. 301–30 (Böhringer Sohn to Interior Ministry, October 16, 18, 1924).

85. III R n.a. (Zeller, Foreign Office: Memorandum of interministerial [Anselmino (Health), Kahler (Interior), Haas (?), Friche (?), and Zeller (Foreign Office)] discussion regarding Böhringer, September 17, 1924). [This entry was located in the III E file.]

86. II 5A R10406, pp. 26–28 (Senate Commission to Interior Ministry, October 25, 1924).

87. II 5A R10406, pp. 54–64 (Interior Ministry to Foreign Office, November 7, 1924), 324–27 (Foreign Office to British Embassy, Berlin, November 13, 1924).

88. II 5A R10406, pp. 324–27 (Foreign Office to British Embassy, Berlin, November 13, 1924).

89. III R 102 (British Embassy, Berlin, to Foreign Office, January 27, 1925). [Located in III E file.] Even new regulations introduced in the aftermath of the MacDonald case in late 1923 had left a possible loophole in German monitoring procedures by holding that "the delivery to a foreign buyer or his agent within German territory inclusive of free ports and free districts is not regarded as an export." 862.114/7 (U.S. consul general, Berlin, to Department of State, December 1923).

90. III R 761 (German Embassy, London, to Foreign Office, August 22, 1927), 35 (German Embassy, London, to British Home Office, December 20, 1927), 35/28 (British Home Office to German Embassy, January 10, 1928). [These entries were all located in III E files.]

91. III R 452 (Interior Ministry to Foreign Office, May 6, 1925), 471 (Interior Ministry to Foreign Office, May 11, 1925, passing on memorandum II 4276 A, May 6, 1925, from Health Office to Interior Ministry; II 5A R10408, pp. 298–303 (Foreign Office to German Consulate, Bern, May 26, 1925). German officials were also concerned with the tendency of the Swiss firm Hoffmann La Roche to transship and to ship goods illicitly through Hamburg. The company's actions had contributed to an anti-German campaign being waged by the French press in late 1924. See, for example, III R 98 (Interior Ministry to Foreign Office, January 23, 1925), 245 (French press translations, February 13, 1925), 257 (Interior Ministry, Hesse, to Interior Ministry and Foreign Office, February 27, 1925), 801 (Interior Ministry to Foreign Office, August 21, 1925).

92. III R 452 (Interior Ministry to Foreign Office, May 6, 1925), 471 (Interior Ministry to German Embassy, Bern, May 26, 1925).

93. III R 577 (German Consulate, Bern, to Foreign Office, June 12, 1925, forwarding Swiss Economic Department to German ambassador, June 10, 1925).

94. II 5A R10408, pp. 298–303 (Foreign Office to German Consulate, Bern, May 26, 1925).

95. III R 588 (Interior Ministry to Fachgruppe Opium und Cocain, June 12, 1925).

96. III R 588 (Interior Ministry to Foreign Office, June 17, 1925), 621 (Foreign Ministry to German Consulate, Bern, June 26, 1925).

97. III R 240/29 (Foreign Office to Interior Ministry, May 14, 1929) [located in the III E file].

98. See, for example, III R 495 (Interior Ministry to Foreign Ministry, May 16, 1925), 155 (Foreign Office to German Consulate, Geneva, December 9, 1925).

99. Taylor, *American Diplomacy and the Narcotics Traffic*, p. 231; Marcel de Kort and Dirk J. Korf, "The Development of Drug Trade and Drug Control in the Netherlands: A Historical Perspective," *Crime, Law, and Social Change* 17 (1992): 130.

100. 511.4A1/2112 (U.S. Legation, the Hague, to secretary of state, February 12, 1929), 2114 (U.S. Legation, the Hague, to secretary of state, March 11, 1929); De Kort and Korf, "The Development of Drug Trade," pp. 130–31.

101. III R 197 (Interior Ministry to State Office for Foreign Affairs, Hamburg, February 25, 1930); III E n.a. [coded as II A 2700/22.7 but in III E file] (Ekstrand, League of Nations, to Kahler, Interior Ministry, passed on to Foreign Office, July 22, 1932). For Böhringer's promise to comply, see III R 270 (State Office for Foreign Affairs, Hamburg, to Interior Ministry, March 12, 1930).

102. For detail on the convention, see Taylor, *American Diplomacy and the Narcotics Traffic*, pp. 255–60; III R 906 (Interior Ministry to Foreign Office, October 11, 1930), 906 (Foreign Office to German Embassy, London, October 16, 1930), 1035 (Interior Ministry to Foreign Office, November 26, 1930), 557 (German delegation to Foreign Office, June 18, 1931). For additional examples of cooperation with league authorities, see III R 174 (Interior Ministry to Foreign Office, February 18, 1930), 174/30 (Interior Ministry to League of Nations, February 18, 1930).

103. III R 38/30 (U.S. Treasury Department to Interior Ministry, December 10, 1929), 41/30 (Department of State, Treaty Division, July 1929), 184/30 (Treasury Department to Health Office, June 26, 1929; Interior Ministry to League of Nations, February 20, 1930), 4ig (German Embassy, Washington, to Foreign Office, April 29, 1931), n.a. (Interior Ministry to Harry Anslinger, May 19, 1931).

104. III R 232 (Interior Ministry to Foreign Office, January 31, 1930), 956/30 (Foreign Office to Interior Ministry, July 24, 1930), 820 (Interior Ministry to Foreign Office, September 15, 1930), 614 (Foreign Office to Interior Ministry, July 9, 1931).

105. The primary trade in question was in esters (for example, Merck's Benzylmorphine sold under the trade name of Peronin) and other derivatives. III R n.a. (Interior Ministry to Foreign Office, September 15, 1930), n.a. (German Consulate, New York, to Foreign Office, April 1, 1931, detail in John D. Farnham and Helen Howell Moorhead, "International Limitation of Dangerous Drugs," *Foreign Policy Reports*, April 1, 1931, pp. 19–47).

106. The German government had notified the league of Merck's actions in 1930. III R 478 (Interior Ministry to Foreign Office, June 6, 1930); Farnham and Moorhead, "International Limitation," pp. 25–26.

107. See, for example, 511.4A1/1186 (Beaupre to secretary of state, August 25, 1911), 1195 (Beaupre to secretary of state, September 7, 1911).

108. I have benefited here from discussions with Peter Katzenstein.

109. See, for example, II 5A R10403, p. 495 (Foreign Office to Interior Ministry, June 24, 1924), R10404, p. 42 (press translation, June 16, 1924). These crackdowns appear to have been facilitated in part by U.S. Treasury officials based in Berlin. German officials, however, also suspected these U.S. agents of industrial espionage. See III R n.a. (commissioner for the oversight of public order to Foreign Ministry, Berlin, July 17, 1925 forwarding report of Senate Police Commission, Bremen).

Chapter 3. Narcotics Trafficking and Japan

1. Arnold H. Taylor, *American Diplomacy and the Narcotics Traffic, 1900–1939: A Study in International Humanitarian Reform* (Durham, N.C.: Duke University Press, 1969), pp. 11, 35, 40–41, 43; Peter D. Lowes, *The Genesis of International Narcotics Control* (Geneva: Droz, 1966), pp. 88, 104; Thomas D. Reins, "Reform, Nationalism, and Internationalism: The Opium Suppression Movement in China and the Anglo-American Influence, 1900–1908," *Modern Asian Studies* 25, 1 (1991): 113.

2. Ian Nish, *Japan's Struggles with Internationalism: Japan, China, and the League of Nations* (London: Kegan Paul International, 1993), pp. 40–41; Michael A. Barnhart, *Japan Prepares for Total War: The Search for Economic Security, 1919–1941* (Ithaca: Cornell University Press, 1987), pp. 58, 65 (quot.).

3. Barnhart, *Japan Prepares for Total War*, pp. 66, 91, 95, 100.

4. Nish, *Japan's Struggles with Internationalism*, p. 6; James B. Crowley, *Japan's Quest for Autonomy: National Security and Foreign Policy, 1930–1938* (Princeton: Princeton University Press, 1966), p. 5; and Alvin D. Coox, "The Kwantung Army Dimension," in Peter Duus, Ramon H. Meyers, and Mark Peattie, eds., *The Japanese Informal Empire in China, 1895–1937* (Princeton: Princeton University Press, 1989), p. 396.

5. Nish, *Japan's Struggles with Internationalism*, p. 6; Albert E. Hindmarsh, *The Basis of Japanese Foreign Policy* (Cambridge: Harvard University Press, 1936), pp. 205–6; Ian Nish, *The Anglo-American Alliance: The Diplomacy of Two Island Empires, 1894–1907* (London: Athlone Press, 1966), pp. 26, 33–34, 50, 111; Barnhart, *Japan Prepares for Total War*, p. 29; Ramon H. Myers, "Japanese Imperialism in Manchuria: The South Manchurian Railway Company, 1906–1933," in Duus, Myers, and Peattie, *The Japanese Informal Empire*, 116–17.

6. Crowley, *Japan's Quest for Autonomy*, pp. 19, 104; Shiroyama Saburo, *War Criminal: The Life and Death of Hirota Koki*, trans. John Bester (Tokyo: Kodansha International, 1977), pp. 81–83; Nish, *Japan's Struggles with Internationalism*, p. 26; Herbert P. Bix, "Japanese Imperialism and the Manchurian Economy," *China Quarterly* 51 (July–September 1972): 427–29, 437; Nish, *The Anglo-Japanese Alliance*, p. 349; William D. Wray, "Japan's Big-Three Service Enterprises in China, 1896–1936," in Duus, Meyers, and Peattie, *The Japanese Informal Empire*, p. 42.

7. Coox, "The Kwantung Army Dimension," pp. 408, 423.

8. Nish, *Japan's Struggles with Internationalism*, p. 122; Bix, "Japanese Imperialism and the Manchurian Economy," p. 434.

9. *Manchuria*, Report of the Commission of Enquiry Appointed by the League of Nations, 1932, pp. 100–101.

10. Nakagane Katsuji, "Manchukuo and Economic Development," in Duus, Meyers, and Peattie, *The Japanese Informal Empire*, pp. 134, 147; Myers, "Japanese Imperialism in Manchuria," p. 125.

11. Nakagane, "Manchukuo and Economic Development," pp. 148–56.

12. Barnhart, *Japan Prepares for Total War*, p. 91.

13. T. J. Pempel, *Policy and Politics in Japan: Creative Conservatism* (Philadelphia: Temple University Press, 1982), p. 27.

14. Ibid., pp. 12–13; and see Robert E. Ward, *Japan's Political System* (Englewood Cliffs, N.J.: Prentice-Hall, 1978), pp. 12–13.

15. Charles Neu, *The Troubled Encounter: The U.S. and Japan* (New York: John Wiley and Sons, 1975), p. 150.

16. Pempel, *Policy and Politics*, pp. 12–13; Ward, *Japan's Political System*, pp. 13, 16.

17. For divisions within the Foreign Ministry over the dynamics of Japan's China policy, see Mark Charles Michelson, "A Place in the Sun: The Foreign Ministry and Perceptions and Policies in Japan's International Relations, 1931–1941" (Ph.D. diss., University of Illinois-Urbana-Champaign, 1979); Barbara J. Brooks, "China Experts in the Giamushō, 1895–1937," in Duus, Meyers, and Peattie, *The Japanese Informal Empire*, pp. 368–94.

18. Nish, *Japan's Struggles with Internationalism*, p. 116; Crowley, *Japan's Quest for Autonomy*, pp. 387–88. For detail on administrative regulations requiring the appointment of active soldiers—generals and lieutenant generals—as army and navy ministers from 1900 to 1913 and from 1936 on, see Meirion Harries and Susie Harries, *Soldiers of the Sun: The Rise and Fall of the Imperial Japanese Army* (New York: Random House, 1991), pp. 65, 108, 193.

19. Harries, *Soldiers of the Sun*, pp. 103–5; Shiroyama, *War Criminal*, p. 76; Crowley, *Japan's Quest for Autonomy*, pp. 85, 96. The power distribution within the military was also affected by several overlapping divisions: regional dynamics (the Choshu dominance of the War Ministry versus Satsuma dominance of the general staff), junior versus more senior officers, and pragmatic differences over the proper approach to bring about change in Japan and abroad (the Imperial Way and Control Factions). See Crowley, *Japan's Quest for Autonomy*, pp. 95–96, 247, 249–79; Harries and Harries, *Soldiers of the Sun*, pp. 169, 180–93; and Wen-hsien Chang, "Dohihara Kenji and the Japanese Expansion into China" (Ph.D. diss., University of Pennsylvania, 1969), pp. 48–50.

20. Coox, "The Kwantung Army Dimension," pp. 397–400; Kitaoka Shin'ichi, "China Experts in the Army," in Duus, Meyers, and Peattie, *The Japanese Informal Empire*, p. 350.

21. Coox, "The Kwantung Army Dimension," pp. 405–6; Nish, *Japan's Struggles with Internationalism*, pp. 25, 85.

22. Nish, *Japan's Struggles with Internationalism*, pp. 158, 161. Administrative control over Manchukuo remained heavily shaped by Japan. In the Manchukuo government, for example, 17 of 27 bureau chiefs and 100 of 135 central officials were Japanese. Coox, "The Kwantung Army Dimension," pp. 411–12; *Manchuria*, p. 99.

23. John H. Boyle, "Japan's Puppet Regime in China, 1937–1940" (Ph.D. diss., Stanford University, 1968), pp. 149–52; International Military Tribunal for the Far East, Photographic Division, *Court Papers, Journals, Exhibits, and Judgements of the International Military Tribunal for the Far East*, Microcopy No. T-918, 1948, cited as IMTFE2, exhibit 389, document 9575. The China Affairs Board was disbanded in 1942 (along with the Colonial Ministry) and incorporated into the Greater East Asia Office. See Okada Yoshimasa, Tatai Yoshio, and Takahashi Masae, eds., *Ahen Mondai* (Opium problem) (Tokyo: Misuzu Shobo, 1986), pp. xxvi–xxvii.

24. Barnhart, *Japan Prepares for Total War*, pp. 71–72.

25. Opium was covered by the Opium Law of 1898, as amended; other narcotics were covered by ordinances of the Home Office. State Department Diplomatic Records, Internal Affairs of Japan, Narcotics, 894.114 Narcotics/N16/2-2745 (League of Nations to Department of State, February 27, 1945).

26. Diet influence was limited primarily to infrequent challenges, usually by the opposition parties, to the government's strategy. See, for example, a summary of a Diet inquiry during the early 1920s in State Department Diplomatic Records, Geneva Conference, 511.4A2/103 (chargé d'affairs, Tokyo, to secretary of state, September 20, 1924).

27. Ibid., State Department Diplomatic Records, International Conferences, Narcotics, 1910–29, 511.4A1/2004 (Shidehara Kijūrō to secretary of state, February 24, 1927); U.S. Embassy translation of article in Tokyo newspaper *Jiji Shimpo*, April 9, 1926, in 894.14 Narcotics/N16/ no number.

28. The committee was empowered to make investigations, inquiries, and representations on questions of opium and manufactured narcotics. Louise Elizabeth Sarah Eisenlohr, *International Narcotics Control* (1934; rpt. New York: Arno Press, 1981), pp. 72–73; *The Opium Trade*, vol. 6 (Wilmington, Del.: Scholarly Resources, 1974), cited as BRIT6, document F 2500/281/87 (British Embassy, Tokyo, to Foreign Office, April 8, 1931); International Military Tribunal for the Far East, *Proceedings, 1946–1948* (Washington, D.C.: Library of Congress, Photo Duplication Service, 1947), cited as IMTFE1, pp. 30624–25.

29. Neu, *The Troubled Encounter*, p. 150. The Home Affairs Ministry was excluded until a December 14, 1937, liaison conference by the Konoe Fumimaro cabinet concerning how Japan should respond to the China Incident. Crowley, *Japan's Quest for Autonomy*, p. 362.

30. Barnhart, *Japan Prepares for Total War*, pp. 71–72. The stated need for the ministry was to address concerns of conscript health and disease threats abroad. The military tasks begun in 1938 included "aid to the military,

military hospitals, and other health and labor problems. 894.114 Narcotics/N16/2-2745 (League of Nations to secretary of state, February 27, 1945).
31. IMTFE1, pp. 30624–25.
32. Sugai Shuichi, "The Japanese Police System," in Robert E. Ward, ed., *Five Studies in Japanese Politics* (Ann Arbor: University of Michigan Press, 1957), pp. 3–4; David H. Bayley, *Forces of Order: Police Behavior in Japan and the United States* (Berkeley: University of California Press, 1976), pp. 185–87.
33. 894.114 Narcotics/N16/2-2745 (League of Nations to secretary of state, February 27, 1945).
34. Japan, Bureau of Foreign Trade, Department of Commerce and Industry, *The Industry of Japan*, 1930 Edition (Tokyo: Maruzen, 1930), p. 66; Yamasaki Kakujiro and Ogawa Gotaro, *The Effect of the World War upon the Commerce and Industry of Japan* (New Haven: Yale University Press, 1929), pp. 277–311; *The Opium Trade*, vol. 4 (Wilmington, Del.: Scholarly Resources, 1974), cited as BRIT4, document 205069 (British Embassy, Tokyo, to Foreign Office, September 12, 1917).
35. 511.4A2/256 (E. R. Dickover to secretary of state, December 16, 1924). 894.114 Narcotics/N16/2-2745 (League of Nations to secretary of state, February 27, 1945) lists the six as Hoshi Drug Manufacturing Company, Sankyo Company, Dai Nippon Drug Manufacturing Company, Takeda Tyobei Syoten Company, Siono Gi Syoten Company, and Koto Drug Manufacturing Company.
36. The government was the sole authorized buyer of opium; coca required only licensing to grow. 894.114 Narcotics/N16/2-2745 (League of Nations to secretary of state, February 27, 1945). Japanese cocaine production initially relied on imports from Java and later Formosa as well as domestic sources.
37. The early history of the Japanese chemical industry, especially pharmaceuticals, is relatively underexplored. Barbara Molony, *Technology and Investment: The Prewar Japanese Chemical Industry* (Cambridge: Harvard University Press, 1990), addresses this gap but gives little detail about the pharmaceutical sector.
38. IMTFE1, pp. 4664–996, 39177–89, and see John C. McWilliams, *The Protectors: Harry J. Anslinger and the Federal Bureau of Narcotics* (Newark: University of Delaware Press, 1990), p. 98; David Bergamini, *Japan's Imperial Conspiracy: How Emperor Hirohito Led Japan into War against the West* (New York: William Morrow, 1971), pp. 528–29; Herbert L. May, "The International Control of Narcotic Drugs," *International Conciliation* 441 (1948): 342–43; Arnold C. Brackman, *The Other Nuremburg: The Untold Story of the Tokyo War Crimes Trials* (New York: William Morrow, 1987), pp. 374, 418–19.
39. "Cynical" is May's term in "The International Control of Narcotic Drugs," pp. 342–43; "dual" is the word used in Fredrick T. Merrill, *Japan and the Opium Menace* (1942; rpt. New York: Arno Press, 1981), pp. 37–40, 72–73.
40. Taylor, *American Diplomacy and the Narcotics Traffic*, p. 49.
41. Reins, "Reform, Nationalism, and Internationalism," pp. 104–5, 139; Harold Traver, "'Opium to Heroin: Restrictive Opium Legislation and the

Rise of Heroin Consumption in Hong Kong," *Journal of Policy History* 14, 3 (1992): 312–13.

42. Reins, "Reform, Nationalism, and Internationalism," p. 139; Taylor, *American Diplomacy and the Narcotics Traffic*, pp. 61, 63; William O. Walker III, *Opium and Foreign Policy: The Anglo-American Search for Order in Asia, 1912–1954* (Chapel Hill: University of North Carolina Press, 1991), p. 16.

43. Taylor, *American Diplomacy and the Narcotics Traffic*, pp. 69–73.

44. See, for example, 511.4A1/709 (Ministry of Foreign Affairs to U.S. Embassy, February 21, 1910), 797 (U.S. Embassy, Tokyo, to Department of State, August 24, 1910), 804 (U.S. Embassy, Tokyo, to Department of State, October 26, 1910), 913 (document contains correspondence among U.S. Embassy, Tokyo, the Department of State, and Hamilton Wright, October–November, 1910), 916 (U.S. Embassy, Tokyo, to Department of State, November 15, 1910), 922 (Ministry of Foreign Affairs to U.S. consul, October 29, 1910), 933 (U.S. consul to Department of State, November 16, 1910), 1098A (Wright to Department of State, May 6, 1911), and 1156 (Ministry of Foreign Affairs, June 5, 1911).

45. Taylor, *American Diplomacy and the Narcotics Traffic*, pp. 82–122; 511.4A1/1283 (Huidekoper, "International Opium Conference," February 28, 1913).

46. Terry Parssinen and Karen Kerner, "An Historical Fable for Our Time: The Illicit Traffic in Morphine in the Early Twentieth Century," *Journal of Drug Issues* (Winter 1981): 49–50. British Foreign Office files reveal that British firms also acted as agents for Japanese importers, purchasing cocaine from Holland (969 pounds in 1915 and 1,278 pounds in 1916) for sale in Japan. The Japanese importers included Iwai and Company, Tokyo Trading Company, Tomada Trading Company (Tokyo), and C. Takeda and Oriental Pharmaceutical Company (Osaka). BRIT4, 37169 (Home Office to Foreign Office, February 15, 1917).

47. See Walker, *Opium and Foreign Policy*, p. 30; Taylor, *American Diplomacy and the Narcotics Traffic*, pp. 138–40; *Peking Gazette*, in Japanese Foreign Ministry Archives, Diplomatic Records Office, 4.2.4.1–2, Regulation and Report of Situation of Opium in China, 1906–24, cited as GA5, no number (October 19, 1915).

48. Walker, *Opium and Foreign Policy*, p. 30; S. D. Stein, *International Diplomacy, State Administration, and Narcotics Control: The Origins of a Social Problem* (Aldershot, U.K.: Gower, 1985), p. 110; BRIT4, 45308 (House of Commons to Board of Trade, February 26, 1917), 44342 (House of Commons to Board of Trade, February 26, 1917), 172112 (regarding Foreign Office to Japanese Ministry of Foreign Affairs, September 6–7, 1917), 158935 (Foreign Office to Japanese Ministry of Foreign Affairs, July 9, 1917).

49. Parssinen and Kerner, "An Historical Fable for Our Time," pp. 52, 55; Stein, *International Diplomacy*, p. 111.

50. 894.114 Narcotics/N16/12 (U.S. Embassy, Tokyo, to secretary of state, October 7, 1919).

51. 894.114 Narcotics/N16/13 (Department of State to U.S. Embassy, Tokyo, October 11, 1919), 14 (U.S. Embassy, Tokyo, to Department of State, October 21, 1919).

52. Japanese Foreign Ministry Archives, 4.2.4.1-1-2, Drug Regulations in Japan, 1906–25, cited as GA6, document 172 (Ishii, Foreign Ministry, to U.S. ambassador, August 29, 1916), 222 (Ishii, Foreign Ministry, to U.S. ambassador, November 14, 1916).

53. Walker, *Opium and Foreign Policy*, p. 31.

54. 894.114 Narcotics/N16/MC (U.S. Consulate, Tokyo, to Department of State, February 28, 1919); and see Walker, *Opium and Foreign Policy*, p. 31; BRIT4/46023 (British Embassy, Tokyo, to Foreign Office, February 10, 1919).

55. 511.4A1/1545 (U.S. Mission, Paris, to Department of State, March 31, 1919); 894.114 Narcotics/N16/5 (U.S. Embassy, Tokyo, to Department of State, March 31, 1919), 7 (Stanley Hornbeck to Department of State, September 15, 1919).

56. See Walker, *Opium and Foreign Policy*, pp. 25–27; 511.4A1/1543 (U.S. Embassy, Tokyo, to Department of State, March 11, 1919), 1545 (U.S. Mission, Paris, to Department of State, March 31, 1919).

57. 894.114 Narcotics/N16/MC (U.S. Consulate, Tokyo, to Department of State, February 28, 1919), 7 (Hornbeck to Department of State, September 15, 1919); Oi Shizuo, "Ahen Jiken no Shinso" (Truth of opium incident), Document reprinted in Okada et al., *Ahen Mondai*, pp. 218–19.

58. Perhaps that is why the U.S. legation in Peking noted that "drastic action" against the Japanese morphine traffic in China was nowhere to be seen. 894.114 Narcotics/N16/2 (Peking Legation to Department of State, March 1, 1919). For reports of instances concerning and steps by Japanese consular officials against opium smuggling from Japanese holdings in China to mainland China, see GA5, 8935 (commissioner of customs, Amoy, to Japanese consul, August 22–23, 1918), no number (commissioner of customs, Chefoo, to Japanese consul, June 21, 1919); and Oi, "Ahen Jiken," pp. 218–19.

59. Walker, *Opium and Foreign Policy*, p. 38.

60. 511.4A1/1560 (British Embassy, Washington, D.C., to Department of State, April 13, 1920), 1562 (Department of the Treasury to Department of State, November 20, 1920); GA6, 409 (Edward Bell, chargé d'affairs, to Uchida, July 14, 1920). In a July note to the Japanese Foreign Ministry, the United States justified its actions to limit exports to Japan under the Harrison Narcotics Act. Foreign Minister Uchida Yasuya in early August noted that the U.S. action was being referred "to the authorities concerned," and by early October he informed the U.S. Embassy that new regulations covering manufactured narcotics were "under compilation." GA6, 409 (Uchida to Bell, August 3, 1920), 119 (Uchida to Bell, October 2, 1920).

61. The new regulations were contained in Home Office Ordinance 41 and were transmitted to the U.S. Embassy on December 14. GA6 159 (Uchida to

Bell, December 14, 1920); BRIT4, F 552/15/10 (British Embassy, Tokyo, to Foreign Office, December 29, 1920).

62. For example, see articles noted in *The Opium Trade*, vol. 5 (Wilmington, Del.: Scholarly Resources, 1974), cited as BRIT5, document F 600/504/10 (British Embassy, Tokyo, to Foreign Office, January 9, 1922), F 1621/504/10 (British Embassy, Tokyo, to Japanese Foreign Ministry, March 29, 1922).

63. The Dairen Kosai Zendo (the Dairen Charity Relief Institute) was granted an exclusive license by Kwantung authorities in April 1915 to import and sell smoking opium. In September 1920 the institute's office for smoking control was reclassified by cabinet order as a pharmacy. In 1928 an imperial ordinance replaced Kosai Zendo with the Kwantung Government Monopoly Bureau, Dairen. State Department Diplomatic Records (Internal Affairs of Japan) 894C.114 narcotics/15 (notes history as detailed in the *Manchuria Mongolia Yearbook*, Sino-Japanese Culture Society, a subsidiary of the South Manchurian Railway Company).

64. 894.114 Narcotics/N16/17 (U.S. Embassy, Tokyo, to Department of State, February 28, 1921).

65. BRIT4, F 1659/15/10 (British Embassy, Tokyo, to Foreign Office, March 24, 1921), F 1672/15/10 (British Embassy, Tokyo, to Foreign Office, March 25, 1921). Although the British and Kenseikai believed the government was complicit in this case, the criminal investigation and subsequent guilty ruling against one Kosai Zendo employee suggests that the authorities were making some efforts. For an example of this interpretation, see Oi, "Ahen Jiken," pp. 218–19.

66. The rationale here included the long-standing purchasing relationship between the company and the Formosa government and the potential damage to the company of ending this relationship "immediately." BRIT5, F 988/452/87 (British Embassy, Tokyo, to Foreign Office, February 27, 1923); 894.114 Narcotics/N16/22 (copy of Diet question, March 15, 1923). The Japanese government relationship with Hoshi was extensive. In 1915 the company was given a monopoly over the disposal of "coarse morphine," and it was the initial licensed producer of refined morphine. Eguchi Keiichi, *Nitchu Ahen Senso* (Japanese-Sino Opium War) (Tokyo: Iwanami Shinsho, 1988), pp. 36–37.

67. BRIT5, F 988/452/87 (British Embassy, Tokyo, to Foreign Office, February 27, 1923); 894.114 Narcotics/N16/22 (copy of Diet question, March 15, 1923). The question of how to integrate crude morphine production in Formosa into Japanese drug policy remained unresolved until 1927, when there were press reports and a court case involving Hoshi Pharmaceutical and Kaku Sagataro ("formerly Director of the Monopoly Bureau, later Civil Governor of Taiwan, and more recently a Japanese delegate" to the Geneva Conference) involving Persian opium imports into Formosa, production of prepared opium, and potential stockpiles of 25,000 pounds of crude morphine. 894.114 Narcotics/N16/no number (Edwin Neville to secretary of state, September 23, 1925).

68. Another link being explored in the transshipment chain included shipments from the United States through Vladivostok. BRIT5, F 553/553/87 (British Embassy, Tokyo, to Foreign Office, January 17, 1923).

69. BRIT5, F 530/452/87 (British Embassy, Tokyo, to Foreign Office, January 23, 1923); 894.114 Narcotics/N16/22 (U.S. consul, Tokyo, to Department of State, July 21, 1923), 31 (Karuizawa to Department of State, August 1, 1924).

70. Thus, the cases did not constitute unlicensed imports or fall under regulations that would have applied had the goods cleared customs. 894.114 Narcotics/N16/22 (U.S. consul, Tokyo, to Department of State, July 21, 1923), 32 (U.S. Embassy, Tokyo, to Department of State, November 7, 1924).

71. This pattern contrasts with disputes over immigration and the Washington Conferences. See Neu, *The Troubled Encounter*, pp. 34–35, 48–59, 79–83, 105–13, 123–25.

72. "Provisional Minutes, Advisory Committee on Traffic in Opium," Second Session, Ninth Meeting (March 24, 1922), in 511.4A1/no number. For a similar pattern in responding to requests from the league, see GA6, no number (League of Nations to Foreign Ministry, November 8, 1923).

73. 511.4A1/1816 (Moorhead report, July 1923).

74. Walker, *Opium and Foreign Policy*, pp. 38–39, notes that the actions of the head of the U.S. delegation reflected the U.S. belief that the Japanese army in China was engaged in the morphine traffic and that the Japanese government in Tokyo was "genuinely concerned."

75. Taylor, *American Diplomacy and the Narcotics Traffic*, pp. 181–82; telegrams to Department of State from Tokyo, Geneva, and Great Britain in 511.4A2/164d (November 20–21, 1924), 164 (November 21, 1924), 173 (December 19, 1924), 214 (December 4, 1924).

76. The committee was deliberating a conference proposal on "white nations bordering on the Pacific." Taylor, *American Diplomacy and the Narcotics Traffic*, pp. 203–4.

77. Ibid., p. 204; and Walker, *Opium and Foreign Policy*, pp. 38–39. These efforts of the Japanese delegation captured the bulk of the reporting on the conference by the Japanese press. 511.4A2/324 (U.S. Embassy, Tokyo, to Department of State, March 17, 1925).

78. Examples of antismuggling efforts include the second meeting of the informal governmental Opium Committee in March 1926 (established in 1924) and the establishment of a formal Opium Committee in March/April 1931. See 511.4A1/2004 (Shidehara to secretary of state, February 24, 1927); translation of April 9, 1926, article in the newspaper *Jiji Shimpo* in 894.114 Narcotics/N16/no number (April 10, 1926); BRIT6, F 2500/281/87 (British Embassy, Tokyo, to Foreign Office, April 8, 1931); IMTFE1, pp. 30624–25.

79. U.S. pressure also tended to reflect a pro-China bias within the State Department. Neu, *The Troubled Encounter*, pp. 67–69, 146–47; Walker, *Opium and Foreign Policy*, pp. 68–71.

80. Neu, *The Troubled Encounter*, pp. 136–41.

81. Walker, *Opium and Foreign Policy,* pp. 51–52; Coox, "The Kwantung Army Dimension," pp. 403–6.

82. What aggrieved the officials in the main was that the assassination had been carried out without the knowledge of the emperor, the prime minister, or the general staff. Coox, "The Kwantung Army Dimension," pp. 405–6. Efforts by the Tanaka Giichi government to punish those involved ran into extensive military opposition. Harries and Harries, *Soldiers of the Sun,* pp. 48–50; Shiroyama, *War Criminal,* pp. 51, 55–61.

83. Because of their close proximity to the civilian government and the emperor, the war minister and chief of the general staff, however, were still left out of the planning. Chang, "Dohihara Kenji," pp. 101–7; Coox, "The Kwantung Army Dimension," pp. 403–6; Crowley, *Japan's Quest for Autonomy,* pp. 114–21. These incidents have been scrutinized by historians and political scientists.

84. Nish, *Japan's Struggles with Internationalism,* p. 25.

85. Crowley, *Japan's Quest for Autonomy,* pp. 127–28.

86. Shiroyama, *War Criminal,* pp. 56–57, 61, 68–69, 70; Nish, *Japan's Struggles with Internationalism,* p. 40; and Crowley, *Japan's Quest for Autonomy,* pp. 105–7.

87. Nish, *Japan's Struggles with Internationalism,* pp. 33, 35–36, 80–82, 85; Chang, "Dohihara Kenji," pp. 66–69, 149–58; Shiroyama, *War Criminal,* pp. 77–79; Brooks, "China Experts in the Gaimushō," p. 388.

88. Still, factions within Seiyukai considered Inukai insufficiently supportive of the army in Manchuria. Crowley, *Japan's Quest for Autonomy,* pp. 168–72; Nish, *Japan's Struggles with Internationalism,* p. 75; and Shiroyama, *War Criminal,* pp. 80–81.

89. Nish, *Japan's Struggles with Internationalism,* pp. 88–89, 124, 138–39, and on the findings of the Lytton Report and Japan's reaction, 186–200.

90. Ibid., pp. 138–39, 151–52; Shiroyama, *War Criminal,* pp. 80–81; Crowley, *Japan's Quest for Autonomy,* pp. 183–85; Charles A. Kupchan, *The Vulnerability of Empire* (Ithaca: Cornell University Press, 1994), pp. 320–21.

91. Nish, *Japan's Struggles with Internationalism,* pp. 205–6, 213–27; and Bergamini, *Japan's Imperial Conspiracy,* pp. 532–40.

92. Taylor, *American Diplomacy and the Narcotics Traffic,* pp. 283–84.

93. Walker, *Opium and Foreign Policy,* pp. 64–71, 85–90, 99. For a similar argument, see Jonathan Marshall, "Opium and the Politics of Gangsterism in Nationalist China," *Bulletin of Concerned Asian Scholars* 8, 3 (1976): 20–24.

94. For example, in 1930 the U.S. Embassy in Tokyo rejected charges appearing in the U.S. press that narcotics were being produced in Japan for illicit export and that such exports, if they occurred, were being sanctioned by Japanese authorities. Moreover, the chargé d'affaires noted that Japanese authorities were trying to reduce transshipment through ports such as Kobe. 894.114 Narcotics/N16/54 (Neville to Department of State, July 26, 1930).

95. Japan's role in the deliberations over the 1931 Convention on the Limitation of Manufactured Narcotics focused primarily on obtaining "an equal

allocation of quotas among manufacturing states." Taylor, *American Diplomacy and the Narcotics Traffic*, pp. 238–51. Questions emerged in the OAC deliberations, however, concerning Japan's (over)stated domestic needs for narcotics such as heroin. Eisenlohr, *International Narcotics Control*, pp. 174–75.

96. State Department Diplomatic Records, Internal Affairs of Japan, 1930–39, 894.114 Narcotics/73 (Memo, Division of Far Eastern Affairs, April 15, 1933); Walker, *Opium and Foreign Policy*, p. 52.

97. 894C.114 Narcotics/26 (U.S. Consulate, Dairen, to secretary of state, August 24, 1931), 171 (U.S. Consulate, Dairen, to secretary of state, January 18, 1933).

98. Kitaoka, "China Experts in the Army," p. 350; Coox, "The Kwantung Army Dimension," pp. 398–400.

99. Nish notes that in the absence of recognition, officials in the new government were not appointed by Tokyo and thus "were capable of independent decision." Nish, *Japan's Struggles with Internationalism*, pp. 124, 158.

100. Document 7 [telegram 576] (consul general, Changchun, to foreign minister, September 7, 1932) in Okada et al., *Ahen Mondai*, pp. 498–99.

101. Walker, *Opium and Foreign Policy*, pp. 58, 64. As General Tanaka Ryukichi testified, "Until 1935 when the opium control board was set up, the opium trade was controlled by various special service organizations of the army," including the Mukden branch. IMTFE1, pp. 15853–58.

102. Crowley, *Japan's Quest for Autonomy*, p. 180.

103. Ibid., p. 110; Nish, *Japan's Struggles with Internationalism*, p. 141.

104. Hirota and his successor, Satō Naotake, would be less supportive of the military approach to China; Ugaki and Arita would shift in the other direction. Brooks, "China Experts in the Gaimushō," pp. 390–92; W. G. Beasley, *The Modern History of Japan* (New York: Praeger, 1963), pp. 248–52; Shiroyama, *War Criminal*, pp. 113, 118–19, 159–61.

105. League of Nations, Advisory Committee on Traffic in Opium and Other Dangerous Drugs, Seventeenth Session, "Provisional Minutes: Third, Fourth, and Fifth Meetings," November 2–3, 1933. O.C./17th Session/P.V.3-5.

106. Westel W. Willoughby, *The Sino-Japanese Controversy and the League of Nations* (New York: Greenwood Press, 1968), pp. 528–31; Taylor, *American Diplomacy and the Narcotics Traffic*, pp. 284–86.

107. Taylor, *American Diplomacy and the Narcotics Traffic*, p. 284.

108. Document 9 [telegrams 688, 689] (Idebuchi, Washington, D.C., to Foreign Minister, December 28–29, 1932), in Okada et al., *Ahen Mondai*, pp. 499–500.

109. 894.114 narcotics/N16/MC (U.S. consul, Tokyo, to Department of State, February 28, 1919); 894C.114 Narcotics/15 (notes history as detailed in the *Manchuria Mongolia Yearbook*, Sino-Japanese Culture Society, a subsidiary of the South Manchurian Railway Company).

110. *Facts Concerning Opium and Other Dangerous Drugs in Manchukuo* (Hsinking: Bureau of Research, Foreign Office, 1937), pp. 2–3; IMTFE1, p. 29117.

111. 894.114 Narcotics/80 (document file note, Tientsin, May 8, 1933); Walker, *Opium and Foreign Policy*, p. 67.

112. 894.114 Narcotics/72 (Anslinger to Stuart Fuller, March 29, 1933), 73 (memo, Division of Far Eastern Affairs, April 15, 1933), 90 (n.a., October 23, 1933), 74 (Anslinger to Fuller, April 18, 1933), 76 (Department of Treasury to secretary of state, April 22, 1933).

113. 894.114 Narcotics/68 (Joseph Grew to secretary of state, February 1, 1933), 76 (Department of Treasury to secretary of state, April 22, 1933).

114. 894.114 Narcotics/92 (U.S. Consulate, Kobe, to secretary of state, August 15, 1933), 89 (U.S. Embassy, Tokyo, to secretary of state, October 2, 1933), 118 (press translation, July 3, 1934), 119 (press translation, June 18, 1934), 134 (U.S. Consulate, Kobe, to Department of State, October 3, 1934). For reports of additional arrests within Japan during 1934–35, see 894.114 Narcotics/155 (press clippings, January 8, 1935), 159 (U.S. Consulate, Kobe, to Department of State, February 5, 1935).

115. Further clarification took place at the behest of the Japanese government in 1937, in part to address the Treasury practice of relying on paid informants. 894.114 Narcotics/283.5 (Department of State to U.S. Embassy, Tokyo, July 7, 1937), 288 (Ministry of Foreign Affairs to U.S. Embassy, Tokyo, July 30, 1937), 297 (U.S. Embassy, Tokyo, to Hornbeck, August 13, 1937).

116. Subsequent reports from Kobe suggested extensive Japanese scrutiny of incoming shipping but less for outgoing; searches were more limited in Yokohama. 894.114 Narcotics/198 (secretary of state to U.S. Embassy, Tokyo, September 18, 1935), 202 (U.S. Consulate, Kobe, to Department of State, October 9, 1935), 203 (U.S. Consulate, Yokohama, to Department of State, October 18, 1935).

117. Document 24 [telegram 491] (Consul General Kurikara, Tientsin, to Hirota, Foreign Ministry, October 11, 1933) in Okada et al., *Ahen Mondai*, pp. 504–5.

118. Okada et al., *Ahen Mondai*, pp. xliv–vii; and Yamanouchi Saburo cited in Eguchi, *Nitchu Ahen Senso*, pp. 41–43.

119. Document 39 [telegram 598] (Yokoyama, Treaty Bureau, to Hirota, Foreign Ministry, September 8, 1934) in Okada et al., *Ahen Mondai*, pp. 522–23.

120. 894.114 Narcotics/N16/135 (press clippings, September 21, 1934). U.S. consular reports through 1935 also noted production by Japanese factories in Manchuria as well as Japanese-backed factories in Jehol. 894.114 Narcotics/171 (May 4, 1935), 172 (May 8, 1935), 173 (May 11, 1935).

121. 894.114 Narcotics/N16/135 (press clippings, September 21, 1934).

122. Japanese Government, *Annual Report on the Traffic in Opium and Other Dangerous Drugs for the Year 1934* (report data submitted to the League of Nations, 1935), p. 44.

123. Merrill, *Japan and the Opium Menace*, pp. 130–31.

124. Walker, *Opium and Foreign Policy*, p. 100, notes that Yokoyama was home on leave and the Japanese representatives present—Hotta Massaki and Inagaki Morikatsu—merely declared their lack of expertise in narcotics

matters. By 1938, however, Inagaki was listed in a Foreign Ministry dispatch as an expert who was to be sent home to Japan to consult on Japan's leaving the OAC. Document 93 (Ministry of Foreign Affairs, August 1, 1938) in Okada et al., *Ahen Mondai*, p. 544.

125. 894.114 Narcotics/218 (Grew to secretary of state, June 24, 1936); Walker, *Opium and Foreign Policy*, p. 100.

126. 894.114 Narcotics/153 (press clippings, December 1–2, 1934). In 1933 concerns with growing addiction problems of Korean laborers in Japan had also led to the establishment of the Association for the Relief of Narcotics Addicts in Japan. 894.114 Narcotics/167 (Department of State to Geneva, April 4, 1935). During 1934 the efforts of the Home Office to deal with addiction concerns included an amendment of existing narcotics ordinances (HOO 5 of May 19, 1930, amended November 20, 1934) and a notification to local governors concerning enforcement of existing regulations on addiction (Home Office Notification 149, November 22, 1934); 894.114 Narcotics/N16/2-2745 (League of Nations to Department of State, February 27, 1945).

127. 894.114 Narcotics/218 (Grew to secretary of state, June 24, 1936), 226 (U.S. Embassy, Tokyo, to Department of State, July 22, 1936).

128. 894.114 Narcotics/267 (n.a., June 5, 1937), 275 (n.a., June 16, 1937). Japan also sent a police official to the United States to study the issue of drug smuggling. 894.114 Narcotics/306 (Customs to Department of State, October 4, 17, 1937). The Kobe Customs Office established a six-man "special narcotics force." 894.114 Narcotics/264 (Anslinger to Department of Treasury, June 3, 1937), 289 (U.S. Embassy, Tokyo, to secretary of state, July 20, 1937).

129. Walker, *Opium and Foreign Policy*, pp. 91, 115–16.

130. Taylor, *American Diplomacy and the Narcotics Traffic*, p. 286. *Facts Concerning Opium* (pp. 4–5, 10–11) declares that the ten-year gradual suppression program was introduced in 1932, with 700,000 addicts registered by 1937.

131. As argued by U.S. Treasury Attaché Martin R. Nicholson, the efforts by the Manchukuo Opium Monopoly Administration (MOMA) to enhance control had leveraged league pressure to force change but were intended more for expanding MOMA control than actually curtailing the trade. IMTFE2, 385, 9534 pp. 1, 4. This revenue dynamic driving control efforts was not limited to Manchukuo. From autumn 1937 through 1939, for example, military authorities and Japanese puppet governments in areas such as Tientsin, Peking, and Shanghai abolished existing drug regulations and replaced them with new tax, monopoly, or licensing schemes. See Walker, *Opium and Foreign Policy*, pp. 115, 120, 124; 894.114 narcotics/330 (document file note, April 11, 1938); BRIT6, F 8960/27/87 (British consul, Peking, to Foreign Office, July 1, 1938), F 10393/27/87 (Sir A. Clark Kerr, Shanghai, to Viscount Halifax, August 31, 1938); Merrill, *Japan and the Opium Menace*, pp. 62–63.

132. Document 46 [telegram 734] (Ueda, Manchukuo, to Hirota, Foreign Ministry, August 18, 1937), and see 44 [telegram 303] (Ueda, Manchukuo, to Arita, Foreign Ministry, April 10, 1936), 49 [telegram 869] (Ueda, Manchukuo, to Hirota, Foreign Ministry, September 27, 1937), in Okada et al., *Ahen*

Mondai, pp. 525–28. Among the imports were 72,000 kilograms of opium in 1936, 108,000 kilograms of opium in 1937, and 2,000 tons of narcotics in 1937.

133. IMTFE2, 405, 9507, November 9, 1934. By 1936 Nicholson was explaining Persian imports by Formosa authorities differently, noting that falling revenue had prompted an expansion of the addict rolls and a need for increased opium to meet demand. See IMTFE2, 407, 9506, April 20, 1936.

134. Walker, *Opium and Foreign Policy*, pp. 96–97.

135. Ibid., pp. 119, 123–25; IMTFE2, 418, 9542.

136. Eguchi, *Nitchu Ahen Senso*, pp. 98–106; document 55 [telegram 8] (n.d.), document 59 [telegram 942] (consul general, Shanghai, to Foreign Ministry, March 22, 1938) in Okada et al., *Ahen Mondai*, p. 532; Walker, *Opium and Foreign Policy*, p. 119.

137. Document 62 [telegram 212] (Ueda, Manchukuo, to Hirota, Foreign Ministry, April 1, 1938) in Okada et. al., *Ahen Mondai*, p. 533. In February the Opium Commission had sent a junior secretary to Manchukuo and north China to address the opium problem in cooperation with "the embassy and the Army Special Service." IMTFE2, 381 (excerpts from "Business Report of 1938," Foreign Ministry Treaty Bureau); Document 63 [telegram 1076] (Hidaka, Shanghai, to Hirota, Foreign Ministry, April 3, 1938), document 66 [telegram 1207] (consul general, Shanghai, to Foreign Ministry, April 13, 1938), in Okada et al., *Ahen Mondai*, pp. 533–35; Marshall, "Opium and the Politics of Gangsterism," pp. 38–40. The situation in Shanghai appears to have stabilized only with the introduction of the China Affairs Board branch in 1939. Walker, *Opium and Foreign Policy*, p. 124. Similarly, the Opium Commission attempted in 1937–38 to broker an agreement between Mitsubishi and Mitsui, but it was reached only in 1939. IMTFE2, 381 (excerpts from "Business Report of 1938," Foreign Ministry Treaty Bureau); and Eguchi, *Nitchu Ahen Senso*, pp. 98–106.

138. Walker, *Opium and Foreign Policy*, p. 126; document 83 [telegram 181] (Usami, consul general to Ugaki, Foreign Ministry, June 25, 1938), in Okada et al., *Ahen Mondai*, p. 541.

139. Walker, *Opium and Foreign Policy*, pp. 126–27.

140. Document 79 [telegram 72] (Japanese minister in Ottawa, Canada, to Ugaki, June 20, 1938), document 85 [telegram 175] (consul general, New York, to Ugaki, Foreign Ministry, June 28, 1938), document 86 [telegram 2087] (Ugaki, Foreign Ministry, to consuls general in China, June 29, 1938), document 93 (Usami, consul general, to Ministry of Foreign Affairs, August 1, 1938), in Okada et al., *Ahen Mondai*, pp. 539, 541–42, 544–45; Eguchi, *Nitchu Ahen Senso*, p. 192.

141. Walker, *Opium and Foreign Policy*, p. 128. In October, for example, the army was seeking ministry support to allow cocaine shipments from Formosa into China. By December the ministry's standing had fallen and Japan had withdrawn from the league; the Opium Committee approved the requests. See documents 102 [telegram 2713] (September 6, 1938), 104 [telegram 2747] (September 8, 1938), and 109 [telegram 2926] (September 26, 1938), in

Okada et al., *Ahen Mondai*, pp. 549–50, 552; IMTFE2, 381 (excerpts from "Business Report of 1938," Foreign Ministry Treaty Bureau).

142. Walker, *Opium and Foreign Policy*, pp. 128–29; Taylor, *American Diplomacy and the Narcotics Traffic*, p. 287; and Merrill, *Japan and the Opium Menace*, p. 132. For detail on Japanese drug policy through the war years, see Okada et al., *Ahen Mondai*, pp. 549–95; Walker, *Opium and Foreign Policy*, pp. 132–59.

Chapter 4. Japan and the Global Partnership

1. William O. Walker III, *Opium and Foreign Policy: The Anglo-American Search for Order in Asia, 1912–1954* (Chapel Hill: University of North Carolina Press, 1991), pp. 167, 172.

2. On the reluctant U.S. movement toward domestic control of stimulants during the 1960s and the efforts of countries such as Sweden to push the stimulant issue into the international agenda (and into the 1971 U.N. Vienna Convention on Psychotropic Substances), see Lester Grinspoon and Peter Hedblom, *The Speed Culture: Amphetamine Use and Abuse in America* (Cambridge: Harvard University Press, 1975); Kettil Bruun, Lynn Pan, and Ingemar Rexed, *The Gentleman's Club: International Control of Drugs and Alcohol* (Chicago: University of Chicago Press, 1975), pp. 243–68.

3. W. G. Beasley, *The Modern History of Japan* (New York: Praeger, 1963), p. 281.

4. Ibid., pp. 281–82.

5. Beasley, *Modern History of Japan*, p. 300; and T. J. Pempel, "Japanese Foreign Economic Policy," in Peter J. Katzenstein, ed., *Between Power and Plenty: The Foreign Economic Policies of Advanced Industrial States* (Madison: University of Wisconsin Press, 1978), pp. 139–90.

6. For example, see the SCAP directive "Exercise of Criminal Jurisdiction," February 19, 1946, in Japanese Government, Foreign Office, Division of Special Records, *Documents Concerning the Allied Occupation and Control of Japan*, vol. 2: *Political, Military, and Cultural*, March 1949, pp. 65–67.

7. Ibid., pp. 84–86, 118, 123–28; "Monograph No. 55, 'Police and Public Safety,'" in Supreme Commander for the Allied Powers, *History of the Nonmilitary Activities of the Occupation of Japan*, Historical Monographs 1945–51 (World War II Records Division, NARS [on microfilm]), pp. 1–39; David E. Kaplan and Alec Dubro, *Yajuza: The Explosive Account of Japan's Criminal Underworld* (Reading: Addison-Wesley, 1986), pp. 44, 47.

8. Forty officials staffed the section in the ministry; an additional 2–20 agents were based at each prefecture. The total number was increased to 250 in 1949, and agents were authorized to carry firearms. "Monograph No. 19, 'Public Health' (September 1945–December 1950)," in Supreme Commander, *History of the Nonmilitary Activities*, pp. 225–26; United Nations, *Annual*

Reports of Governments for 1946 [under the *1931 Convention as Amended by 1946* Protocol]: *Japan*, Communicated by the Government of the United States of America, p. 5, located in 894.114 Narcotics/12-147, cited as UN1946; United Nations, *Annual Reports of Governments for 1947* [under the *1931 Convention as Amended by 1946 Protocol*]: *Japan*, Communicated by the Government of the United States of America, found in 894.114 Narcotics/5-2748, cited as UN1947, p. 5.

9. National Police Agency, *Anti-Drug Activities in Japan, 1989* (Tokyo: NPA, 1990), cited as NPA1989, pp. 2–3; Grinspoon and Hedblom, *The Speed Culture*, pp. 18–19; "Energy in Pills," *Business Week*, January 15, 1944, pp. 40–44; "Putting the Brakes on Speed," *Business Week*, October 28, 1967, pp. 92–93.

10. The ministry had been reorganized by SCAP directive in 1946 and given "full responsibility for the production and distribution of all medical and sanitary supplies and equipment, including the control of narcotics." "Monograph No. 19," pp. 10, 221–23; Japanese Government, Ministry of Foreign Affairs, *Japan and Narcotic Drugs*, February 1950, p. 15; UN1946, p. 7.

11. UN1946, p. 6; United Nations, *Annual Reports of Governments 1948* [under the *1931 Convention as Amended by 1946 Protocol*]: *Japan*, Communicated by the Government of the United States of America, filed in 894.114 Narcotics/8-1549, cited as UN1948, p. 8.

12. NPA1989, pp. 2–3; *Japan Times*, February 9, 1980; Florence Rome, *The Tatooed Men* (New York: Delacorte Press, 1975), pp. 90–91, 136.

13. Walker, *Opium and Foreign Policy*, p. 167; UN1948, pp. 71–73; 894.114 Narcotics/10-1245 (SCAP to Imperial Japanese Government, October 12, 1945).

14. Tamura Masayuki, "Japón: Passado y presente de las epidemias de estimulantes," *Boletín de Estupefacientes* 16, 1–2 (1989): 94–95; Yokoyama Minoru, "Development of Japanese Drug Control Laws towards Criminalization," Paper presented at the International Conference on Crime, Drugs, and Social Control, Hong Kong 1988, pp. 3, 6; Japanese Government, Ministry of Health and Welfare, *Brief Account of Drug Abuse and Countermeasures in Japan*, 1989, cited as Health and Welfare 1989, p. 8; Japanese Government, Ministry of Health and Welfare, *Brief Account of Drug Abuse and Countermeasures in Japan*, 1972, cited as Health and Welfare 1972, pp. 5–6; Bruun et al., *The Gentleman's Club*, p. 138. For detail on Harrison Narcotics Act, see David F. Musto, *The American Disease: Origins of Narcotics Control* (New Haven: Yale University Press, 1987).

15. Tamura, "Japón," p. 95; and Yokoyama, "Japanese Drug Control," p. 6.

16. NPA 1989, pp. 2, 20; Tamura, "Japón," p. 95.

17. See Katzenstein, *Between Power and Plenty*.

18. United Nations, Asia and the Far East Institute for the Prevention of Crime and the Treatment of Offenders, *The International Seminar on Drug Problems in Asia and the Pacific Region* (Tokyo: UNAFEI, 1987), p. 53; Health and Welfare, *1989*, p. 9.

19. This section is drawn from interviews conducted in Japan during 1990 and 1991; H. Richard Friman, "The United States, Japan, and the International Drug Trade: Troubled Partnership," *Asian Survey* 31 (September 1991): 875–90; H. Richard Friman, "Awaiting the Tsunami? Japan and the International Drug Trade," *Pacific Review* 6, 1 (1993): 41–50; H. Richard Friman, "International Pressures and Domestic Bargains: Regulating Money Laundering in Japan," *Crime, Law and Social Change* 21 (December 1994): 253–66.

20. Friman, "United States, Japan," p. 887.

21. *Asahi Evening News*, June 12, 1991; *Daily Yomiuri*, June 6, 1991; *Japan Times*, October 19, 1991; interviews (Japan, 1991).

22. *Japan Times*, October 20, 1991; interviews (Japan, 1991); *Japan Times*, weekly edition, August 24–30, 1992.

23. UN1948, p. 14; UN1947, p. 9; United Nations, *Annual Reports of Governments for 1949* [*under the 1931 Convention as Amended by 1946 Protocol*]: *Japan*, Communicated by the Government of the United States of America, found in 894.53/10-1550, p. 21, cited as UN1949.

24. 894.53/3-1254 (Anslinger to George A. Morlock, Department of State, March 12, 1954); 894.53/3-3054 (John Foster Dulles to U.S. Embassy, Tokyo, March 30, 1954); and 894.53/4-3054 (Kent Lewis, Treasury representative in Japan, to Department of Treasury, May 20, 1954).

25. UN1949, p. 4.

26. UN1948, p. 8; UN1949, pp. 8–19.

27. Friman, "Awaiting the Tsunami?" p. 43.

28. Health and Welfare 1972, pp. 5–6, 14.

29. Ibid., p. 4; NPA 1989, p. 21; Yokoyama, "Japanese Drug Control," p. 6. Possession for gain was punished by a limited term of not less than one year and a fine of not less than ¥3 million. Simple possession carried a maximum ten-year sentence. Health and Welfare 1989, p. 18.

30. Kaplan and Dubro, *Yakuza*, pp. 46–49, 57–63; Jonathan Marshall, "Opium, Tungsten, and the Search for National Security, 1940–52," *Journal of Policy History* 3, 4 (1991): 453–54. Shikita and Tsuchiya note that Japanese police began to crack down on organized crime groups in the late 1940s, subsequently lowering the rate of gangster violations of the penal code. But in the absence of a consolidated national police force, these figures may not provide an entirely accurate representation of the effectiveness of such efforts. See Shikita Minoru and Tsuchiya Shinichi, eds., *Crime and Criminal Policy in Japan from 1926 to 1988: Analysis and Evaluation of the Showa Era* (Tokyo: Japan Criminal Policy Society, 1990), p. 81.

31. Kaplan and Dubro, *Yakuza*, pp. 48, 76.

32. Tamura, "Japón," pp. 95–96; Yokoyama, "Japanese Drug Control," pp. 5–6; NPA 1989, pp. 2–3, 20, 32.

33. Ibid.

34. Tamura Masayuki, "The Yakuza and Amphetamine Abuse in Japan," in Harold H. Traver and Mark S. Gaylord, eds., *Drugs, Law, and the State*

(Hong Kong: Hong Kong University Press, 1992), pp. 99–118; NPA 1989, p. 3; interview (Japan, 1990).

35. Shikita and Tsuchiya, *Crime and Criminal Policy in Japan*, p. 84; Kaplan and Dubro, *Yakuza*, p. 90; Iwai Hiroaki, "Organized Crime in Japan," in Robert J. Kelly, ed., *Organized Crime: A Global Perspective* (Totowa, N.J.: Rowman and Littlefield, 1986), p. 209.

36. The *yakuza* came quickly to the conclusion that the heroin trade offered fewer domestic market opportunities (because of weak demand for the drug, especially within the organizations themselves) and greater risk (because of the Narcotics Control Law) than the stimulant trade. Friman, "Awaiting the Tsunami?" pp. 43–44.

37. Kaplan and Dubro, *The Yakuza*, p. 96.

38. David H. Stark, "The Yakuza: Japanese Crime Incorporated" (Ph.D. diss., University of Michigan, 1981), p. 32.

39. Ibid.; *Japan Times*, Weekly International Edition, April 27–May 3, 1992.

40. NPA 1989, pp. 3, 22–23; Tamura, "Japón," p. 96; Rome, *The Tattooed Men*, pp. 201–5.

41. NPA 1989, pp. 22–23; Tamura, "The Yakuza and Amphetamine Abuse," p. 5; Kaplan and Dubro, *The Yakuza*, pp. 193–200; Iwai, "Organized Crime in Japan," p. 210; Stark, "The Yakuza," p. 36. By the early 1990s, this figure had decreased slightly to 34.8 percent. "Organized Crime Control Today and Its Future Tasks," unpublished paper received by the author from the NPA, 1991.

42. For more detail, see Friman, "Awaiting the Tsunami?" pp. 44–46. At the time of writing, it was too early to assess the impact of the 1992 boryokudan legislation.

43. Interviews (Japan, 1991); U.S. Department of Justice, DEA, Office of Intelligence, *A Special Report: ICE*, October 1989, p. 4.

44. U.S. Congress, House, Hearings before a subcommittee of the Committee on Ways and Means, *Trafficking in and Control of Narcotics, Barbiturates, and Amphetamines* (Washington, D.C.: Government Printing Office, 1956), pp. 200–203; United Nations, *The International Seminar*, p. 56; and Health and Welfare 1989, p. 13.

45. *Japan Times*, February 9, 1980; Rome, *The Tattooed Men*, pp. 204–5; interview (Japan, 1990).

46. For detail on the leadership role played by the United States in expanding international drug control during the postwar period, see Bruun et al., *The Gentleman's Club*.

47. Health and Welfare 1989, p. 13; and United Nations, *The International Seminar*, p. 56.

48. Interviews (Japan, 1990); U.S. Congress, Senate, *Convention on Psychotropic Substances*, Message from the President of the United States Transmitting a Copy of the Convention on Psychotropic Substances (Washington, D.C.: Government Printing Office, 1971).

49. *Asahi Evening News*, May 6, 1985; *Mainichi Daily News*, April 20, October 24, 1985.

50. NPA 1989, p. 5; interviews (Japan, 1990).
51. *Mainichi Daily News,* May 5, 1983; *Japan Times,* May 18, 1983.
52. NPA 1989, p. 5; interviews (Japan, 1990).
53. "Reagan Takes Steps to Blunt Hill Drive," *Congressional Quarterly Weekly,* September 14, 1985, p. 1795; Yoichi Funabashi, *Managing the Dollar: From the Plaza to the Louvre* (Washington, D.C.: Institute for International Economics, 1988).
54. *Mainichi Daily News,* October 24, 1985; *Asahi Evening News,* May 6, 1985; *Japan Times,* January 24, 1987; and *Daily Yomiuri,* July 31, 1987.
55. *Japan Times,* September 10, 1988; White House, *National Drug Control Strategy* (Washington, D.C.: Government Printing Office, 1989), pp. 66–67, 70.
56. *Mainichi Daily News,* May 20, October 24, 1985; *Asahi Evening News,* May 6, 1985.
57. *Japan Times,* October 10, 1986; and see *Asahi Evening News,* October 14, 1986; *Daily Yomiuri,* September 26, 1986.
58. *Japan Times,* September 20, 1988.
59. *Japan Times,* January 19, 1985, December 11, 1986; *Daily Yomiuri,* January 19, 1985, December 11, 1986; interviews (Japan, 1990, 1991).
60. Interview (Japan, 1990); *Mainichi Daily News,* November 10, 12, 1987.
61. *Mainichi Daily News,* November 12, 1987; interview (Japan, 1990).
62. *Daily Yomiuri,* January 4, 1989; *Japan Times,* February 19, 1990.
63. *Japan Times,* February 19, 1990; Baker quoted in *Daily Yomiuri,* December 23, 1989; interview (Japan, 1990).
64. *New York Times,* September 2, 1989.
65. For example, see *New York Times,* September 2, 4, 1989.
66. Interviews (Japan, 1990); *Daily Yomiuri,* September 27, 1989.
67. *Daily Yomiuri,* September 27, 1989; *New York Times,* September 26, 1989. The Japanese Foreign Ministry disclosed the contents of Kaifu's written response to Bush soon after Quayle's announcement. *Japan Times,* September 30, 1989.
68. Interviews (Japan, 1990).
69. *Daily Yomiuri,* September 1, 1989; *Japan Times,* weekly international edition, August 27–September 2, 1990.
70. This comparison remains valid even if one assumes, as do most law enforcement officials, that seizure rates capture roughly 10 percent of the actual drug trade.
71. Interviews (Japan, 1990).
72. *Daily Yomiuri,* November 29, 1989; *Japan Times,* December 7, 1989; *Japan Times,* weekly international edition, April 27–May 3, 1992; and interviews (Japan, 1990).
73. *Daily Yomiuri,* November 29, 1989; *Japan Times,* December 7, 1989; interviews (Japan, 1990).
74. Interviews (Japan, 1990).
75. Ibid.

76. Ibid.; *Japan Times*, weekly international edition, August 27–September 2, 1990.

77. *Japan Times*, weekly international edition, August 27–September 2, 1990; and see *Mainichi Daily News*, February 24, 1990.

78. *Japan Times*, February 19, 1990; *Daily Yomiuri*, January 18, 1990; *Mainichi Daily News*, October 28, 1989, February 24, 1990.

79. *Mainichi Daily News*, February 24, 1990; *Japan Times*, May 17, 1990; *Daily Yomiuri*, May 17, 1990; *Japan Times*, weekly international edition, August 27–September 2, 1990.

80. For example, see *Mainichi Daily News*, August 3, 1991; *Japan Times*, August 3, 19, October 19, 1991.

81. *Mainichi Daily News*, August 3, 1991; *Japan Times*, March 17, 1990, August 3, October 19, 1991. For a discussion of the factors shaping the cocaine trade in Japan, see Friman, "Awaiting the Tsunami?" pp. 46–49.

82. *Asahi Evening News*, June 12, 1991; *Daily Yomiuri*, June 6, 1991; *Japan Times*, October 19, 1991; interviews (Japan, 1991).

83. *Japan Times*, October 20, 1991; interviews (Japan, 1991).

84. Interview (Japan, 1991); National Police Agency, "Organized Crime Control Today and Its Future Tasks," unpublished paper prepared for Asian Organized Crime Seminar, 1991, p. 13.

85. Interview (Japan, 1991). External sources of supply clearly exist for cocaine as does the potential for Japanese involvement. In 1990, for example, Colombian and Italian authorities seized two Japanese-registered freighters sailing from Colombia to Europe carrying a total of 745 kilograms of cocaine. *Asahi Evening News*, September 18, 1990; *Japan Times*, September 22, 1990.

86. *Daily Yomiuri*, September 8, November 6, 1990, January 7, June 12, 1991; *Japan Times*, February 27, September 9, 1990, February 20, August 3, 1991; and *Asahi Evening News*, April 1, September 8, 1990.

87. Robert Delfs, "Feeding on the System," *Far Eastern Economic Review*, November 21, 1991, pp. 28–35.

88. *Mainichi Daily News*, November 21, 1991.

89. Even among smaller advanced industrialized states, Switzerland has made greater strides against money laundering than Japan through extensive revisions in bank secrecy legislation. On money laundering and Switzerland, see Jean Ziegler, *Die Schweiz wäscht weisser: Die Finanzdrehscheibe des internationalen Verbrechens* (Munich: Piper, 1990).

90. Delfs, "Feeding on the System," pp. 28–30; Shikita and Tsuchiya, *Crime and Criminal Policy in Japan*; Aron Viner, *Inside Japan's Financial Markets* (Homewood, Ill.: Dow Jones-Irwin, 1988); Kaplan and Dubro, *Yakuza*; Stark, "The Yakuza."

91. Friman, "Awaiting the Tsunami?" p. 48.

92. *Daily Yomiuri*, January 7, 1990; and see Friman, "United States, Japan," pp. 880, 885.

93. These provisions were contained under the Kerry Amendment in the 1988 Anti–Drug Abuse Act. See "Election-Year Anti-Drug Bill Enacted," *Congressional Quarterly Almanac* 1988, pp. 85–86, 88, 108; and "Follow the Money," *Economist*, October 21, 1989, p. 29.

94. David P. Stewart, "Internationalizing the War on Drugs: The UN Convention against Illicit Traffic in Narcotic Drugs and Psychotropic Substances," *Denver Journal of International Law and Policy* 18 (1990): 387–404.

95. Friman, "United States, Japan," p. 886; *Mainichi Daily News*, October 14, 1989; *Asahi Evening News*, October 12, 1989; *Japan Times*, October 7, 1989.

96. *Daily Yomiuri*, January 7, April 21, 1990; *Japan Times*, March 14, April 20, 1999; *Nihon Keizai Shimbun*, February 15, 1990; *Japan Times Weekly*, April 23, 1990; *Tokyo Shimbun*, February 12, 1990; interview (Japan, 1990).

97. *Mainichi Daily News*, October 14, 1989; *Asahi Evening News*, October 12, 1989; *Japan Times*, October 7, 1989.

98. The common argument was that most Japanese retail stores would fall in the category of the $10,000 break point, but the U.S. regulations allowed exemption lists for large retail stores. *Nihon Keizai Shimbun*, February 15, 1990; *Japan Times*, March 14, 1990.

99. Francis McCall Rosenbluth, *Financial Politics in Contemporary Japan* (Ithaca: Cornell University Press, 1989), pp. 168–99; Friman, "International Pressures and Domestic Bargains," pp. 256–57.

100. *Japan Economic Journal*, May 19, 1990.

101. Ibid.; *Japan Times*, June 9, 1990.

102. *Asahi Evening News*, September 7, 1990; *Asian Wall Street Journal*, September 7, 1990; *Japan Times*, September 30, 1990, August 28, 1991; interview (Japan, 1991).

103. *Asian Wall Street Journal*, September 7, 1990. By 1991 only two incidents of money laundering had been reported in the Japanese press and these involved Colombian and Bolivian narcotics cartels laundering funds internationally through what the press portrayed as unwitting bank branches. *Asahi Evening News*, September 7, 1990; *Japan Times*, September 9, 1990; *Japan Economic Journal*, September 15, 1990; interview (Japan, 1991).

104. *Japan Times*, April 21, 1991; *Asahi Evening News*, April 19, 1991; *Daily Yomiuri*, April 15, 1991. According to one report, the legislation had been presented to the Diet in late 1990 but was "shelved due to lack of time." *Japan Times*, August 28, 1991.

105. Implementing ordinances were to be in place within a year. NPA, "Organized Crime Control Today," p. 13; *Japan Times*, October 3, 1991; *Mainichi Daily News*, October 3, 1991; *Daily Yomiuri*, October 3, 1991; interviews (Japan, 1991). Pressure had continued during the Diet deliberations with demands from the Financial Action Task Force in June that countries comply with its earlier recommendations. *Mainichi Daily News*, June 30, 1991; *Yomiuri Shimbun*, July 22, 1991; and *Daily Yomiuri*, June 19, 1991.

106. The question of what happens to seized assets, especially those seized as a result of cooperative international investigations, remains unclear and a potential source of international conflict. Interviews (Japan, 1991).

107. Banking industry representatives themselves noted that it would be very difficult to determine what "suspicious transactions were." Interviews (Japan, 1991). To solve this problem, the bankers' association and the Ministry of Finance introduced an information manual as the laws went into effect in August 1992. *Japan Times,* weekly international edition, August 10–16, 1992.

108. NPA, "Organized Crime Control Today," p. 13; *Japan Times,* October 3, 1991; *Mainichi Daily News,* October 3, 1991; *Daily Yomiuri,* October 3, 1991; interviews (Japan, 1991).

109. For example, see DEA, *ICE;* and Michael Isikoff, "America's Drug: Crank Vies to become the U.S. Stimulant of Choice," *Washington Post,* national weekly edition, April 3–9, 1989, p. 10.

Chapter 5. Germany and the American Agenda

1. Ethan A. Nadelmann, *Cops across Borders: The Internationalization of U.S. Criminal Law Enforcement* (University Park: Pennsylvania State University Press, 1993), pp. 130–33.

2. Wolfgang Storz, *Suchtpolitik: Eine Untersuchung zum Verhältnis von Staat und Wohlfahrtsverbanden in Baden-Württemberg* (Bielefeld: Kleine, 1987), pp. 71–74.

3. Helen Howell Moorhead, "International Narcotics Control, 1939–1946," *Foreign Policy Reports,* July 1, 1946: 99. These provisions reflected deliberations within the drug control agencies of the League of Nations. See *Times* (London), May 16, 1944.

4. United Nations, *Annual Reports of Governments: Germany, 1946* [under the Convention for Limiting the Manufacture and Regulating the Distribution of Narcotic Drugs of July 13, 1931, as amended by the Protocol of December 11, 1946], communicated by the Allied Control Authority, p. 5, cited as UNG1946, located in 862.114 Narcotics/12–147.

5. United Nations, *Annual Reports of Governments: Germany (United States Zone), 1947* [under the Convention for Limiting the Manufacture and Regulating the Distribution of Narcotic Drugs of July 13, 1931, as amended by the Protocol of December 11, 1946], communicated by the Military Government for Germany (U.S.) Allied Control Authority, p. 10, cited as UNG1947, located in 862.114 Narcotics/11–3048.

6. Moorhead, "International Narcotics Control," p. 99. According to U.S. occupation officials (UNG1947, p. 13), the central police records in Berlin had been "deliberately destroyed."

7. UNG1947, p. 10.

8. UNG1946, p. 5. Given the pattern of Soviet expropriation of industrial and other supplies from occupied territories (for example, see *Times*, September 28, 1946) a similar seizure of stockpiles within East Germany was likely.

9. UNG1947, p. 9.

10. Moorhead, "International Narcotics Control," p. 99.

11. Administration within the Soviet zone was carried out on the Länder rather than zone level. Armin Linz, *German Opium Legislation* (Control Commission for Germany, Printing and Stationery Office, 1947), p. 2 [located in 862.53/2-2750]; UNG1946, p. 5.

12. UNG1946, p. 10; 862.114 Narcotics/5-1247 (J. H. Hilldring, Department of State, to Robert Murphy, Berlin, May 12, 1947).

13. UNG1946, pp. 6–7; UNG1947, p. 5.

14. UNG1947, p. 6.

15. Ibid., pp. 13, 32.

16. Günter Amendt, *Sucht Profit Sucht* (Hamburg: Rowahlt Taschenbuch, 1990), pp. 51–52; "Energy in Pills," *Business Week*, January 15, 1944, pp. 40–44. Such drugs—Dolantin, Actedron, Benzedrine, Pervatin, Elastonon— were put under the act's strict licensing provisions for production, sale, and trade. Amendt, *Sucht*, pp. 51–52; and Linz, *German Opium Legislation*, p. 15. Cannabis drugs—specifically marijuana and hashish—were added to the Opium Act in 1959. Friederich-Christian Schröder, *Rauschgift: Bekämpfung des Drogenmißbrauchs* (Berlin: Walter de Gruyter, 1973), p. 115.

17. These steps were reinforced by tighter pharmaceutical regulations under section 9 of the Pharmacy Regulations. Yet, through the 1960s, some stimulants such as Aponeuron, Captigon, Rosinon, and diet pills containing amphetamines were not covered by such regulations or the Opium Act. Günther Bauer, *Rauschgift: Ein Handbuch über die Rauschgiftsucht, den Rauschgifthandel, die Bekämfungsmaßnehmen und die Hilfen für die Gefährdete* (Lübeck: Max Schmidt-Römhild, 1927), pp. 44–45, 119–22; "Was Wissen wir über Amphetamine?" *Drogen-Report* (February 1972): 8.

18. Amendt, *Sucht*, pp. 52–54.

19. Nelson Gross, "Bilateral and Multilateral Efforts to Intensify Drug Abuse Control Programs," *Department of State Bulletin* April 3, 1972, p. 510; Brian Freemantle, *The Fix: Inside the World Drug Trade* (New York: Tom Doherty, 1987), pp. 40, 192.

20. The military divisions included the army's Criminal Investigative Division (CID, Detachment A), the Naval Investigative Service (NIS), and the Air Force Office of Special Investigation (AFOSI). Heinz Schulz, *Die Bekämpfung der Rauschgiftkriminalität: Handbuch für die Praxis* (Heidelberg: Kriminalistik Verlag, 1987), p. 663; and Nadelmann, *Cops across Borders*, pp. 125–26.

21. E. N. Earley, "Politics of Heroin for GIs, Germans," *In These Times*, January 24–30, 1979, pp. 19–20; "Berlin as a Heroin Transit Point," *Drug Enforcement* (July 1978): 37; Laura M. Wiconski, "Europe Awash with Heroin," *Drug Enforcement* (Summer 1981): 14–16.

22. Bundestag committees active on drug issues include the Legal Committee for Youth, Women, and Health (therapy and treatment issues) and the Committee for the Interior (enforcement questions). Interview (Germany, 1990).

23. Hans-Jörg Albrecht, "Drug Policy in the Federal Republic of Germany," in Hans-Jörg Albrecht and Anton van Kalmthout, eds., *Drug Policies in Western Europe* (Freiburg: Max-Planck-Institut, 1989), pp. 175–78; Schröder, *Rauschgift*, pp. 112–13.

24. Hans-Dieter Schwind, *Kriminologie: Eine praxisorientierte Einführung mit Beispeilen* (Heidelberg: Kriminalistik Verlag, 1993), pp. 387–88, 435.

25. Interviews (Germany, 1990, 1991); "Antworten der Bundesregierung auf die 'Additional GAO Questions,'" unpublished correspondence dated October 1989, p. 5, received by the author from the Family Ministry.

26. Schultz, *Die Bekämpfung der Rauschgiftkriminalität*, pp. 322–24; Annemarie Griesinger, "Drug Abuse and Counter-measures in Germany," *North Atlantic Assembly: Reports of the Working Group on Narcotics, Science, and Technical Committee*, T 152 STC/WGN (76) 4, November 1976, p. 21; Hubert Meyer and Klaus Wolf, *Kriminalistisches Lehrbuch der Polizei* (Hilden: Deutsche Polizeiliteratur, 1994), p. 12.

27. Schultz, *Die Bekämpfung der Rauschgiftkriminalität*, p. 412; interview (Germany, 1990).

28. Interviews (Germany, 1990); Schwind, *Kriminologie* (1993), p. 385.

29. Interviews (Germany, 1990); Narcotics Act, reprinted in *Strafgesetzbuch* (Munich: Beck-Texte im Deutscher Taschenbuch, 1994), pp. 207–33.

30. For example, see Schröder, *Rauschgift*, pp. 101–4; Griesinger, "Drug Abuse and Countermeasures," p. 21; Gross, "Bilateral and Multilateral Efforts," p. 510; and Ralf Beke-Bramkamp, *Die Drogenpolitik der USA, 1969–1990* (Baden-Baden: Nomos Verlagsgesellschaft, 1992), p. 145.

31. Beginning in 1992, these agencies also included Germany's antiterrorist forces. Schwind, *Kriminologie* (1993), pp. 387–88; Drug Enforcement Administration, Office of Intelligence, Strategic Section, *Country Briefs: Western Europe*, October 1988, p. 19.

32. Nadelmann, *Cops across Borders*, pp. 204–5; "Antworten der Bundesregierung," p. 24.

33. "Berlin as a Heroin Transit Point," p. 37.

34. Harold Becker and Donna Lee Becker, *Handbook of the World's Police* (Metuchen, N.J.: Scarecrow Press, 1986), p. 174.

35. "Antworten der Bundesregierung," p. 24.

36. Interview (Germany, 1990). New German drug legislation during the early 1990s called for the expansion of the division by an additional four hundred members over the next four years. Federal Ministry for Health and Federal Ministry of the Interior, *National Programme on Drug Abuse Control* (1990), pp. 34–35; interview (Germany, 1990). Subsections within the drug division by the early 1990s included those focusing on international cooperation (RG1), regional issues (RG2), and money laundering and amphetamines (RG26). Interview (Germany, 1990).

37. "Antworten der Bundesregierung," p. 19.

38. Health and Interior, *National Programme*, p. 72; interviews (Germany, 1990).

39. Nadelmann, *Cops across Borders*, pp. 236–38; "Antworten der Bundesregierung," p. 5; interview (Germany, 1990). The 1990 Drug Plan proposed joint investigative groups of customs and police officials in areas including money laundering. Health and Interior, *National Programme*, pp. 34–35.

40. Interview (Germany, 1990).

41. Alexander Niemetz, *Die Kokain-Mafia: Deutschland im Visier* (Munich: C. Bertelsmann, 1990), p. 276; Peter J. Katzenstein, "Coping with Terrorism: Norms and Internal Security in Germany and Japan," in Judith Goldstein and Robert O. Keohane, eds., *Ideas and Foreign Policy: Beliefs, Institutions, and Political Change* (Ithaca: Cornell University Press, 1993), pp. 289–90; Butz Peters, *Die Absahner: Organisierte Kriminalität in der Bundesrepublik* (Hamburg: Rowohlt, 1990), pp. 229–30; interview (Germany, 1990).

42. "Antworten der Bundesregierung," pp. 46, 50; interview (Germany, 1990).

43. For example, CELAD was established in December 1989 to improve European coordination and reduce overlap. Germany's representative to CELAD is from the Interior Ministry. Commission of the European Communities, "Recommendation for a Council Decision on Community Participation in the Preparatory Work and the International Conference on Drug Abuse and Illicit Trafficking," COM(86) 457 final, Brussels, August 5, 1986, pp. 7, 11; interviews (Germany, 1990); Health and Interior, *National Programme*, pp. 43, 67–68.

44. Schulz, *Die Bekämpfung der Rauschgiftkriminalität*, p. 418. Additional working groups at the enforcement level link Germany and France and Germany and the Netherlands. Moreover, German liaison officers work with Interpol and more recently with the European efforts against organized crime through Europol's European Drug Unit. Health and Interior, *National Programme*, pp. 44, 68–69; interview (Germany, 1990); private correspondence to author from Federal Criminal Office, November 4, 1991.

45. UNG1946, pp. 8–10; UNG1947, p. 29.

46. UNG1947, pp. 27–28.

47. Ibid., pp. 7, 39.

48. Ibid., p. 11.

49. Amendt, *Sucht*, pp. 65–66.

50. Griesinger, "Drug Abuse and Counter-measures," pp. 19–20.

51. For examples of this range, see Karl-Heinz Reuband, "Drug Addiction and Crime in West Germany: A Review of the Empirical Evidence," *Contemporary Drug Problems* 19 (Summer 1992): 333; Hans-Dieter Schwind, *Kriminologie: Eine praxisorientierte Einführung mit Biespeilen* (Heidelberg: Kriminalistik Verlag, 1986), p. 315; Schwind, *Kriminologie* (1993), p. 373; DEA, *Country Briefs*, p. 17; Kommission der Europäischen Gemeinschaft, "Bericht unter Nationale Programme zur Reduzierung der Drogennachfrage in der Europäischen Gemeinschaft," KOM (90) 527 endg., November 8, 1990, p. 8; Health and Interior, *National Programme*, pp. 12–13.

52. For example, the addict population numbers used by scholars (and by enforcement officials) often reflect official government figures multiplied by a factor of anywhere from 1.5 to 6. Peters, *Die Absahner*, p. 215; and Schwind, *Kriminologie* (1986), p. 315.

53. Interviews (Germany, 1990, 1991). According to "Als hättest du eine Rakete im Kopf" *Der Spiegel* 46 (1988): 149, the first year of official statistics on drug-related deaths was 1973. The article notes that the official figures are probably understated.

54. Larry Collins and Dominique LaPierre, "The French Connection in Real Life," *New York Times Magazine*, February 6, 1972, pp. 14–15, 51–55; Griesinger, "Drug Abuse and Counter-measures," pp. 19–20; Schwind, *Kriminologie* (1986), pp. 319–22.

55. Schwind, *Kriminologie* (1993), pp. 424–36; Peters, *Die Absahner*, p. 225; Hans Leyendecker, Richard Rickelmann, Georg Bönisch, *Mafia im Staat: Deutschland fällt unter die Räuber* (Munich: Knaur, 1993), pp. 193–207; Meyer and Wolf, *Kriminalistisches Lehrbuch*, pp. 393–397; *Christian Science Monitor*, June 19, 1989.

56. *New York Times*, January 9, 1978; Earley, "Politics of Heroin," pp. 19–20; "Berlin as a Heroin Transit Point," p. 37; Schwind, *Kriminologie* (1986), pp. 319–22; and Leyendecker et al., *Mafia im Staat*, pp. 90–94.

57. Schwind, *Kriminologie* (1986), p. 326.

58. Eileen M. Brooke, "Activities in the Field of Drug Dependence," Ad hoc Committee on Drug Dependence, Public Health Division, Council of Europe, Strasbourg, May 1975, p. 38; interview (Germany, 1990).

59. Stephan Quensel, *Drogeneland: Cannabis, Heroin, Methadon: Für eine neue Drogenpolitik* (Frankfurt: Campus, 1982), pp. 10, 269–84; Albrecht, *Drug Policy*, pp. 182–83.

60. For example, see Bundesverband für akzeptierende Drogenarbeit und humane Drogenpolitik, e.V., *Menschenwürde in der Drogenpolitik: Ohne Legalisierung geht es nicht!* (Hamburg: Konkret Literatur, 1993); Christine Bauer, *Heroin Freigabe: Möglichkeiten und Grenzen einer anderen Drogenpolitik* (Hamburg: Rowohlt, 1992); Heiner Gatzemeier, *Heroin vom Staat: Für eine kontrollierte Freigabe harter Drogen* (Munich: Knaur, 1993); Beke-Bramkamp, *Die Drogenpolitik der USA*, p. 145; "Common Market of Crack?" *Newsweek*, September 18, 1989; "Null Toleranz," *Der Spiegel*, December 10, 1990, pp. 70, 73; "Sinnvolle Ergebnisse," *Der Spiegel* February 15, 1993, p. 96; "Krieg Staat Hilfe," *Der Spiegel* November 16, 1992, pp. 98–101; Schwind, *Kriminologie* (1993), p. 377.

61. John C. McWilliams, "Through the Past Darkly: The Politics and Policies of America's Drug War," in William O. Walker III, ed., *Drug Control Policy* (University Park: Pennsylvania University Press, 1992) pp. 20–21; Freemantle, *The Fix*, pp. 22–23. For a brief history of the rise of the DEA, see Nadelmann, *Cops across Borders*, pp. 140–41.

62. McWilliams, "Through the Past Darkly," p. 21; David F. Musto, *The American Disease: Origins of Narcotics Control* (New Haven: Yale University

Press, 1987), pp. 254–58; Alfred W. McCoy, with Cathleen B. Read and Leonard P. Adams II, *The Politics of Heroin in Southeast Asia* (New York: Harper and Row, 1973).

63. Turkish opium cultivation would resume in 1975, although new harvesting methods reduced the threat of illicit diversion. McWilliams, "Through the Past Darkly," p. 21; Gross, "Bilateral and Multilateral Efforts," pp. 506–7; Musto, *The American Disease*, p. 257; Catherine Lamour and Michael R. Lamberti, *The International Connection: Opium from Growers to Pushers* (New York: Pantheon, 1974), pp. 17–36, 201–21.

64. Christopher Mathew, "Joint Drive against Drug Abuse," *European Community* 151 (December 1971): 20, and on the Pompidou Group, see 20–21. See also Collins and LaPierre, "The French Connection," pp. 15, 51–55; McCoy et al., *The Politics of Heroin*, pp. 30–57; Peter Rodino, "Progress Report on the Control of Narcotics," North Atlantic Assembly, Scientific and Technical Committee, November 1972, pp. 4–5.

65. Berndt Georg Thamm, *Drogen Report: Und nun auch noch Crack!* (Bergisch Gladbach: Gustav Lübbe, 1988), pp. 153–55. LSD was most popular in the large urban centers. Wolfgang Metzner and Berndt Georg Thamm, *Drogen* (Hamburg: Sternbuch im Gruner und Jahr, 1989), pp. 38–39.

66. Bernd Ruland, *Geschäft ohne Erbarmen: Rauschgift, Menschen, und der Liebe* (Zurich: Schewizer, 1965), pp. 240–46, 270–71.

67. For broader social explanations of this wave of drug consumption, see Volker Meudt, "Drogenpolitik in der Bundesrepublik," in Thomas Kutsch und Günter Wiswede, eds., *Drogenkonsum: Einsteig, Abhaengingkeit, Sucht* (Königstein: Anton Hain Meisenheim, 1980), pp. 195–215; Arthur Kreuzer, "Kriminologische, kriminalpolitische, und strafjustitielle Aspekte des Drogenwesens in der Bundesrepublik," in Herbert Schäfer, ed., *Rauschgiftmißbrauch, Rauschgiftkriminalität*, Grundlagen der Kriminalität 9 (Hamburg: Steintor, 1972), p. 258.

68. Metzner and Thamm, *Drogen*, pp. 38–39; and Griesinger, "Drug Abuse and Counter-measures," pp. 19–20. Hermann P. Voight, *Zum Thema: Kokain* (Basel: Sphinx, 1982), p. 40, argues that cocaine's resurgence can be attributed to growing concern about the dangers of amphetamines (especially Methedrine) within the German drug culture. As suggested by Bauer, *Rauschgift* p. 43, the limited extent of resurgence reflected the prohibitive street price of the drug.

69. Schröder, *Rauschgift*, pp. 113–14.

70. Griesinger, "Drug Abuse and Counter-measures," pp. 18–23.

71. Gross, "Bilateral and Multilateral Efforts," p. 510.

72. Schulz, *Die Bekämpfung der Rauschgiftkriminalität*, pp. 322–24; "Aufklärungskampagne der Kriminalpolizei," *Drogen-Report*, January 1972, p. 6; Rodino, "Progress Report," p. 6.

73. Rodino, "Progress Report," p. 6; Schröder, *Rauschgift*, pp. 113–14. On the convention ratified by Germany in 1976, see Kettil Bruun, Lynn Pan, and

Ingemar Rexed, *The Gentlemen's Club: International Control of Drugs and Alcohol* (Chicago: University of Chicago Press, 1975), pp. 243–68.

74. Schröder, *Rauschgift*, pp. 113–15; Albrecht, "Drug Policy," pp. 176–77.

75. Schröder, *Rauschgift*, pp. 197–217.

76. Nadelmann, *Cops across Borders*, pp. 130–33.

77. Bruun et al., *The Gentleman's Club*, pp. 142–43.

78. Rodino, "Progress Report," p. 6; Gross, "Bilateral and Multilateral Efforts," p. 511. The Munich office was closed and agents assigned to the Federal Criminal Office in Wiesbaden as part of the centralization undertaken by the United States and Germany during the 1970s.

79. Gross, "Bilateral and Multilateral Efforts," pp. 510–11.

80. Ibid.

81. The amphetamine issue would remain partially unresolved. According to a 1978 congressional task force investigation, nonprescription amphetamines were still being abused by U.S. servicemen. Earley, "Politics of Heroin," pp. 19–20. Early steps included a joint declaration of new regulations in March 1972 by the Ministries of Economics and Finance, including tighter monitoring of border traffic, special customs units, drug-sniffing dogs, and cooperation among the Federal and Länder Criminal Offices and customs to deal with the illicit arms and drug trades. Schröder, *Rauschgift*, pp. 182–85.

82. U.S. authorities thought the morphine traffic by auto and truck was overwhelming customs personnel in southern Germany. In addition, German police were reputed to be more interested in the hashish traffic. Lamour and Lamberti, *The International Connection*, pp. 26–27; Editors and Staff of *Newsday*, *The Heroin Trail* (New York: Signet Books, 1974), pp. 67–68.

83. German authorities gradually expanded the working group into Working Group South to investigate drug trafficking throughout southeastern Europe. Schulz, *Die Bekämpfung der Rauschgiftkriminalität*, pp. 415–17.

84. Ibid., pp. 418–19; William J. Stoessel Jr., "U.S.-German Cooperation in Narcotics Control," *Drug Enforcement* (February 1979): 9–10.

85. "Special Report: Western Europe's Latest Worry: A Growing Army of Junkies," *U.S. News and World Report*, December 13, 1976, pp. 43–47; *New York Times*, January 9, 1978; Schwind, *Kriminologie* (1986), pp. 319–22; Freemantle, *The Fix*, p. 191; Musto, *The American Disease*, p. 257.

86. Earley, "Politics of Heroin," pp. 19–20.

87. Ibid.

88. *New York Times*, January 9, 1978.

89. Stoessel, "U.S.-German Cooperation," p. 9; interview (Germany, 1990).

90. The army had claimed that 12.5 percent of U.S. forces were using hard drugs, and 31 percent were smoking hashish. "Are Drugs Crippling Our Armed Forces?" *U.S. News and World Report*, August 14, 1978, pp. 18–20; Earley, "Politics of Heroin," pp. 19–20.

91. Earley, "Politics of Heroin," pp. 92–93.

92. "A Half-Won War," *Time*, March 30, 1981, p. 41.

93. "Antworten der Bundesregierung"; interviews (Germany, 1990); Schwind, *Kriminologie* (1986), p. 324.

94. Bundesministerium für Jugend, Familie, Frauen, und Gesundheit, "Report on the Drug Policy of the Federal Ministry for Youth, Family Affairs, Women, and Health," March 1989, pp. 1, 3–6; Albrecht, "Drug Policy," pp. 178–79; Schwind, *Kriminologie* (1986), p. 324. Exemptions from punishment were also allowed in cases where "minor amounts of drugs" were at issue and the drugs were "intended for personal use." Subsequent court decisions during 1982–84 clarified these levels as up to 0.15 grams of heroin, 6 grams of hashish, and 300 micrograms of cocaine. Albrecht, "Drug Policy," p. 178.

95. For example, see "Christine F.," *Time*, May 4, 1981, p. 41.

96. Nadelmann, *Cops across Borders*, pp. 220–36. By the early 1980s, German enforcement methods extended to drug control included the use of undercover agents, paid informants, wiretaps, and observation. Peters, *Die Absahner*, p. 338.

97. Roger Lewis, "European Markets in Cocaine," *Contemporary Crises* 13 (1989): 46; Niemetz, *Die Kokain-Mafia*, pp. 229–36; B. Bieleman et al., *Lines across Europe: Nature and Extent of Cocaine Use in Barcelona, Rotterdam, and Turin* (Amsterdam: Swets and Zeitlinger, 1993), pp. 22–23; "The Coming Cocaine Plague in Europe," *U.S. News and World Report*, February 20, 1989, pp. 34–36.

98. Metzner and Thamm, *Drogen*, pp. 42, 44, 47; interview (Germany, 1990); Henner Hess, "F. Der illegale Drogenhandel," in Henner Hess, ed., *Drogen und Drogenpolitik* (Frankfurt: Campus, 1989), p. 469.

99. Information provided to the author by the Federal Criminal Office, 1990; *New York Times*, July 27, 1989; Beke-Bramkamp, *Die Drogenpolitik der USA*, p. 37.

100. Commission of the European Communities, "Recommendation for a Council Decision," p. 7.

101. Ibid.; Sir Jack Stewart-Clark, "Report Drawn Up on Behalf of the Committee of Enquiry into the Drugs Problem in the Member States of the Community," *European Parliament Working Documents*, Document A 2-114/86/Corr., October 2, 1986, pp. 39–57; "Drugs: European Community Action," *British Information Services*, October 21, 1986; *New Statesman*, October 17, 1986.

102. Commission of the European Communities, "Proposal for a Council Decision," COM (89) 654 final, December 21, 1989; Health and Interior, *National Programme*, p. 43; interview (Germany, 1990).

103. From 1980 to 1990, Germany had contributed approximately DM 30 million through UNFDAC. The annual allocation was to be increased in 1991 from DM 3 million to DM 5 million. Health and Interior, *National Programme*, p. 48.

104. The remaining 32 to 44 percent of funds went to multilateral assistance programs such as UNFDAC. "Antworten der Bundesregierung," pp. 46, 50, 86.

105. "Anti-Drogenstrategie der Bundesrepublik Deutschland," manuscript and correspondence, October 1989, p. 9, received by author from the Family Ministry; interviews (Germany, 1990).

106. Interviews (Germany 1990, 1991); "Rede von Bundesinnenminister Dr. Wolfgang Schäuble anlässlich des Besuchs beim Bundeskriminalamt in Wiesbaden," June 26, 1989, p. 5. For information on the EC Commission's four-year aid package to Latin America (ECU credits, preferential trade status, and a pledge to coordinate member-country aid), see "The Commission Presents Its Proposal for a Response to Colombia's Special Cooperation Plan," press release, IP (90) 473, June 13, 1990; "The Council Adopts a Commission Proposal," press release, IP (90) 866, October 30, 1990.

107. Interviews (Germany, 1990).

108. Interviews (Germany, 1991).

109. Other possible reasons include the increased financial pressures of German reunification or the EC development of a coordinated aid program, but these factors were not cited as primary in interviews with either German or U.S. officials. Interviews (Germany, 1991).

110. For example, see "Der Stoff versaut das Land," Der Spiegel, July 9, 1990, pp. 32–45; "Der Gegner überschätzt uns," Der Spiegel, July 16, 1990, pp. 47–57.

111. Bundeskriminalamt, Rauschgift Jahresbericht, 1990 (Wiesbaden: BKA, 1991), pp. 45–47.

112. This age group has tended to account for over 50 percent of drug consumers since 1977–78 (followed by the 18–21 and 30–40 age brackets). Ibid., tables 12, 20, 21; Health and Interior, National Programme, p. 13.

113. Health and Interior, National Programme, pp. 3–4.

114. In general, Länder proponents of prevention came from the northern areas of Berlin, Hamburg, Northrhein-Westfalia, and Schleswig-Holstein. Beke-Bramkamp, Die Drogenpolitik der USA, p. 145; interviews (Germany, 1990); Frankfurter allgemeine Zeitung, March 31, 1990.

115. Health and Interior, National Programme, pp. 3, 17–30; Beke-Bramkamp, Die Drogenpolitik der USA, p.146.

116. Health and Interior, National Programme, pp. 37–38.

117. Schwind, Kriminologie (1993), pp. 387–88.

118. "Zuruck zum Krieg," Der Spiegel, May 23, 1994, p. 33; "Wie Essen, Trinken, und Sex," Der Spiegel, March 2, 1992, pp. 18–20. For more recent shifts in this direction, see also "Der Geruch des Bösen," Der Spiegel, May 2, 1994, pp. 38–44; and New York Times, May 3, 18, 1994.

119. Leyendecker et al., Mafia im Staat, pp. 122–23.

120. "Dreckiges Geld, sauber Helfer," Der Spiegel, February 24, 1992, pp. 130–44. This article is partially reprinted in Leyendecker et al., Mafia im Staat, pp. 84–108, 120.

121. Niemetz, Die Kokain-Mafia, p. 286; "Community Action against Money Laundering," Information Memo, IP (90) 16, January 11, 1990. The EC provisions would lead to a directive in 1991 calling on member states to adopt

money-laundering regulations by 1993. "Germany's Brash New Import: Dirty Money," *Business Week*, April 6, 1992, p. 42.

122. One U.S. official said awareness of German sensitivity over national sovereignty served as a check on the use of threats by U.S. policy makers, but clearly they were not dissuaded on the issue of precursor chemicals. Interview (Germany, 1991).

123. "Anti-Drogen Strategie der Bundesrepublik Deutschland," pp. 6–7, 9.

124. *Frankfurter allgemeine Zeitung*, March 31, 1990; Health and Interior, *National Programme*, pp. 53–61.

125. Health and Interior, *National Programme*, pp. 40–41; private correspondence from Federal Criminal Office to the author, November 4, 1991.

126. Schwind, *Kriminologie* (1993), pp. 434–35. For example, see sec. 43a (asset penalties) and sec. 261 (money laundering) of the German Penal Code, in *Strafgesetzbuch* (Munich: C. H. Beck, 1994), pp. 24, 120–21.

127. Health and Interior, *National Programme*, p. 41.

128. Interviews (Germany, 1991); *Frankfurter allgemeine Zeitung*, June 13, 1991.

129. "Dreckiges Geld, sauber Helfer," pp. 130–44; "Ab 50,000 Mark nur mit Ausweis," *Der Spiegel*, March 2, 1992, p. 152. According to *Business Week* ("Germany's Brash Import," p. 42), the German banking industry by early 1992 was also seen as being "extremely uncooperative" in dealing with police investigations of money laundering.

130. Law over the Discovery of Proceeds from Major Criminal Acts, also known as the Money Laundering Law. *New York Times*, November 30, 1993; *Wall Street Journal*, September 27, 1993; Meyer and Wolf, *Kriminalistisches Lehrbuch*, p. 399.

131. Leyendecker et al., *Mafia im Staat*, p. 135; Health and Interior, *National Programme*, p. 38.

132. Bruce M. Bagley, "Myths of Militarization: Enlisting Armed Forces in the War on Drugs," in Peter H. Smith, ed., *Drug Policy in the Americas* (Boulder, Colo.: Westview, 1992) pp. 139–40.

133. Niemetz, *Die Kokain Mafia*, pp. 295–99; Interview (Germany, 1991).

134. Recurrence to these charges is even more interesting in light of reports that Merck was one of the firms involved. Niemetz, *Die Kokain-Mafia*, pp. 295–99.

135. Interview (Germany, 1990); and "Anedridi asit asitik," *Der Spiegel*, September 3, 1990, pp. 59, 62.

136. Gatzemeier, *Heroin vom Staat*, p. 38; and Leyendecker et al., *Mafia im Staat*, p. 132.

137. Leyendecker et al., *Mafia im Staat*, p. 129; "Anedridi asit asitik," pp. 59, 62.

138. Private correspondence from Federal Criminal Office to author, November 4, 1991.

139. Health and Interior, *National Programme*, pp. 38–39.
140. "The Commission Extends Its Action to Combat Drug Abuse," *Information Memo*, P-35, May 30, 1990; Council Regulation (EEC) No. 3677/90, printed in *Official Journal of the European Communities*, no. L 357/1, December 20, 1990.
141. See sec. 18a of the Narcotics Act in *Strafgesetzbuch*, p. 219. The measures basically prohibit the unauthorized import, export, and transit of materials that can facilitate the unauthorized production of narcotics or other illicit drugs. According to Leyendecker et al., *Mafia im Staat*, pp. 136–37, proposals by the Health Ministry in 1992 included penalties of five years' imprisonment for violation of these regulations.

Chapter 6. Capacity and Compliance

1. H. Richard Friman, "Awaiting the Tsunami? Japan and the International Drug Trade," *Pacific Review* 6, 1 (1993): 41–51.
2. See, for example, the strategies and alternatives discussed in Peter Andreas et al., "Dead-End Drug Wars," *Foreign Policy* 85 (Winter 1991–92): 106–28; Rensselaer Lee, "Making the Most of Colombia's Drug Negotiations," *Orbis* 35 (Spring 1991): 248–49.
3. See, for example, the discussion in Donald J. Mabry, "The Role of the Military," in Raphael F. Perl, ed., *Drugs and Foreign Policy: A Critical Review* (Boulder, Colo.: Westview, 1994), pp. 101–30.
4. David R. Decker and Ignacio Duran, *The Political, Economic, and Labor Climate in Colombia* (Philadelphia: Wharton School, 1982), p. 13; Robert H. Dix, *The Politics of Colombia* (New York: Praeger, 1987), p. 59; Rensselaer W. Lee, *The White Labrynth: Cocaine and Political Power* (New Brunswick, N.J.: Transaction, 1989), pp. 22, 191–92.
5. Dix, *The Politics of Colombia*, p. 59.
6. Scott B. MacDonald, *Mountain High, White Avalanche: Cocaine and Power in the Andean States and Panama* (New York: Praeger, 1989), pp. 54–55.
7. Francisco E. Thoumi, "The Economic Impact of Narcotics in Colombia," in Peter H. Smith, ed., *Drug Policy in the Americas* (Boulder, Colo.: Westview, 1992), pp. 62–64.
8. Lee, *The White Labyrinth*, pp. 10–11, 121, 126–27, 135–36.
9. Ibid., p. 113, 124; Tina Rosenberg, *Children of Cain: Violence and the Violent in Latin America* (New York: William Morrow, 1991).
10. *New York Times*, August 21, September 15, 1995; "Drugsgate, Bogota," *Economist*, August 5, 1995, p. 39; "In the Mire," *Economist*, August 12, 1995, pp. 38–39.

INDEX